Management
for Visual Resources
Collections

The Visual Resources Association

MANAGEMENT FOR VISUAL RESOURCES COLLECTIONS

2d Edition

NANCY SHELBY SCHULLER
Curator of Visual Arts
and
Senior Lecturer
The University of Texas at Austin

Graphics by
F. TERRY ARZOLA
Humanities Research Associate
The University of Texas at Austin

LIBRARIES UNLIMITED, INC.
Englewood, Colorado
1989

Copyright © 1989, 1979 Visual Resources Association
All Rights Reserved
Printed in the United States of America

No part of this publication may be reproduced, stored in a retrieval system, or transmitted, in any form or by any means, electronic, mechanical, photocopying, recording, or otherwise, without the prior written permission of the publisher.

LIBRARIES UNLIMITED, INC.
P.O. Box 3988
Englewood, CO 80155-3988

Library of Congress Cataloging-in-Publication Data

Schuller, Nancy S.
　Management for visual resources collections / Nancy Shelby Schuller ; graphics by F. Terry Arzola. -- 2d ed.
　　xii, 169 p. 22x28 cm.
　　At head of title: The Visual Resources Association.
　　"This publication evolved from the earlier Guide for management of visual resources collections, 1979 edition"--Acknowledgments.
　　Includes bibliographical references.
　　ISBN 0-87287-612-8
　　1. Libraries--Special collections--Pictures. 2. Libraries--Special collections--Photographs. 3. Libraries--Special collections--Slides (Photography) 4. Slides (Photography)--Collectors and collecting. 5. Photographs--Collectors and collecting. 6. Visual aids--Collectors and collecting.
7. Pictures--Collectors and collecting. 8. Art libraries--Administration.   I. Visual Resources Association.   II. Guide for management of visual resources collections. III. Title.
Z692.P5S38   1989
025.177--dc20
　　　　　　　　　　　　　　　　　　　　　　　89-13229
　　　　　　　　　　　　　　　　　　　　　　　CIP

Contents

PREFACE..ix

ACKNOWLEDGMENTS...xi

1 – PLANNING GOALS AND OBJECTIVES.......................................1

2 – FACILITIES PLANNING...3
   Getting Started..3
      Statement of the Objective or Purpose of the Visual Resources Collection...4
      Analysis of Activities: Users and Staff........................5
      Specifications for Space Requirements, Present and Projected...6
      Development of a Physical Proximity and Accessibility Plan....16
      General Architectural Interior Features.......................18
      Final Plan..19
      Furnishings and Equipment.....................................20
      Moving In...23
   Critique of Physical Facility.....................................24
   Notes...25

3 – BUDGETING...26
   Budget Systems..26
   Types of Expenses...29
   Development of a Cost Accounting System...........................31
   Budget Planning Cycle...32
   Managing the Budget...34
   Use of Microcomputers for Budgeting...............................34
   Notes...34

4 – STAFFING..35
   Staffing Categories...35
      Administrative and Professional/Curatorial Category...........36
      Technical Category..38
      Clerical/General Category.....................................38

4—STAFFING (*continued*)

- Staff Size ... 39
- Job Descriptions ... 40
- Recruiting and Interviewing ... 41
  - Interviewing ... 42
- Staff Training ... 46
  - Staff Appraisals ... 46
- Volunteers ... 47
- Communication ... 47
- Final Thoughts on Staffing ... 48
- Notes ... 48

5—REPORTS AND STATISTICS ... 49

- Methodology and Terminology ... 49
- Annual Report: Quantitative Portion ... 52
  - Identification of the Collection/Type of Collection ... 52
  - Income ... 52
  - Expenditures ... 52
  - Circulation ... 54
  - Acquisitions and Holdings ... 54
  - Staff Make-up and Size ... 54
- Annual Report: Nonquantitative Portion ... 55
  - Staff Development and Professional Pursuits ... 55
  - Special Projects: Accomplished and Planned ... 55
  - Collection Strengths and Weaknesses ... 56
  - Short- and Long-Range Goals ... 56
- Collection and Use of Statistics ... 56
  - Counting the Collection ... 58
- Notes ... 59

6—POLICIES AND PROCEDURES MANUALS ... 61

- General Information ... 62
  - Description of the Resources of the Collection ... 62
- User Information ... 62
  - Circulation and Access to the Collection and Audiovisual Equipment ... 62
  - Services Provided ... 62
- Collection Development and Maintenance ... 62
- Administrative Functions ... 66
  - Staffing ... 68
- Records and Reports ... 68
- Supplies, Equipment, and Services ... 69
- Notes ... 69

7—CIRCULATION AND CONTROL ... 71

- Policies ... 71
- Circulation Systems ... 72
  - Manual Systems ... 72
  - Automated Systems ... 73

Contents / vii

 Maintenance and Control...74
  User Orientations..74
  Circulation Desk..74
  Shelflists...74
  Inventory and Shelf Reading...75
  Sorting and Filing Procedures...75
  Weeding, Replacement, and Collection Development..............76
  File Arrangement and Other Access...77
  Security..78
  Fees, Overdue Notices, and Fines...78
 Notes..78

8 – MICROCOMPUTER APPLICATIONS...80
 Historical Background...80
 Microcomputers...81
 Needs Assessment..82
 Establishing Priorities...83
 Selection..83
 Purchase vs. In-house Development of Software..............................84
 Implementation: Standards for Data Entry...84
  Subject Thesauri..86
 System Documentation...86
 Future Trends..87
 Summary..87
 Notes..87

APPENDIX A – SAMPLE FLOOR PLANS..89
APPENDIX B – SAMPLE JOB DESCRIPTIONS....................................97
 Administrative and Curatorial Examples..97
 Curatorial and Curatorial Assistants..103
 Technical Services..107
 Clerical Services...111
APPENDIX C – GLOSSARY...113
APPENDIX D – MISCELLANEOUS ADMINISTRATIVE FORMS..........119
 Photographic Services Forms..119
 Staff-Related Forms..123
 Statistics Forms..128
APPENDIX E – AUDIOVISUAL CIRCULATION FORMS.....................133
APPENDIX F – SAMPLE STANDARD RECORD FORMATS................143

BIBLIOGRAPHY...151
 General..151
 Facilities Planning...151
 Budgeting..152
 Staffing..152
 Reports and Statistics..153
 Policies and Procedures Manuals...154
 Circulation and Control..154
 Microcomputers..155
  General...155
  Authorities and Subject Access...157
  Interactive Videodisk, Optical Disk Use.................................159

INDEX...161

Preface

The term *visual resources collection* has evolved as a description for what was formerly called a photograph and/or slide library or collection. The most likely reasons for this transition are to reflect the increasing variety in visual formats being collected today and to avoid the impression that such a collection provides the same kind of access and service as a book library. A visual resources collection is any organization or unit having as its primary function the collection of photographic images for such purposes as research, teaching, or historical documentation. Because collections of slides and photographs have been associated with the teaching and study of art and architecture since the latter part of the nineteenth century, it is only natural that collections in the visual arts and architecture are the focus not only of this publication, but also of much of what has been published regarding collecting and managing such materials. However, the subjects covered in this publication apply to similar collections for fields such as history, classics, anthropology, zoology, geology, and other scientific collections.

In the United States, visual resources collections exist anywhere that art or architecture is taught or practiced and increasingly in other academic disciplines. They are found in galleries and museums, not only of art, but also of history and science. Such collections frequently began modestly, without a curator or plans for development or management. It has not been unusual for these collections to have attained a substantial size before users realized the value of the resource and the need for management and direction.

During the past decade, the profession of visual resources curatorship has been established. Currently it has its own professional organization (with an international membership of about 800), a growing number of publications, and opportunities for professional development through national conferences, workshops, and seminars.[1] This organization has provided increased communication among curators and the definition of numerous issues common among collection managers.

Although there are probably as many types of visual resources collections as there are collections, activities classed as administrative are common to most operations. Anyone responsible for a visual resources collection will need to be able to make the most efficient use of physical facilities or plan for new or renovated ones; propose and manage a budget; recruit, hire, train, and supervise a staff or volunteers; collect statistics and make reports; prepare and maintain a policies and procedures manual; deal with collection circulation and control; and consider the use of computers in the collection. These are the issues addressed in this publication.

Many of the administrative functions common to book libraries and archives can be applied in visual resources collections, with modifications. For example, budgets, both for the whole operation and for special projects and proposals, can, with adjustments, be utilized in visual resources collections. Staffing practices for libraries and visual resources collections are similar, with the exception that visual collections may produce particular materials entirely in-house, requiring staff with special training, skills, and knowledge. Visual resources collections and libraries share the need for control of the materials contained in them. Although their circulation policies and procedures vary greatly, the practice of recording the removal and return of items is common to both in many cases, as is the practice of weeding and developing the collections. Gathering and reporting of statistics is a usual practice in book libraries and one that this author believes should become routine in visual resources collections in order to advance the communication of highly useful information. Although the physical facilities required for visual resources collections and libraries differ considerably, the motives underlying planning—that of providing a convenient and efficient space for users and safe and efficient storage for the materials contained in the collection—are similar.

The chapters in this publication address management activities practiced in most visual resources collections. They are indispensable for daily as well as long-term planning for collections. Unlike such activities as classification and cataloging; conservation and maintenance; collection development for slides, photographs, and other formats; and audiovisual equipment management, which are specialized functions of visual resources curators, the topics in this guide are more general in nature.

The objective here is to provide the visual resources curator with a framework and examples for planning and decision making in management of the collection. The overall focus is on the general administrative and management fundamentals germane to those responsibilities that the curator must address while developing and coordinating an effective visual resources collection operation. These basic management techniques can be effective in improving and simplifying procedures in collections.

It is the nature of visual resources collections that there is no single "right way" that things must be done. Much of the administration and management of these collections can be characterized as "problem solving activities." It is as an approach to "problem solving" that this publication is offered.

NOTES

[1] The Visual Resources Association was formed in 1983. Information on membership, publications, and meetings can be obtained from Joy Alexander, ed., *International Bulletin for Photographic Documentation of the Visual Arts*, University of Michigan, Department of the History of Art, Tappan Hall, Ann Arbor, MI 80723.

Acknowledgments

This publication evolved from the earlier *Guide for Management of Visual Resources Collections*, 1979 edition, issued by the Mid-America College Art Association, Slide Curators Special Interest Group. During a three-year period, that group published six guides providing information relative to visual resources curatorship.[1] The steady demand for these guides, the production and distribution of which has been very capably managed by Zelda Richardson at the University of New Mexico at Albuquerque, underscores the need in the profession for the information they contain.

As a contributing author and the editor for the *Guide to Administration and Management of Visual Resources Collections*, I am pleased that the Visual Resources Association invited me to undertake the revised and expanded version of this earlier issue. The project has been enlightening and rewarding in many ways. As I researched each chapter, I found myself making use of what I learned almost daily as Visual Resources Curator for the Department of Art at The University of Texas at Austin. I wish to thank Dr. Maurice Sevigny, Chairman of our department, the users of our collection, and my staff members who have been supportive of this project and patient with my distracted attention; I trust they will benefit from what I have learned in the process.

I am grateful to Nancy DeLaurier, Slide Curator at the University of Missouri at Kansas City, who has influenced my professional development and provided me with many important opportunities during my career. The annual Workshop in Basic Training for Slide Curators, which she began in 1976 and which has continued here at The University of Texas at Austin each year here since 1984, has helped to develop many of the ideas presented in this publication.

The two readers for this manuscript, Susan Hoover, Assistant Director of The Center for the Study of American Architecture at The University of Texas at Austin School of Architecture, and Christine Sundt, Slide Curator, Architecture and Allied Arts Library, University of Oregon, have worked long and patiently to help me approach their very high editorial standards. Their levels of assistance and encouragement have been essential to the completion of this project.

The graphics throughout the publication are the creation of F. Terry Arzola, Humanities Research Associate II at The University of Texas at Austin, Department of Art, Slide and Photograph Collection. His mastery of the Macintosh graphics programs is reflected in the very professional quality of the diagrams, plans, and charts. I am indebted to his diligence, for the scope of this project increased each time we conferred. He has turned my scribbled and scratched out ideas into effective results.

One of the highlights of this endeavor has been the overwhelming response from curators to my requests for examples for forms, floor plans, job descriptions, and other documents used for administrative purposes in their collections. I am grateful to those listed here for taking the time and effort to send materials and suggestions and respond to my questions. Elizabeth Alley, School of Architecture, University of Maryland; Donald Beetham, Rutgers University, Department of Art History; Mark Braunstein, Connecticut College, Department of Art History; Bette Rae Callow, Memphis College of Art; Eileen Coffman, Dallas Museum of Art; Nancy DeLaurier, Department of Art and Art History, University of Missouri at Kansas City; Leigh Gates, Art Institute of Chicago; Lise Hawkos, School of Art, Arizona State University; Mary M. Jacoby, Virginia Museum of Fine Arts; Marilyn Kerner, College of Design, Iowa State University; Jean Krchnak, School of Architecture, University of Houston; Eileen Krest, Department of Art, Queens College; Mireille Lavigne, Audio-Visual Media Library, University of Ottawa; Micheline Nilsen, University of Pennsylvania; Astrid Otey, School of Fine Arts, Miami University; Jonny Prinz, Bird Library, Fine Arts Department, Syracuse University; Anne Renaud, Department of Art History, University of California at Santa Barbara; Martha Steward, School of Architecture and Environmental Design, Instructional Resources Center, California Polytechnic State University; Sherrie Rook, Department of Art and Art History, George Mason University; Gary Seloff, TGS Technology, Johnson Space Center, Houston; Maryly Snow, College of Environmental Design, Department of Architecture, University of California at Berkeley; Christine Sundt, Architecture and Allied Arts Library, University of Oregon; Tina Updike, Art Department, James Madison University; Sandy Walker, Art Department, University of Tennessee; Margaret Webster, College of Architecture, Cornell University; and Linda S. White, Fiske-Kimball Fine Arts Library, University of Virginia.

Throughout the process of researching, writing, and revising, my husband Brian and daughter Nicole have filled in for me in more ways than I can describe. Without their understanding and patience I could never have indulged myself in the luxury of writing this book. I thank them with all my heart.

NOTES

[1] Nancy Schuller, ed., *Guide to Management of Visual Resources Collections* (1979); Gillian Scott, ed., *Guide to Equipment for Slide Maintenance and Viewing* (1978); Nancy Schuller and Susan Tamulonis, eds., *Guide for Photograph Collections* (1978); Zelda Richardson and Rosemary Keuhn, eds., *Guide to Copy Photography for Visual Resources Collections* (1980); Eleanor Collins, ed., *Guide to Collections without Curators* (1978); Zelda Richardson and Sheila Hannah, eds., *Introduction to Automation* (1980).

1
Planning Goals and Objectives

There must be clear objectives involving the purposes of the visual resources collection that, once established, will promote its effective and efficient operation. Any planning for the routine operation of the collection relies on generally accepted goals. From a broad statement of objectives, a series of policies can be established to provide guidelines for decisions on priorities, timetables, and allocation of resources. Such decisions as what will be collected, the purposes for which it can be used (e.g., research, reference, teaching), and who it will serve must be established for the successful implementation of the administrative activities described in this publication.

Of primary importance in the planning process is the identification of the user group or groups. Frustration and confusion on the part of patrons and staff result when a system devised for a particular group of users begins to be utilized by others. The users, their needs, and how they are determined should be formalized. It is also necessary to designate the formats to be collected, the subject areas to be covered, and the sources or methods employed to obtain these resources. Involving users and staff in this planning will ensure that the policy is known and understood by all associated with the collection and that it provides complete coverage. These two procedures—that of establishing who is to use the collection and what is to be collected—are instrumental in eliminating misunderstandings and reducing dissatisfaction and frustration experienced by both users and staff.

The established objectives should be reflected in policies and procedures developed for the following broad activities:

1. acquisitions and collection development
2. circulation and procedures for control and conservation
3. management of the documentation of and access to collection items
4. use of equipment and facilities
5. recruitment, training, supervision, and responsibilities of staff
6. reports and proposals

For the curator to provide the most professional services for the users, there must be a clear understanding of authorities and responsibilities and the curator's relationship to the larger administrative unit. The curator must be able to negotiate directly with the administrative head in matters concerning the collection. Although the curator serves the users of the collection and may work with a committee of interested users on matters of policy, this is not the body to whom the curator is officially answerable. The communication with the policy committee for developing and implementing policies is lateral, but separate from this should be one supervisor or director who gives instructions; receives reports, plans, and proposals; and acts on budgets.

1 – PLANNING GOALS AND OBJECTIVES

The curator's authorities, such as hiring (and firing) of collection staff, and responsibilities, such as reports, budgets, and upholding policies, should be officially designated, not assumed. The clear definition of what is expected becomes critical when performance appraisals occur. Definition of these requirements will eliminate uncertainty and free the professional to work efficiently and without the apprehension of leaving something undone or failing to meet some unknown or misunderstood standard. The curator's standing within the administrative unit (and within the profession as well) can affect the way the collection is perceived by its users.

There are other factors to be considered when handling the management responsibilities covered in this publication. Planning is an indispensable part of management. It involves goal setting, but also the use of delegation to accomplish desired results. Much of the hands-on work in the visual resources collection is done by someone other than the curator. This means that the curator supervises either full- or part-time staff, or both. Often the staff members are college students, some of whom have little work experience. To gain the maximum from the staff and to provide a postive situation in which they can develop and learn is the responsibility of the curator.

Study of current theories, experiences in all areas of management, attendance at professional meetings, and continuing education seminars are important activities for the professional visual resources curator. A person knowledgeable and interested in contemporary ideas and trends provides innovative and creative approaches to problems, whether dealing with administrators, users, other professionals, or staff.

The standard response to these suggestions for management is "but there is not enough time for all of that!" On the contrary, one cannot afford to neglect such activities. Hours spent in planning, reporting, record keeping, and staff development will prevent crises before they occur, and will result in improved collection management.

2
Facilities Planning

In the recent past, traditional library literature has provided vital information on the physical planning and building of book libraries as well as media and audiovisual centers. While much of this available material is generally applicable to visual resource collections, it is the purpose here to review the specific physical requirements of such collections, to modify existing techniques that address these requirements, and to provide specific information to aid the curator in creating an adequate and successful physical facility.

By developing a step-by-step approach to the physical design of the visual resources area, the curator can ensure the results of a successful and workable space for users, staff, and managers of the facility. A good and effective design will not only improve the functions of the collection, but also enhance the recognition given to the collection. Aspects of the facility that must be addressed from the beginning of the planning process include storage and work spaces, technical facilities, security, environmental controls, graphics, furniture, lighting, acoustics, and traffic patterns. Throughout the examination of each of the elements, both function and aesthetics must be emphasized in order to achieve the desired results.

Whether planning a new facility, renovating an older one, or merely rearranging an existing space, the curator must be prepared to spend significant time and energy on the project. Continuous collaboration between curator and architect or designer is mandatory so that the designer will be fully aware of the needs of the collection. The curator may be called on to participate as part of a planning committee or merely requested to report on various aspects of the collection design. Whatever the situation, adequate preparation and presentation will go far in achieving a space that ultimately will be suitable for all of the requirements of the collection. The method proposed here is simple: begin at the beginning and take nothing for granted.

GETTING STARTED

Initially the curator needs to provide a preliminary but reasonably complete statement of the visual resources collection requirements. This should include input from staff and user representatives who, with the curator, should comprise a facility planning committee. This will be followed by a series of more detailed statements, scale drawings and calculations required for the layout, work areas, capacities, communications, lighting, acoustics, climate controls, furniture, and equipment. The architect or designer will want to know the purpose for each area in the plan. A description of the services, routines, staffing accommodations, and equipment needed in each activity area and the relationship of each activity to all the others is also necessary. These data should be presented with consideration not only for present conditions but also for future objectives.

4 / 2 — FACILITIES PLANNING

Effective planning begins with a facilities planning program that consists of the following basic elements:

1. Statement of the objective or purpose of the collection.

2. Analysis of the staff and users of the collection as well as the furniture and equipment necessary to occupy the spaces for each activity or function.

3. Specifications of space requirements (i.e., number of square feet required for the various areas and activities), preferable space shapes (e.g., square, rectangle, circle), growth projections, inventory of spaces, storage and seating capacities.

4. Development of a physical proximity and accessibility plan (i.e., what needs to be adjacent to or *not* adjacent to what).

5. Architectural features (i.e., ambiance or environment: how the user or staff is to feel or act in this area; comfort of furnishings, behavior patterns, lighting, signs, noise control, floor covering, walls, environmental controls, outside views, etc.).

6. A final plan based on the above criteria.

7. A specifications list of needed equipment; furniture and other special requirements; and what current furniture and equipment will be utilized in the new space, including heating, cooling, venting, and other electrical requirements.

8. Moving day plans.

Development of the planning worksheet requires outlining and describing, as fully as possible, the elements listed above.

Statement of the Objective or Purpose of the Visual Resources Collection

A statement of this type is important to help the architect, designer, or project manager understand the major focus for the plan as a whole. It should include what is housed (i.e., formats collected), the projected annual growth of the collection, and how it serves the sponsoring institution (school, library, museum, educational institution, corporation, government service, etc.). It should include numbers of users, current and projected, both regular and occasional, and their activities while utilizing the collection, necessary interaction with staff, and estimate of occupancy levels of users and staff. The statistics for the formats housed may be collected in a form such as that in figure 2.1.

	Year 1	Year 2	Year 3	Year 4
Regular users				
Occasional users				
Staff: full-time equivalent				
Holdings: slides				
Holdings: other formats				
fiche				
video				
films				
reference material				
photographs				
Circulation: slides				
Circulation: other formats				
fiche				
video				
films				
reference materials				
photographs				

Figure 2.1. Sample format to describe activity levels, current and projected.

Analysis of Activities: Users and Staff

The second step in the development of the planning program is preparing the description of precisely what takes place and what the requirements are (equipment, supplies, furnishings, architectural features, etc.) for the performance of each activity. An example of format and outline for describing visual resources collection activities and their requirements follows:

Inventory of spaces or activity areas

Name and description of specific activity or purpose: What happens in this area. What users and/or staff members are to do in this area.

Size: Number of square feet.

Capacities: seating required, storage required: Storage for numbers of slides, photos, audiovisual equipment. Seating for numbers of staff and users. Other formats, equipment, etc.

6 / 2 – FACILITIES PLANNING

Occupancy: Staff: in groups or one at a time.
              Users: in groups or one at a time.

Furniture and equipment required for this area: A complete listing of each piece of equipment or furniture, such as files, bookshelves, chairs, etc.

Electrical and communications outlets: Numbers and locations where these are needed; special requirements for both high voltage or where electrical outlets or computer hook-ups should be located.

Dimensions for area: Total square footage for area; preferable proportions, e.g., square, rectangle, circle, etc.

Lighting requirements: Types of lights, areas where lights should be selectively controlled.

Proximity to other areas: Close proximity or areas to be situated nearby; close proximity not desired, i.e., functions best suited to remote areas.

Environmental controls: Air conditioning, temperature and humidity controls, cold storage.

Surfaces: Floors, walls, ceilings, other special requirements.

Architectural features: Ambiance or environment. Comfort of furnishing, lighting, signs, noise control, colors. Security and storage needs.

Specifications for Space Requirements, Present and Projected

From the analysis of the activities and functions of the collection, the conversion into physical terms begins. This involves the determination of necessary square footage for each function, resulting in the computation of total ideal square footage required for the entire space.

The four main categories for which space is needed are collection space (files and storage units), user space (carrels, viewers, sorters, tables, chairs, reference files and shelves, files and circulation area), staff space (work stations, technical processes, administration, circulation, user space), and support space (copier, photographic darkroom, copy stand, computer equipment, audiovisual equipment).

COLLECTION SPACE— SLIDE STORAGE

The size of the collection depends not only on the numbers of slides in the collection, but also on the kind of storage files used. For example, the five-drawer Neumade File (model SF-5-S), filled to capacity, holds 2,500 glass-bound slides or 5,000 cardboard mounted slides. Figure 2.2 lists comparative capacities for several commonly used slide storage units. To calculate how much space is required for slide storage, convert the size of the storage units used and those projected to be needed to accommodate future growth into linear feet and multiply by the number of units. Double-faced, long ranges of slide files provide more efficient storage than small groupings or short ranges of slide files. Running single-faced files around the walls reduces storage efficiency, but may be necessary because of structural load limits of the floors.

Unit	Capacity	Dimensions	Capacity / Linear Feet
Drawer Storage:			
Neumade #SF-5-S			
metal cabinet	5 drawer unit	w. 15 1/2"	30,000 slides / 6'6"
metal dividers	2,500 slides/unit	h. 13"	(4 units stacked 3 high)
	(500 slides/drawer)		
Library Bureau #97515			
wood	15 drawer unit	w. 10 1/2"	18,000 slides / 5'3"
	3,000 slides/unit	h. 33"	(6 units)
	(200 slides/drawer)	d. 17"	
Luxor #39-84037			
metal cabinet	4 drawer unit	w. 39"	33,600 slides / 6'6"
plastic inserts	5,600 slides/unit	h. 11 1/4"	(2 units stacked 3)
	(1,400 slides/drawer)	d. 17 1/2"	
Remington Rand			
metal cabinet	8 drawer unit	w. 18"	38,592 slides / 4'6"
custom inserts	12,864 slides/unit	h. 51"	(3 units)
	(1,608 slides/drawer)	d. 28"	
Rack Storage:			
Abodia #5000			
metal racks	50 rack unit	w. 69"	5,000 slides / 5'8"
wood cabinet	5,000 slides/unit	h. 19"	(1 unit)
	(100 slides/rack)	d. 28"	
Multiplex #4010			
metal racks	33 rack unit	w. 18 1/4"	11,880 slides / 4'7"
metal cabinet	3,960 slides/unit	h. 27"	(3 units)
	(120 slides/rack)	d. 30"	

Figure 2.2. Comparison of storage capacities of slide storage units.

In a book library, aisle passages between ranges can be as little as three feet wide. However, in slide collections, because drawers or racks must be pulled out for selection of slides, considerably more space between ranges is required. Sufficient space must be provided for drawers to pull out, for people to stand, as well as space for narrow tables and chairs or stools between the ranges and aisles. Figure 2.3, p. 8, illustrates space required for slide storage racks and files.

Floor loads, a major consideration in libraries, are often overlooked when planning the visual resources collection facility. Calculations of floor loads should be the responsibility of the engineer or architect, but in renovations, it is possible that such professionals will not be called in. Even in planning a new building, it is possible that the weight potential of cabinets containing thousands of glass-bound slides will not be fully realized. A Neumade Model SF-5-S five-drawer slide cabinet loaded with approximately 2,500 glass-bound slides divided by thirty slides per pound equals a weight of sixty-two pounds. Add thirty-six pounds shipping weight for the cabinet, and the total weight for each is ninety-eight pounds. Stacked three-high on a wooden or metal base or cabinet in which supplies are stored, the load averages approximately 400 pounds per square foot.[1] In a typical library, the standard "live load" is 150 pounds per square foot (or 300 pounds per square foot for compact shelving). *Live load* refers to elements that can be moved

8 / 2—FACILITIES PLANNING

around inside a building, such as desks, equipment, other furnishings, and even people. Thus, with typical library books, shelves, files, and other furnishings on the floor should not exceed 150 pounds per square foot, averaged across the floor.[2] Most office buildings in the United States are designed for only fifty to eighty pounds per square foot, depending upon the local building codes.[3] By comparison, film materials are very heavy. This important factor must be considered in the planning process.

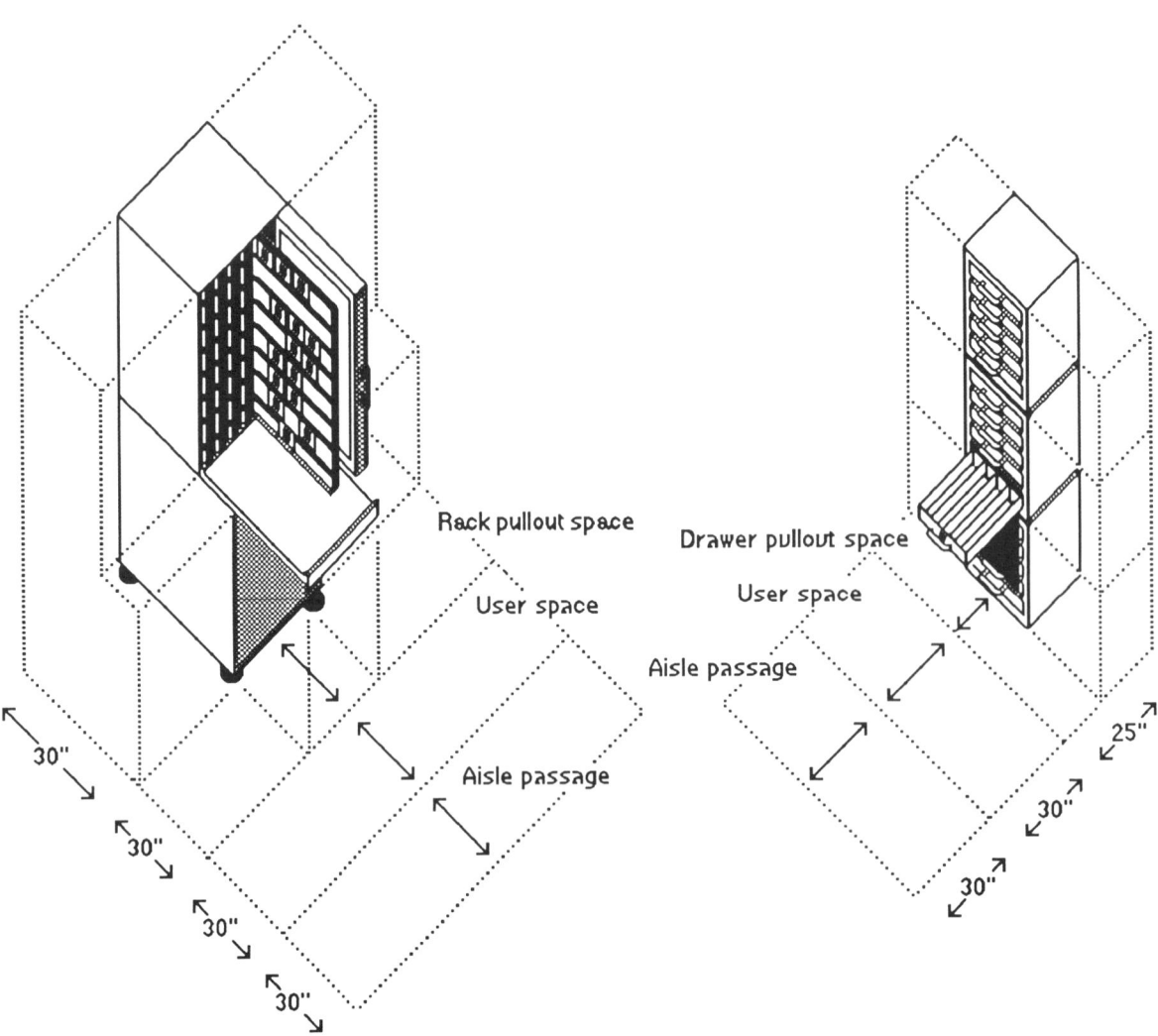

Figure 2.3. Space required for slide storage racks and files.

COLLECTION SPACE—PHOTOGRAPH COLLECTION AREA

Collecting and housing photographs may or may not be a function of the visual resources collection. Very often it is, and such collections require a vast amount of floor space. As with the slide storage area, the floor load capabilities must be considered. Most mounted photo collections are stored either in legal-sized file cabinets (requiring ten square feet each) or utilizing a flat storage system with the photographs placed in document cases. As with slides, long ranges back to back offer the most efficient capacity in the least amount of space; however, lining the outside walls may be required to distribute the weight more safely.

Photo users need large table surfaces to spread out and examine groups of photographs. A table designed to accommodate four or six readers will most likely be used by only one person at a time examining photographs. Therefore, if the collection is used by a large number of people, adequate table space must be provided.

If the technical services for the collection are provided in the same area where the photographs are housed, additional table space will be required for sorting, processing, and to accommodate a drymount press (if photographs are mounted) and a large paper cutter. Also needed is storage space for supplies, particularly the large mounting boards. In addition, space of approximately 150-200 square feet for a desk, typewriter, computer, storage, and supplies should be included. The usual electrical and communications outlets are needed.

USER AREA

Visual resources collections and archives commonly house very large collections, but require seating for relatively few users when compared with a book library. However, a large percentage of these users need long-term study or work space for work in progress, with storage for personal belongings. User space should include space for both long-term or regular patrons as well as those who use the collection less frequently. Both user types require slide viewing or sorting space. However, the spaces designated for occasional users can be shared spaces.

For regular or long-term users the goal should be a reserved carrel within the collection providing a viewing or sorting surface with sufficient storage for work in progress. Adequate work space in the collection promotes better control of the collection. The user space should be contiguous to the collection storage space.

Slide viewers or sorters and carrels vary in size. If the specifications for the equipment to be used are known, these measurements should be used in calculating the spaces. If not, one can estimate that an individual carrel requires about fifteen square feet of space, a table-top light table or slide sorter about twenty-five square feet, and a slide viewer about ten square feet. These measurements each include chair space. Figure 2.4 represents space requirements for table and carrel users.

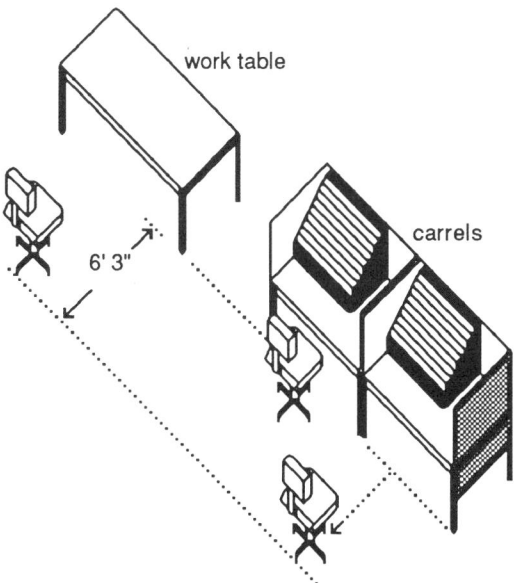

Figure 2.4. Space requirements for carrel and table users.

Storage spaces for regular, long-term users is somewhat more difficult to calculate. Allowing enough space for individuals to store their personal image collections helps keep collection materials out of private offices, while also providing environmentally safer storage for private collections. A small amount of storage space is also needed for books and other materials used in research or lecture preparations. These spaces do not need to be locked, but it is desirable for them to be somewhat secluded from the public areas to ensure some quiet and privacy. Light neutral colors are best for work surfaces in both the public and work areas. These provide reflection needed for easy viewing of transparencies.

Projection facilities should be designed so that the equipment can be easily serviced. Projection housings, for example, should provide security, but should not inhibit access and replacement when a breakdown occurs. Instructions for users, including diagrams, should be posted prominently. Machines and sorters are best located near a staff work area where supervision and assistance can be provided.

USER AREA – CIRCULATION/ INFORMATION/REFERENCE AREA

This activity area should be planned for the convenience of staff and general users, and both should have direct access to the collection storage area as well. The circulation counter and the space immediately surrounding it should be close to the main entrance. This is an area that requires immediate visibility and constant control by the staff. Staff should be easily accessible for user orientations, reference questions, circulation activities, searches, and to help occasional users find viewing space.

A well-designed circulation desk or counter is important for effective functioning. A design for a multi-purpose circulation center is provided in figure 2.5. Determine what activities will occur in this area, and the equipment or supplies necessary for these activities: circulation files (manual or automated), containers for slide circulation, and audiovisual equipment circulation (storage for projection equipment, trays, extension cords, etc., reserve materials, orientation brochures, other descriptive material, slide/tape orientations). To make the best use of staff, include a work station such as data entry, label typing, or sorting at the circulation desk; make the design fit a variety of needs. Because of the nature of the materials stored in the circulation area, it is best that storage compartments be lockable. The circulation counter should include designated spaces for circulation forms; reserve materials; slide containers, projectors, and slide trays; a computer terminal or typewriter; and a copier, if one is utilized for circulation.

STAFF

Depending upon the size of the staff and the services performed, there may be need for several staff-designated areas within the user areas. Obviously some of the technical functions, such as slide and/or photo mounting and slide production, and some of the clerical functions (label and card production, for example) should be separate from the public areas because of acoustical requirements. The nature of each of these activities is tedious, and sufficient "psychological" space for each worker is essential to promote concentration and accuracy. Some activities can take place in the presence of conversation (e.g., slide or photo mounting), while others need to be done without distractions (data entry, card and label typing, cataloging); therefore, these activities should be separated from one another.

A general *technical services area* should provide flexible work space for all activities associated with processing, classifying and cataloging, labeling, sorting, and filing new materials, as well as for various collection maintenance projects. This area can also be suitable for housing the collection records and all work in progress, as well as related supplies. Approximately 150 square feet of floor space per worker or a minimum of 200 square feet of storage and work space per worker is recommended.[4]

A *multi-purpose work area* could be combined with the technical services area, or located in the professional support staff area to accommodate a variety of tasks. Work with slides and photographs requires space for spreading out images and reference materials. Rarely will the average-sized desk provide enough space to process images into the permanent collections. A work surface, or table, approximately thirty-six square feet in size; a slide-sorting-selecting and programming table, horizontal or tilted, approximately twenty-five square feet in size; and a multi-purpose work table with a two-sided work area, sixty-five square feet in size, are recommended. This technical services area should be located to provide easy access to slide and public card files and may even be part of the public user area if space is suitable.

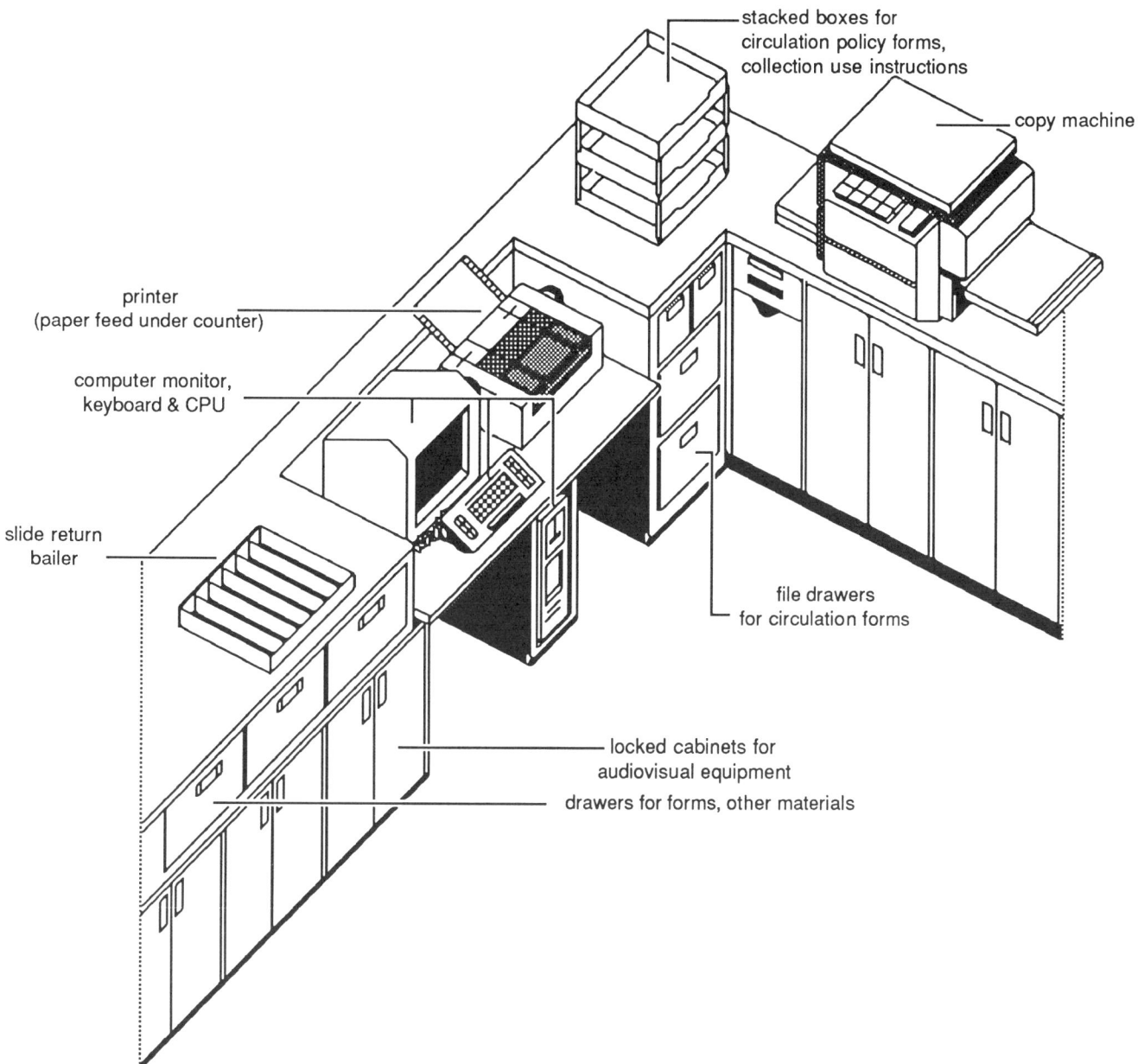

Figure 2.5. Design for a circulation counter.

The rest of *staff space* can be calculated as follows: approximately eighty-seven square feet per person, which includes a five-by-three-foot desk, three-by-four-foot sitting space, six square feet of personal file and storage space, a walkway around the desk, and two feet to pull a chair out.[5] Sample layouts for desk and chair and computer terminal and storage space are provided in figures 2.6 and 2.7, p. 12. Space for shared equipment such as storage shelves, a computer terminal, and storage for office and clerical supplies is calculated separately. These spaces should be close to the user and storage areas. They should also provide enough separation from the public areas so that both the staff member and the public user will not be

12 / 2—FACILITIES PLANNING

disturbed. Proximity should allow for some surveillance of the public spaces. The lighting in these areas should be good; natural lighting is desirable. Standard electrical and communications outlets must be provided.

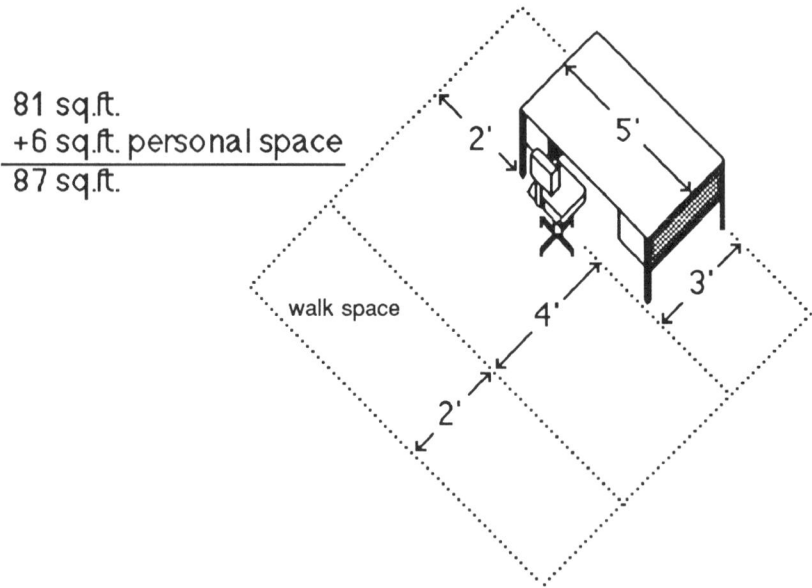

Figure 2.6. Diagram of space requirements for staff desk and chair.

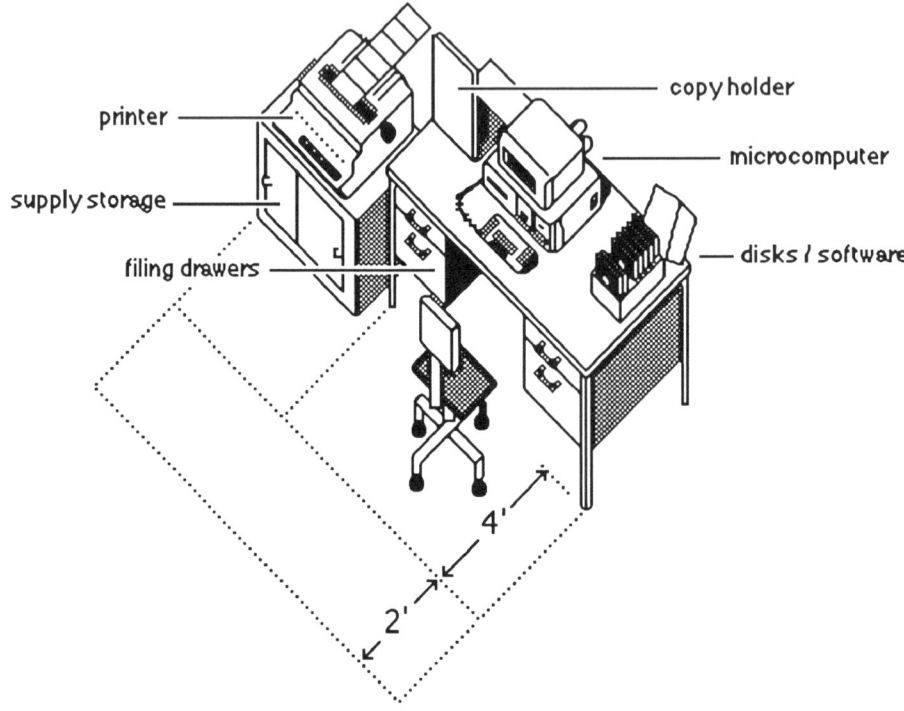

Figure 2.7. Diagram of space requirements for computer work station.

The *slide binding area* requires good light, clean air circulation, electrical outlets, storage space, opaque and lighted counter or table surfaces, and comfortable seating. This area should be easy to keep clean—dust- and clutter-free. It should be acoustically separate from other areas because conversation can be permitted. Lighted surfaces for slide mounting with storage cabinets below for supplies are required.

CURATOR'S OFFICE

The *curator's or administrator's office* should be no less than approximately 200 square feet, since this area will need to double as a conference room. Located to allow the curator the ability to oversee the collection storage, user, staff, and circulation areas, this room should also offer quiet and privacy when needed. Lighting should be the same as in the other user areas, and daylight is desirable. Built-in storage should include shelving and a cabinet or closet. There should be adequate space for several (at least two) letter-sized filing cabinets (each requiring eight and one-half square feet), an office-type desk and chair, seating for four to six people, a computer terminal and printer, a typewriter, viewing equipment, and sufficient electrical and communications outlets.

SUPPORT SPACE

A *darkroom or copy studio* is necessary if photographic services are to be performed by the staff. The nature and extent of the services will determine how much space and equipment are needed. Although it is not absolutely necessary that this area be housed within the visual resources collection, it is much more convenient and easier to supervise when the darkroom is adjacent to or within the visual resources collection area. Often in small operations, a single staff member may be assigned multiple tasks, including photography. To leave the area to do this work would be an inconvenience. Even when there is a designated photographer, it is far more efficient to have this work occurring at a location close to the other activities. A separate room where overhead lights can be regulated without disturbing other users, staff, or members is essential for copy photography.

A photographic darkroom for processing both slides and photographs should be at least nine by twelve feet in size, allowing for minimum cabinet space, a sink, and copy stand equipment. The door to the darkroom must be light-tight; a foyer preceding the actual darkroom provides an additional safeguard against light exposures. In situations that do not allow for the foyer space, a revolving light-tight door may be used. (See figure 2.8, p. 14, for an example of such a door.) Standard features should include electrical outlets, an exhaust fan, tungsten lights, running hot and cold water (with mixing valves for temperature control), and a safe light (if printing and developing are done). There should be a deep water-resistant counter surface for photograph printing, space for an enlarger and trays, a slide duplicator, a print drier, a copy stand, and lights, as well as over- and under-counter shelves and cabinets for supply storage. Floors should be water-resistant and the walls should be painted white to maximize illumination from the safe light. There should be space in an adjacent work room for a refrigerator to store film and dry chemicals, counter space for a slide viewer or sorter, and storage space for books and other work in progress. This should be a secure area because of the photographic equipment. If a separate copy stand is to be provided for outside users, an additional thirty square feet of space should be allocated in a secure area where lights can be individually controlled.

14 / 2—FACILITIES PLANNING

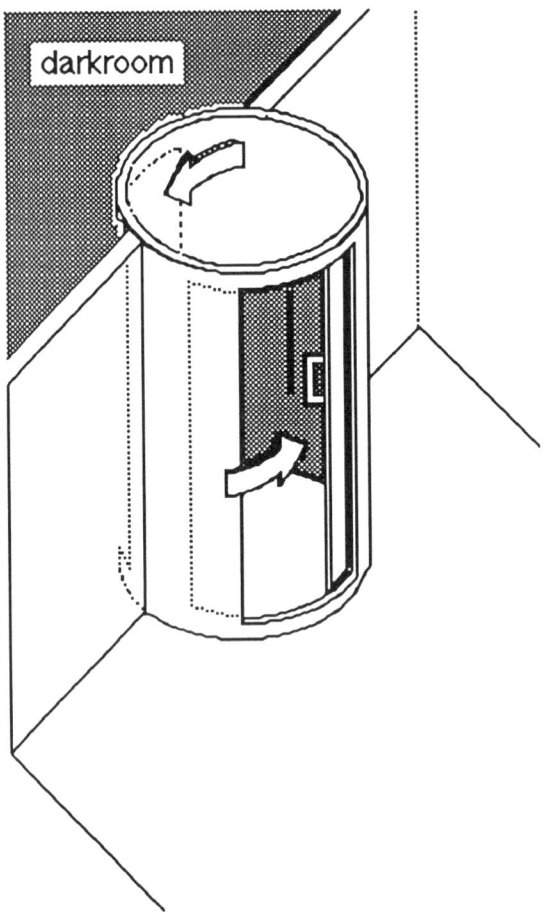

Figure 2.8. Diagram of a rotary darkroom door. From Kreolab Laboratory Systems, Inc., 715 E. 10th St., P.O. Box 2099, Wichita, KS 67201-2099.

If management of *audiovisual equipment* is the responsibility of the visual resources collection, space for its storage is necessary. The equipment may include slide and movie projectors, video equipment, overhead and opaque projectors, and even various kinds of camera equipment, as well as power extension cords, a supply of projection lamps, trays, and other accessories. Although there should be space at the circulation desk to store slide trays and some projection equipment, a larger, more secure area should be provided for the major part of the inventory of audiovisual equipment. From 100 to 300 square feet are needed, depending on extent of equipment housed. The storage area must be secure.

Having described all the activity areas and approximated their needed square footage, it is helpful to develop a summary of the spaces (see figure 2.9). This will help the architect or designer to understand size ratios and functional relationships before developing a floor plan.

GRAPHIC ANALYSIS OF ACTIVITY AREAS
SLIDE AND PHOTOGRAPH COLLECTION

1. **Circulation / Reference / information**
   - approximate square footage: .... _____
   - capacity reference books: .... _____
   - capacity card file: .... _____
   - anticipated square footage 5 years: .... _____
   - anticipated square footage 10 years: .... _____

2. **Slide Storage Area**
   - approximate square footage: .... _____
   - back-to-back slide file/rack
     storage capacity: .... _____
   - aisle space w/ table seating for: .... _____

3. **Slide User Area**
   - approximate square footage: .... _____
   - single carrel capacity-
     - assigned: .... _____
     - unassigned: .... _____
   - large slide sorter capacity-
     - assigned: .... _____
     - unassigned: .... _____
   - individual storage spaces: .... _____

4. **Photograph Storage Area**
   - approximate square footage: .... _____
   - back-to-back steel legal files
     for photo storage-
     capacity (10 sq.ft./legal file): .... _____

5. **User / Staff Photo Area**
   - approximate square footage: .... _____
   - a. work table space along outside
     walls; seating capacity: .... _____
   - b. work tables for processing and
     mounting photos: .... _____
   - c. staff desk: .... 100 sq.ft

6. **Staff Area Slide Collection:** approx. square footage:_____
7. **Copy Studio and Adjacent Work Area:** approx. square footage:_____
8. **Professional Curator's Office:** approx. square footage:_____

TOTAL SQUARE FEET:_____

Figure 2.9. Summary of spaces.

Development of a Physical Proximity and Accessibility Plan

Once the basic requirements and activities have been established, several techniques may be used to ensure a functional physical space that facilitates internal traffic flow and access to all areas. Flow charts, bubble diagrams, and access charts all serve to define relationships between areas. Figures 2.10 and 2.11 provide examples.

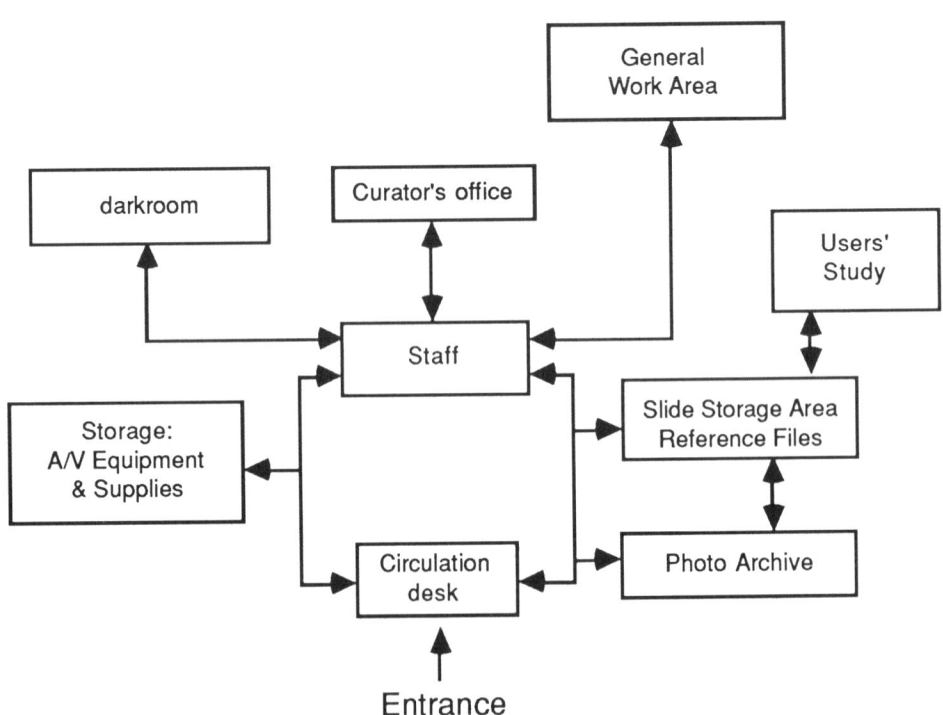

Figure 2.10. Flow chart defining spatial relationships.

Getting Started / 17

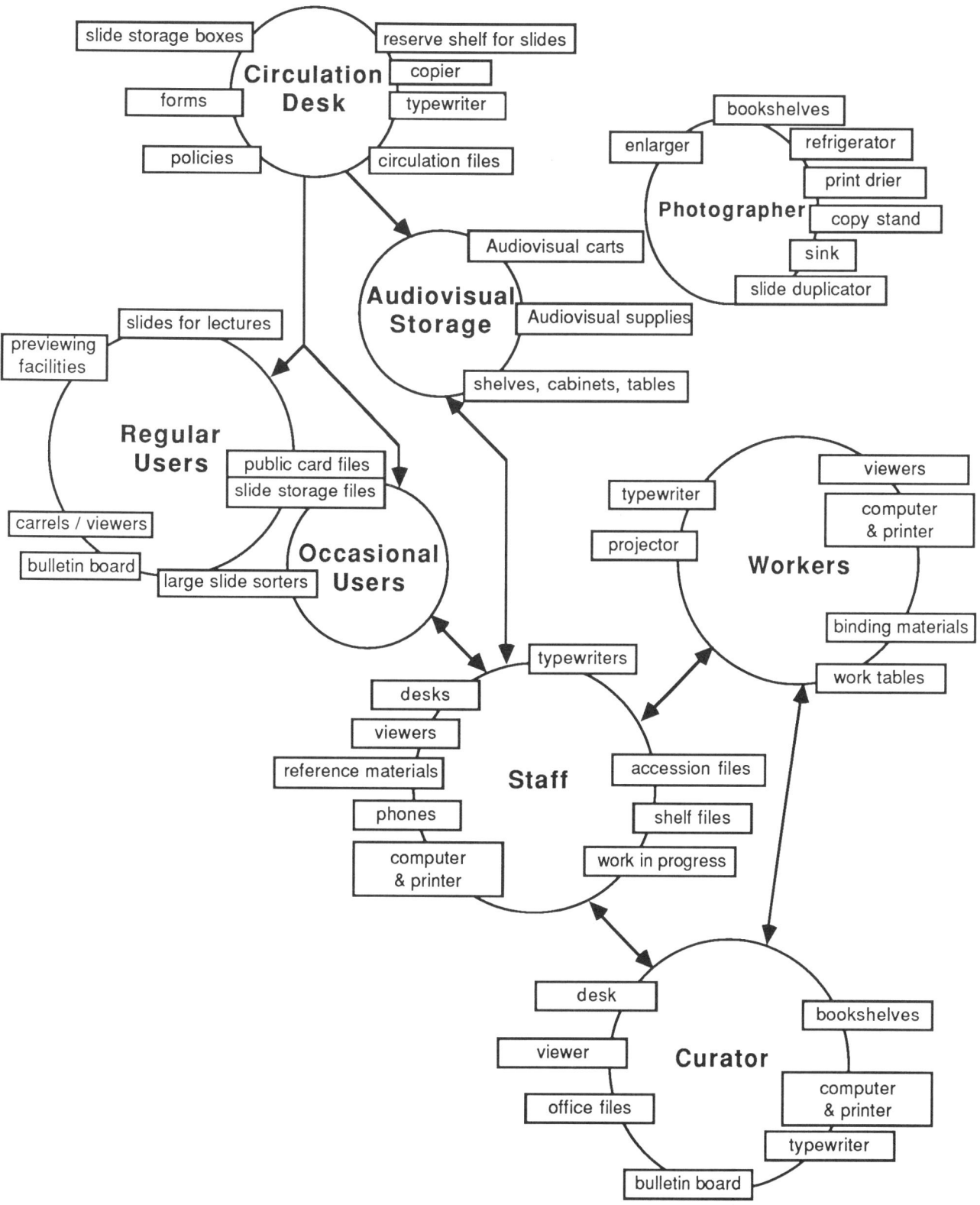

Figure 2.11. Bubble diagram defining spatial relationships as well as furniture and equipment associated with each area.

18 / 2 – FACILITIES PLANNING

Still another approach useful for relating visual resources collections spaces is the "charting method" developed by Richard Munther and John D. Wheeler to indicate relationships of various areas to each other.[6] A series of circles represents activity areas, which are then connected by a series of lines describing their relationship in space. Four connecting lines mean absolutely necessary proximity; three, necessary; two, not so important; one, not necessary. This enables the architect or designer to develop a sense for the essential services, and to decide which functions require proximity and which should be farther apart. It is also important that the arrangement of spaces promote efficient staffing. Beware of areas that may be difficult to supervise. Figure 2.12 is an example of the Munther charting method applied to a visual resources collection.

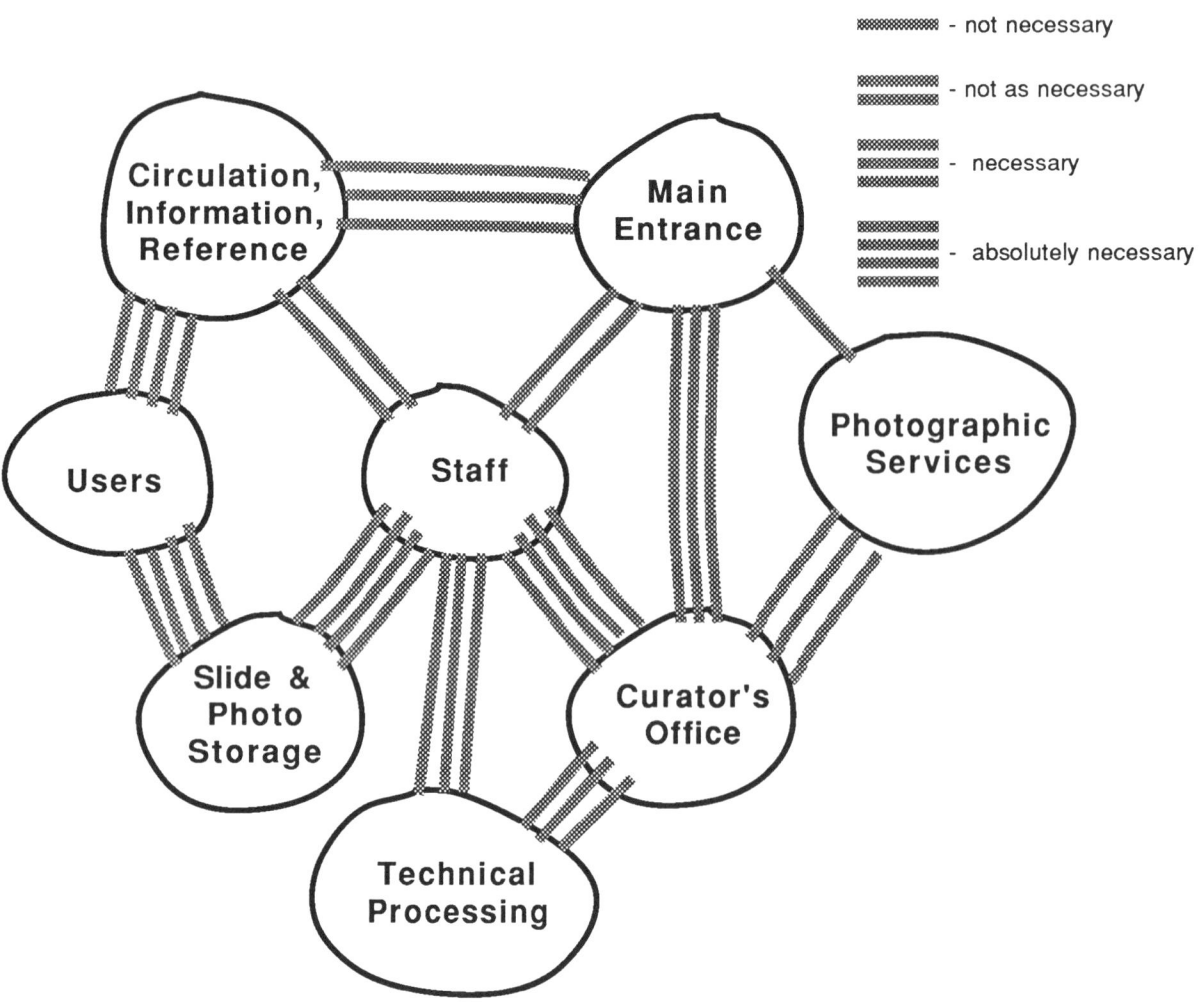

Figure 2.12. The Munther Charting method applied to a visual resources collection.

General Architectural Interior Features

The interior features of the space are a central part of the function and effect of the facility. Elements such as the *temperature control system, humidity, and ventilation* affect the comfort of the people who work in the visual resources collection as well as the well being of the items in the collection. Although safe storage of photographs and slides requires a temperature lower than comfortable for users and staff, a compromise of around 70 degrees Fahrenheit with relative humidity of around 50 percent can be achieved if planned for.[7] Specifications for a hydrothermograph should be included for permanent installation so that temperature and relative humidity conditions can be tracked continuously. It is important that air conditioning ducts are insulated so they do not produce condensation. Temperature should be regulated so that it is distributed evenly. Windows transmit heat and cold, and this should be considered in the planning. Exterior masonry walls should not be used inside because they transfer humidity. Placement of sprinkler systems should be noted.

Acoustics are important in a visual resources collection in which simultaneous activities require areas for quiet study, conversations, and equipment noise (printers, metal file drawers, typewriters, telephones, etc.). Control of noise in contiguous spaces can be effectively achieved with ceiling, wall, and floor coverings, as well as use of wood rather than metal furnishings where practical. Acoustical tile ceilings are standard in many public buildings. Carpeting for the floors may seem at first a luxury, but its advantages far outweigh its disadvantages. It is easier to maintain than other floor finishes, and in addition to reduced noise, carpet minimizes slide breakage. Nylon carpeting is extremely durable, but it can build up static in cold, dry weather, requiring antistatic treatment in the slide binding area. The pile height as well as use or omission of padding is of importance if rolling heavy equipment or carts is necessary in the carpeted areas.

Electricity is an important consideration in today's visual resources collections because of the use of equipment such as computers, mainframe terminals, audiovisual equipment, closed circuit television, copy machines, photographic equipment, drymount press, typewriters, and telephones. This requires advance planning for electrical, telephone, and computer cables which are run through walls, ceilings, floors, and columns.

Lighting is the third important element in visual resources planning. Light, heat, and relative humidity are factors that cause deterioration of photographic images.[8] Direct sunlight in areas where photographic images are displayed should be avoided entirely. Pure ultraviolet light passing through transparencies should be avoided. If fluorescent lights are to be used in ceilings of the visual resources collection, sleeves that filter ultraviolet light can be installed, though they alter color somewhat. Another option is to utilize lamps that emit low levels of ultraviolet light while still providing the needed color temperature and light quality. Also, plexiglass used on slide sorters or light tables can help in filtering ultraviolet light somewhat. The common use of fluorescent lighting is due to its high lumen output per watt of electricity, which makes it highly energy efficient; however, it must be filtered in areas where photographic materials are displayed.

Fire specifications should be discussed with the designers. Proper exits and alarms should be provided, as well as alternatives to ceiling sprinklers where film is stored. *Plumbing* requirements for the darkroom, such as hot and cold water supply, floor drains, sinks, and other features should be researched and determined in advance.

Access and security are also considerations to be discussed with the architect or designer. Access to the visual resources collection is often quite different than that to archives and book libraries. With careful planning it is possible to allow regular, security-approved users access to the slide storage areas while maintaining security for audiovisual equipment, the darkroom, and work in progress areas. Under these circumstances, security for the collection is an issue that must be handled separately.

Final Plan

The preceding analyses should be clearly defined and sufficiently developed before the actual design or arrangement is done. Such an analysis provides an objective foundation, the actual facts and figures that support the final decision making. The curator who has done this thorough "homework" will be prepared with the necessary tools for making effective decisions and suggestions.

Interior planning for the visual resources collection might be compared to factory planning on a small scale. There, the layouts require the best possible positioning of equipment and furnishings to produce the most functional results. One problem for the curator is that file cabinets for slides and photographs are basically uninteresting shapes. Designers may be tempted to rearrange slide file space by creating a layout in more interesting patterns. The results can be wasted space and arrangements that are confusing to users. Space is an important commodity; collections with little space for users, and confusing, illogical arrangements, discourage use (and consequently support).

20 / 2 – FACILITIES PLANNING

Flexibility is another important feature for the final plan. The most versatile shape for a visual resources collection is a square or large rectangle. Good lighting is easier to achieve within a square shape. The square shape minimizes walking, is easier to oversee from a central location, and is also simple to subdivide and rearrange. Designing a collection to occupy more than one level should be avoided.

The architect or designer usually makes the final plan; however, if the project is a small one, such as a renovation or simply relocation to a new space, the curator may have to take the responsibility. If so, the following steps can be helpful guides:

1. Make a scale drawing of the basic shape of the new space, using graph paper and a scale ruler.

2. Divide it into simple blocks for users, staff, and collection storage (i.e., the major activity areas).

3. Designate the entrance and establish traffic paths to the various areas.

Plans should be reviewed to assure that:

1. Handicapped requirements are met.

2. Locations for electrical, telephone, and computer outlets are functional.

3. Window placements do not create glare, direct sunlight where images will be used, or interfere where wall space is needed.

4. Doors are sufficiently wide to accommodate audiovisual equipment.

5. Lighting can be regulated as needed.

6. Security is adequate.

7. Environmental controls (heating, air conditioning, humidity, and pollution controls) will be sufficient to protect the collection.

All of these factors must be taken into consideration before construction begins. Changes which occur during construction require "change orders" which generally result in added cost.

When the final plans have been decided upon, the next job is to decide on locations for furniture and equipment and its coordination with electrical outlets, telephones, and lighting. Again, this may be done by the architect, but, if not, the curator must assume this responsibility. Using measurements provided by the manufacturers for the furniture and equipment to be used, make scale cut-outs for everything that will take up floor space. A computer software design program can make this process much easier. Extra space must be allowed for chairs to be pushed back from desks and tables, and for file drawers to be pulled open. This modeling process is tedious, but essential in planning for space, furniture, and equipment. For examples of how various collections have handled furniture placement and floor plans, see appendix A.

Furnishings and Equipment

An inventory of furniture and equipment to include both items to be purchased as well as items to be reused should be included as part of the planning. With the items to be purchased, a complete description, cost, and manufacturers' names and addresses should be included. A single inventory list of all electronic equipment to be purchased should also be prepared. Figure 2.13 is an example of a chart for an inventory of new and reusable equipment.

Factors to consider in furniture selection should include durability, function, and ease of maintenance. If carpet is used, its color should camouflage dirt. For chairs and tables, sharp or brittle corners that will either snag clothing or chip should be avoided. The curator also should know exactly what types of user and staff furniture exist and what should be ordered. Figure 2.14, p. 22, is designed to aid in outlining this information.

Equipment Inventory Diagram

EQUIPMENT DESCRIPTION	EXISTING QUANTITY	QUANTITY NEEDED	NUMBER OF STAFF USERS	NUMBER OF COLL. USERS	COMMENTS
35 mm projectors					
16mm projectors					
overheads					
videocassette recorders					
videodisk player and monitor					
microfiche readers					
microfilm readers					
copystands					
typewriters					
microcomputers					
terminals					
carrels					
large sorters					
light tables					

Figure 2.13. Sample chart for inventory of needed and reusable equipment.

Furniture Inventory Diagram

EQUIPMENT DESCRIPTION	EXISTING QUANTITY	QUANTITY NEEDED	NUMBER OF STAFF USERS	NUMBER OF COLL. USERS	COMMENTS
desk (size)					
work table (size)					
bookcase (size)					
file cabinets (legal-size)					
file cabinets (letter-size)					
file cabinets (lateral)					
credenza					
chairs (executive)					
chairs (secretarial)					
computer desk					
typing table					
bases for files					
carrels					
slide storage files					
storage cabinets					

Figure 2.14. Sample chart for inventory of needed and reusable furniture.

Getting Started / 23

From these inventories the final, complete list of furniture and equipment to be purchased can be established. The list should be alphabetical by item and contain complete specifications and prices. Because revisions must often be done, each inventory produced should be dated. A helpful extension of this is an alphabetical listing of the names, addresses, and telephone numbers of each supplier and what each is supplying (see figure 2.15). This serves as a handy reference not only in the planning stages, but in the future for servicing and reordering.

Name of Institution
Department
Collection Name
Furniture & Equipment Specifications
Prepared by:_____
Date:_____

NAME OF ITEM (list in alphabetical order)	DESCRIPTION (include sizes, model numbers, manufacturers & addresses, etc.)	PRICES (include discounts)

Figure 2.15. Sample format for furniture and equipment specifications.

Moving In

The floor plan of the new space, showing furniture and equipment placement, will be a valuable guide on moving day. Copies should be supplied to the movers and staff supervisors before the move. Added to it should be general area designations (e.g., audiovisual storage, work area, photo work room, photo collection, etc.) where furniture and equipment to be reused from the old facility will be placed. Those pieces of furniture and equipment should each be tagged with their respective destinations. It takes several days of planning and preparation to accomplish this. Depending upon the kind of slide storage units, some can be moved while full and others, such as rack units, cannot. The cabinets moved while full must be securely taped closed and numbered sequentially as they are to be stacked so that restacking can be accurate. (See figure 2.16, p. 24, for the numbering of storage files for moving and restacking.) Supplies as well as contents of each staff member's work area must be boxed and labeled for their area destinations. Items to be stored or discarded should be marked accordingly. Staff members should be assigned posts in both old and new facilities to give directions to the movers. For the new facility, all locations for furniture and equipment should be decided in advance to prevent movers having to place items more than once.

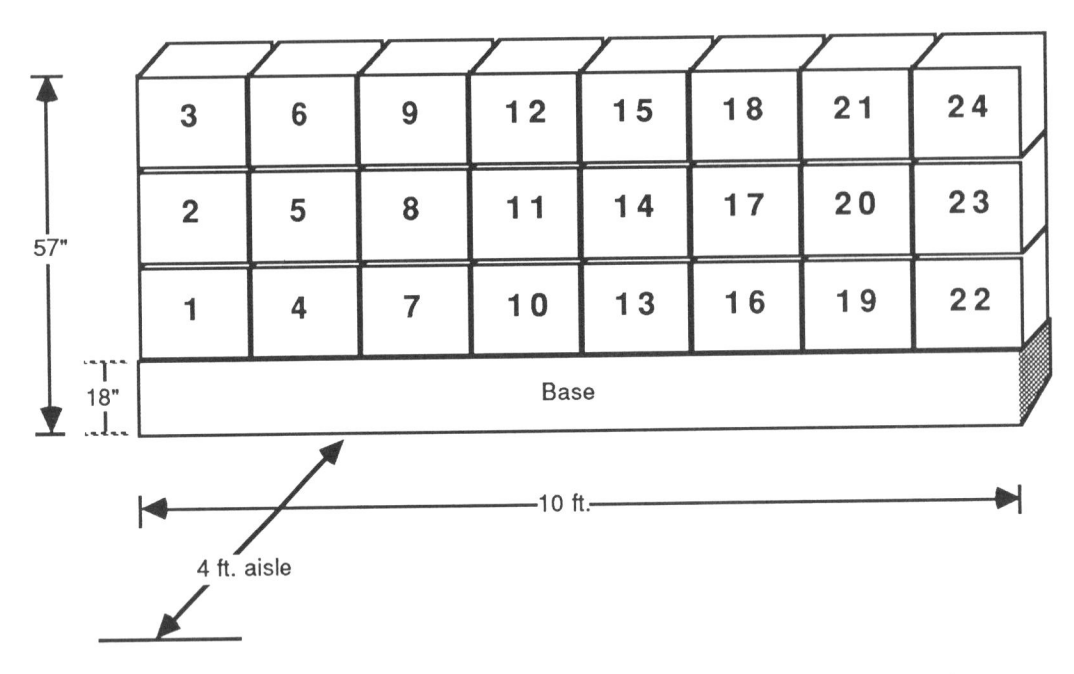

Figure 2.16. Diagram of drawer-type slide storage files numbered for moving and restacking.

CRITIQUE OF PHYSICAL FACILITY

After a set period of time following the occupancy of the new facility, an evaluation with the architect or designer is useful. For some projects, funds are set aside to rectify problems that surface after move-in day. A checklist for evaluating a new facility follows.

1. Tour the visual resources collection as if you were a user, asking yourself the following questions and doing the following:
   — Is the collection easy to find; are there directional signs?
   — Upon entering, is an information point easy to find?
   — Are reference aids for using the collection readily available?
   — Is it easy to figure out how to find slides, photographs, work space, etc.?
   — Visit with collection users.
   — Visit with staff.

2. View the facility from the aspect of a staff member.
   — Is it easy to see users entering the visual resources collection and needing help?
   — Is there one clearly marked entrance/exit?
   — Is the view down the slide storage aisles clear?
   — Are the reference files and books in a convenient location?
   — Can staff perform reference, orientation, and check-out functions from one work station?
   — Is there adequate storage and counter space at this staff location?
   — Can staff efficiently assist users with audiovisual equipment?

— Is it possible for staff to work quietly while supervising the user area?
— Is there a place where staff can have privacy for work or conferences?

If the answers to most of these questions are positive, the facilities planning program has served its purpose.

NOTES

[1] Christine Sundt, Letter to author, 13 August 1987.

[2] Aaron Cohen and Elaine Cohen, *Designing and Space Planning for Libraries: A Behavioral Guide* (New York: Bowker, 1979), 89.

[3] Ibid., 91.

[4] Nolan Lushington and Willis N. Mills, Jr., *Libraries Designed for Users, a Planning Handbook* (Hamden, CT: Library Professional Publications, 1980), 182.

[5] Cohen and Cohen, *Designing and Space Planning for Libraries*, 82.

[6] Richard Munther and John D. Wheeler, *Simplified Systematic Layout Planning* (Kansas City, MO: Management and Industrial Research Publications, 1977).

[7] Eastman Kodak, *Preservation of Photographs* (Rochester, NY: Eastman Kodak, 1979), 24.

[8] Ibid.

3
Budgeting

The budget is a translation of the plans, goals, and the staff required into financial terms; it is a pragmatic statement of services, activities, and their costs. Obtaining, managing, and maintaining an adequate budget for the visual resources collection is one of the most significant administrative duties of the curator. The budget request should originate with the person responsible for carrying it out once approval is given, that is, the visual resources curator. The budget request is based upon the specified missions and goals set for the collection, and is the management tool with which to control, develop, and coordinate each year's activities.

It is necessary to implement sound budgetary procedures such as proposals, reports, and allocations in order to assert the role of the visual resources collection as a functional member of the departmental (or other administrative unit) budgeting structure, as well as to foster operational and administrative efficiency. Every visual resources collection curator is responsible for being well informed on current budgeting practices for developing financial plans to match the level of service expected. Although each situation is unique, this chapter will present several techniques that may be employed to aid the curator in successful budget planning.

To begin the development of a budget, accurate knowledge not only of the missions and goals developed for the collection, but also of current and past activities and expenses is necessary. The maintenance of detailed records of expenses will facilitate budget preparation and facilitate accurate projections of future expenses. It is important to be able to refer to previous budgets from the past several years.

BUDGET SYSTEMS

Described here are four budget systems frequently utilized in business as well as in nonprofit organizations such as libraries and archives that may easily be adapted for use in visual resources collections. There are other types of budget systems, but these seem particularly well suited to visual resources collections.

The *lump sum budget* is one in which a flat sum is presented to the curator, who then is responsible for managing it to meet the needs of the collection. Although entirely flexible, it provides no accountability in terms of how the funds are to be used.

The *line item budget* is a commonly used system due to the ease with which one year's expenses can be compared with those of the past or future. It is based on categories in which expenses are made. Figure 3.1 is an example of a visual resources line item budget. This type of budget can be designed to summarize a four-year expense period, covering two years past, the current year, and the request for the coming year. It is necessary to develop line item categories for the expenses incurred annually. See figure 3.2 for a sample four-year line item budget.

1.0 Supplies & Materials

    1.1 Collection development: Commercial sources
    1.2 Collection development: In-house photography
    1.3 General supplies
    1.4 Audiovisual expenditures
    1.5 Services & repairs
    1.6 Computer software & supplies

2.0 Personnel

    2.1 Permanent staff
    2.2 Hourly, temporary staff

3.0 Capital Expenditures

    3.1 Audiovisual equipment
    3.2 Storage files
    3.3 Typewriters
    3.4 Computers
    3.5 Other furniture

Figure 3.1. Line item budget.

Item #	Description	Expenditures 1985-86	Expenditures 1986-87	Expenditures 1987-88	Expenditures 1988-89	Request 1988-89
1.0	Supplies & Materials	$	$	$	$	$
1.1	Collection development: Commercial sources					
1.2	Collection development: In-house photography					
1.3	General supplies					
1.4	Audiovisual expenditures					
1.5	Services & repairs					
1.6	Computer software & supplies					
2.0	Personnel	$	$	$	$	$
2.1	Permanent staff					
2.2	Hourly, temporary staff					
3.0	Capital Expenditures	$	$	$	$	$
3.1	Audiovisual equipment					
3.2	Storage files					
3.3	Typewriters					
3.4	Computers					
3.5	Other furniture					

Figure 3.2. Four-year line item budget.

28 / 3—BUDGETING

Line item budgets focus on "resources, not results."[1] They do not describe what services or other results were achieved with the money expended. However, an asset to the line item budget is its infinite flexibility and ease of expansion. For example, a general line for materials may be utilized as a whole, or may be subdivided into binding supplies, clerical supplies, reference materials, printed materials, etc. A general line for personnel can be used, or it can be subdivided into narrower categories such as clerical, technical, professional, hourly, etc. Another flexible feature is that although you may underspend in the professional subdivision and overspend in the clerical, it will not matter so long as the total allocation for personnel is not surpassed.

The *program budget*, unlike the line item budget, focuses on direct results, showing the outcome achieved with the money spent. With the program budget it is possible to show how much each service costs. The program budget incorporates the line item budget format into a grid of visual resources collection services and activities. Each service or function has line item amounts assigned to it for the resources required.

The advantage of the program budget is that it tells more, i.e., coordinates funds and functions. It is extremely useful when expansions of activities or services are being considered. If charges are made for specific services, it identifies what the charge needs to be. This type of budget system is useful for developing a budget for special projects or grants. Figure 3.3 represents a sample program budget.

Activities / Programs

Line Items:	Audiovisual services	Photographic services	Circulation	Slide Binding
1.0 1.1 1.2 1.3 1.4 1.5 1.6				
2.0 2.1 2.2				
3.0 3.1 3.2 3.3 3.4 3.5				
Totals:				

Figure 3.3. Program base budget.

The *zero base budget* is particularly useful in times of financial stress when cut-backs must be made. The zero base budget requires that the cost of each program or activity (current and proposed) be justified at the beginning of each fiscal year. Programs and their costs are arranged in priority order, from top to bottom. All programs that fall below the point on the list where the total funds available run out are dropped. This requires that each new budget be started from scratch annually and each activity and service be evaluated each year and then either be approved as submitted, approved with increased funding, decreased funding, or cut. Figure 3.4 represents a proposal for a zero base budget for audiovisual activities.

Priority	Unit: Audiovisual Services	Full-time employed Staff	Supplies	Amount
1.	Services and equipment for scheduled classes.	.40	$	$
2.	Circulation of equipment to occasional users.	.10	$	$
3.	Services for special programs and lectures.	.05	$	$
4.	Services to other departments.	.05	$	$
5.	Videotape special lectures.	.25	$	$
6.	Projection services for weekly film series.	.05	$	$

Figure 3.4. Zero base budget for audiovisual services.

The zero base budget is particularly useful if you do not have objective data available from past years on which to base a budget proposal. However, once done, it is very time consuming to have to repeat this entire procedure annually.

TYPES OF EXPENSES

The annual expenses are usually divided into three areas: (1) operating expenses, (2) capital expenses, and (3) specially designated expenses. Again, it is important to know just how the administrative budgeting unit to which the visual resources collection reports defines each of these categories.

Operating expenses usually include personnel (both permanent and hourly), materials and supplies, and services. Items for the collection such as slides, photographs, videotapes, films, reference materials, or computer software may be assigned to this category, or designated as capital expenses (described below) depending upon administrative policy. In some cases the division may not be so distinct, with some capital expenses being taken from operating expenses and some from capital budget.

As cost effectiveness and financial accountability become increasingly important, the curator must be able to produce sufficient justifications for programs and activities. The maintenance of unit cost figures and production rate records provide a tangible basis for decision making. The *unit cost* is an average cost determined by dividing a specific cost figure by the total of services delivered. For example, the total salaries of filers divided by the number of slides circulated equals the unit cost of slide circulation. Figure 3.5, p. 30, demonstrates how unit costs are determined.

A *cost group* is a concept for gathering costs for a particular work group or activity, such as slide binding, slide filing, or photographic services. All the costs (materials and salaries) associated with this work group are gathered to produce an accurate account of total costs involved in carrying out the work of the group. Figure 3.6, p. 30, illustrates how cost groups are calculated.

Capital outlay refers to items of long-term use, such as audiovisual equipment, furniture, light tables, slide and/or photograph storage files, card files, computer terminals, microcomputer hardware, typewriters, and expenses for physical plant improvements or remodeling. Sometimes the distinction between operating and capital expenses is made between expendable versus nonexpendable supplies. However, this cannot be used literally because, for example, slide projectors do have a limited life span.

30 / 3—BUDGETING

$$\frac{\text{Unit cost}}{\text{Total services delivered} \overline{)\text{Total cost of services}}}$$

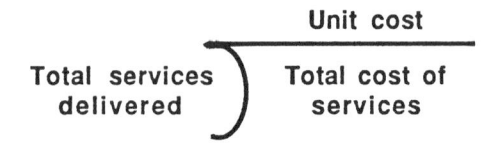

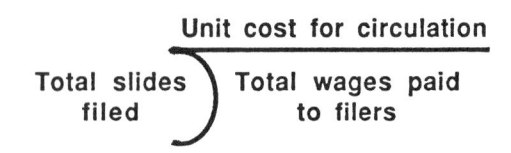

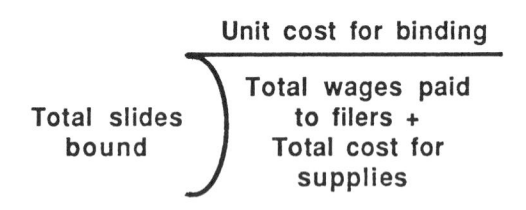

$$\frac{\text{Unit cost for circulation}}{\text{Total slides filed} \overline{)\text{Total wages paid to filers}}}$$

$$\frac{\text{Unit cost for binding}}{\text{Total slides bound} \overline{)\text{Total wages paid to filers + Total cost for supplies}}}$$

Figure 3.5. Unit costs.

The costs of binding materials for year: _____

Binder's salary for year + _____

Total cost of binding slides: _____

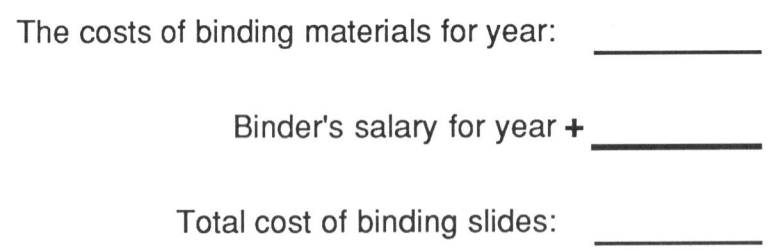

Figure 3.6. Method to calculate cost groups.

This distinction introduces the subject of capitalization and depreciation. "*Capitalization* is a system designated to handle items purchased that would give value for a number of years in the future."[2] When equipment is purchased, it is necessary to establish the useful life of that item. (This is usually available from the manufacturer.) Then the purchase price of that item is prorated over its years of useful life. This annual purchase price write off is called *depreciation*. (Figure 3.7 describes how annual depreciation is determined.)

$$\frac{\text{depreciation / year}}{\text{Years of useful life} \overline{)\text{total purchase price}}}$$

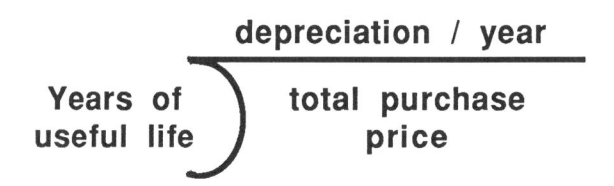

Figure 3.7. Calculation of capitalization and depreciation for capital expenses.

If a visual resources collection does not capitalize and depreciate its audiovisual equipment purchases, but rather reports them in full in the year that the equipment is purchased, a somewhat distorted view of the costs of running the collection is given. Most libraries capitalize and depreciate audiovisual equipment, other equipment, and furniture, and many do so for books (useful life of three to ten years[3]) as well. Visual resources collections should consider the budgetary merits of this same practice for slides and photographs (perhaps a useful life of seven to twelve years for slides). Even with today's more stable color transparency films that declare a shelf life of forty to fifty years, it is unrealistic to suggest that with the heavy use that many color slides receive in collections used primarily for teaching the shelf life will be that long.

Categorical or designated funds should be reported in the budget, but are handled somewhat differently from the others discussed. These are funds with designated purposes, such as grants, endowments, or donations. These may also be funding received for exceptions to the budget that arise and for which outside funding must be sought. Therefore, these funds are designated for a specific, often one-time-only purpose and should be reported separately.

Making projections must always play a part in any budget planning. It is necessary in doing this to obtain all the information possible regarding uses of budgeted money over the past two years and the current year. In addition to the information compiled in the four-year line item budget diagram, it is necessary to know both the approved budget and the final budget (they are usually *not* the same). The approved budget shows what was authorized, and the final, what was actually spent. In making these projections, consideration must be given to whether or not programs and activities requiring visual resources collection services are going to continue to increase. Do the statistics for visual resources activities reflect activities or services that are declining or increasing which will make it impossible to reduce or increase a service's line?

Staff input is not to be overlooked as a source for information on demands for services, collection development, and equipment. Information on increases in costs for supplies and equipment can be obtained from vendors and other suppliers. It might be useful to find out if the sponsoring institution has official guidelines for inflation and acceptable levels for budget increases. This information can also be useful in projecting salaries. As all these data are brought together for each line item, they become the foundation for the new budget proposal.

In dealing with expenses, one other factor merits discussion: fixed and variable costs. *Fixed costs* are those committed over a long-range period, usually more than one fiscal year. For example, fixed costs are salaries, service contracts, and depreciation of capital equipment. *Variable costs* increase or decrease in proportion to the volume of activity. It is useful to understand which line items are fixed and which are variable in order to be able to make reductions when necessary.

DEVELOPMENT OF A COST ACCOUNTING SYSTEM

In formulating a budget, one of the most important resources is information regarding past expenditures. It is vital to have an accurate method for recording data. The documents for reporting expenses such as work orders, purchase requests, purchase vouchers, shipping receipts, invoices, time sheets, personnel appointment records, expense account records, and travel requests are often retained outside the visual resources collection. It is important, therefore, for the curator to develop a simple accounting system for accurately recording costs each year. Such a system provides data for use in budgeting as well as cost control. It can provide a basis for management decisions. It also provides an audit record.

Since most visual resources collections have maximum budgets that cannot be exceeded, and because they are usually part of larger bureaucracies, purchases are not direct, across the counter transactions. Rather, the curator, after determining specifications for an item and its approximate cost, turns the actual purchasing over to another agent. The item is delivered at a later time, with the final cost often differing from the original cost estimate. For this reason, an *encumbering accounting system* is useful. This method reserves costs or expenses that are committed but not yet expended, and therefore minimizes the chances of overspending the budget. Care must be taken to delete encumbered amounts when the actual charge is entered in order not to double charge. The curator may want to set up a notebook for maintaining records of expenditures. Figure 3.8, p. 32, is a sample diagram of an encumbering system.

32 / 3—BUDGETING

Item Description	Quantity	Area Source	date encumbered	amount encumbered	date received	freight	actual amount	Balance
slide mounts	7,000	Ace Supply	8/5/88	$1,252.00	10/2/88	$8.00	$1299.68	$13,100.00
slide files	3	Education Aids	8/5/88	$525.00	10/7/88	$21.00	$546.00	$12,554.46

Figure 3.8. Sample encumbrance accrual system.

A similar system can be developed for hourly employee salaries as well. If the budget for such wages is allocated for the entire fiscal year, but the need for hourly help fluctuates throughout the year, it is useful to be able to plan in advance for the entire year so as not to expend the total allocation before the year's end. Figure 3.9 represents a diagram for recording the part-time employee expenditures.

Total Budget:$_____

Name	Title/Duty	Hourly Wage	Total Hours (month; semester)	Total allocation	Balance

Figure 3.9. Encumbrance system for hourly or part-time staff.

BUDGET PLANNING CYCLE

In preparing the budget presentation, it is helpful to become familiar with the budget system of the administrative unit. It is also necessary to understand how the visual resources collection unit relates to the overall budget unit and its importance to the users. Administrators are looking not only for the total funds requested, but also for the benefits that will come to the users. The curator is responsible for adequate funding to the collection and also for meeting the *real* needs of the users.

The curator may be asked to submit a budget in writing or appear for an annual budget interview. In either case, the budget request should be condensed into a format that concisely represents the requirements of the collection. This aspect of budgeting is highly individual and variable; however, in budget presentation, the curator should consider the following points:

Are the administrators interested in every minute detail of the budget, or would a broadly categorized budget be more appropriate? (Remember it is easier to cut budget items that are listed separately. If materials are itemized too specifically, the budget administrator may take issue with some items and cut them. If it is known that the budget is to be reduced by a certain percentage, it may be advantageous to lump some items together so that cuts can be across the board and the curator can then decide which items to cut.)

Is the format of the budget in accordance with the overall budget format used within the institution or the budget unit?

Are the amounts requested reasonable within the overall framework of the department or budget unit? Are they too high, or too low?

If funding requested is approved, will the collection deliver the services and results promised? In other words, is the budget requested realistic?

The actual budget preparation cycle should be in progress throughout the entire year. This mission involves many aspects of the daily routine of the visual resources curator. The time when the final presentation is due may vary; however, the curator can save a great deal of last minute pressure if the production of the budget request is spread out throughout a longer portion of the year. The flow chart represented in figure 3.10 is a recommended schedule for a fiscal year beginning September 1.

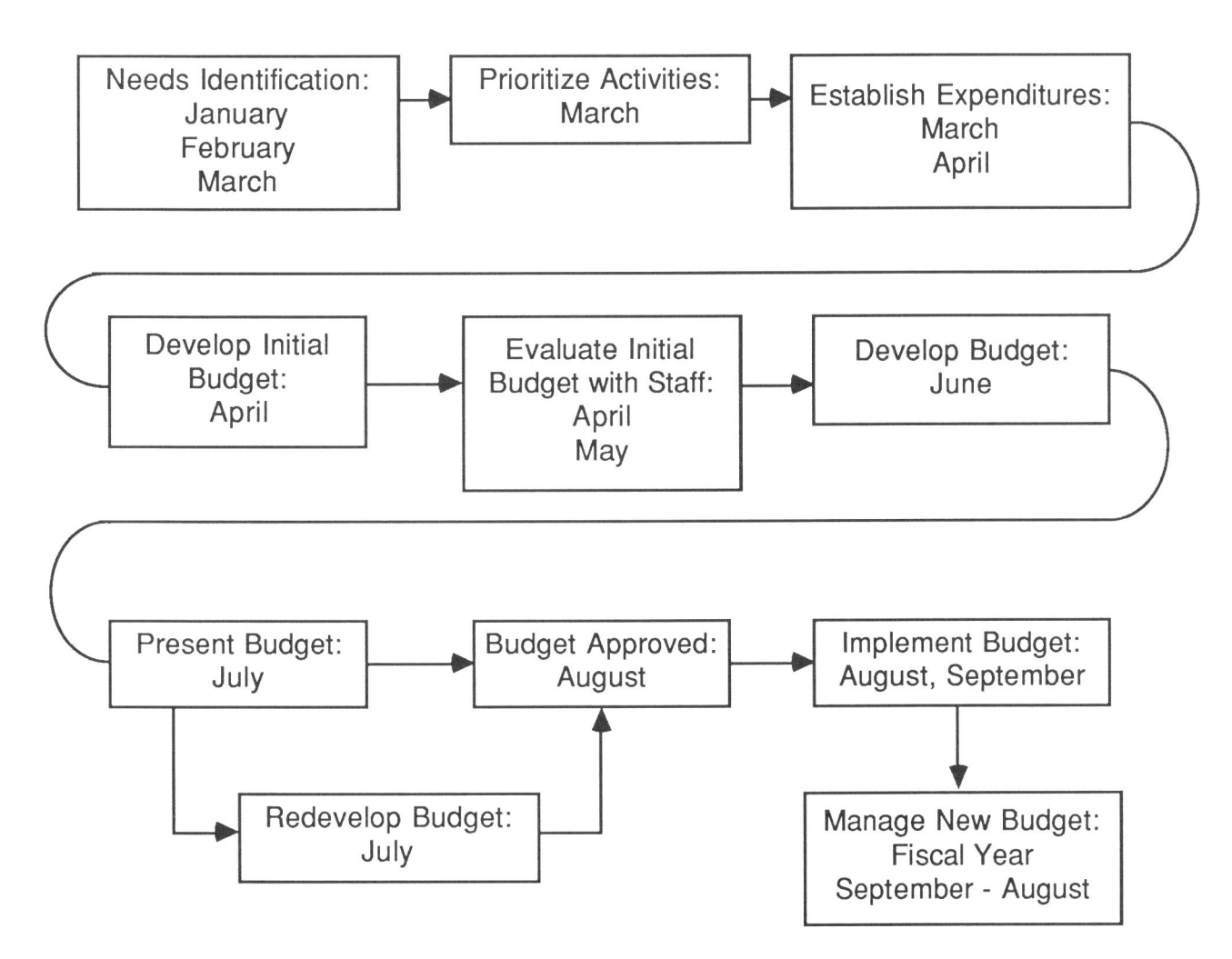

```
Needs Identification:        Prioritize Activities:      Establish Expenditures:
   January          ──▶           March           ──▶           March
   February                                                      April
   March

Develop Initial              Evaluate Initial            Develop Budget:
  Budget:         ──▶        Budget with Staff:  ──▶         June
   April                         April
                                 May

Present Budget:              Budget Approved:            Implement Budget:
    July           ──▶            August          ──▶     August, September
     │                             ▲                             │
     ▼                             │                             ▼
Redevelop Budget: ─────────────────┘                      Manage New Budget:
    July                                                     Fiscal Year
                                                          September - August
```

Figure 3.10. Annual budget cycle: Flowchart.

The advantages gained through a *personal budget interview* definitely outweigh the anxiety experienced by the curator who must do it. The purpose of such a presentation is to provide decision makers with information about the proposal. The personal interview allows two-way communication and is an excellent way to assure that the administrators understand the visual resources collection programs and the funding requirements. Administrators' questions can be addressed directly. This interview is a prime opportunity to promote the importance of the visual resources collection in the overall program and to influence decisions.

MANAGING THE BUDGET

As stated earlier, the budget is a management tool which, for one thing, helps reduce expenditure decision making during the fiscal year. In managing the budget, the curator must spend the appropriated funds in the way proposed. It is prudent to spend all the funds allocated so as not to suggest to administrators that there were miscalculations or errors in the budget presentation. Such actions might adversely affect future budget requests. To overspend reflects inadequate management and can also be illegal. The curator is obligated to spend the allocated funds as proposed in the budget.

USE OF MICROCOMPUTERS FOR BUDGETING

What has been presented in charts for recording expenditures and costs, etc., can also be handled with a computer spreadsheet software program. The computer can be effectively employed only *after* all the planning and data gathering has taken place, however. If the concepts are not already clear, the use of a computer spreadsheet program cannot improve the budget process. However, once established manually, the budget process is one that repeats itself each year and, therefore, the computer will eliminate much repetitious work for the curator.

NOTES

[1] Margo C. Trumpeter and Richard S. Rounds, *Basic Budgeting Practices for Libraries* (Chicago: American Library Association, 1985), 44.

[2] Inez L. Ramsey and Jackson E. Ramsey, *Library Planning and Budgeting* (New York: Watts, 1986), 25-26.

[3] Ibid., 27.

4
Staffing

The first part of this chapter describes the categories of staffing generally required in the visual resources collection. Included are the activity divisions requiring staff as well as the duties and responsibilities associated with each. The second section deals with many of the administrative responsibilities associated with staffing performed by the curator of the visual resources collection. Issues such as selecting the right staff, effective interviewing, job descriptions, performance standards, training, supervising, evaluating, using volunteers, and communications will be considered.

Many visual resource collections have developed randomly, relying on faculty members, part-time clerical staff, or students for management. Unfortunately, as such collections increased in size, services, and users, makeshift staffing patterns continued. If the expanding functions, objectives, and holdings had been analyzed along the way, the need for a full-time professional curator as well as permanent staffing patterns would have been evident. Today, the problems of understaffing, reliance on temporary, part-time help, and lack of professional recognition are shadows cast by earlier practices and constitute one of the most prevalent problems faced by visual resources professionals today.

The problems of chronic understaffing were first officially confirmed in a Mid-America College Art Association (MACAA) staffing survey in 1977.[1] This survey recorded multiple staffing combinations of full-time professional, technical, clerical, graduate, and undergraduate student assistants. The most revealing aspect of the study showed that the staffing solution for larger collections was not addition of permanent full-time staff, but increasing numbers of part-time, temporary help. Clearly, the collection that has reached a certain size and complexity (over 30,000 slides) and is still managed by part-time temporary students is not being managed effectively. The situation can lead to inconsistency, lack of continuity in the work produced, and increasing opportunities for errors and collection losses. Valuable time is wasted in having to continuously recruit and train the constantly changing part-time staff, resulting in inefficient and ineffective overall operations.

The success of any visual resources collection is dependent upon its staff: their knowledge, skills, and attitudes. The staff members are the people with whom the users meet and deal. The logical consequence of this fact is that each curator's success can be measured in the level of talent selected for the staff.

STAFFING CATEGORIES

Staffing patterns vary in visual resources collections depending upon the type and size of the collection, administration or governance, funding levels, and the technical resources available to the collection. Throughout the profession, there is considerable contrast in the ratio of professionals to nonprofessionals, definitions of duties and responsibilities, and the use of specialists. Since the visual resources collection is a production as well as a service facility, the importance of a staffing balance of professional, technical, and clerical personnel for maximum effectiveness needs to be recognized.

36 / 4—STAFFING

Staffing for visual resources collections falls into three distinct categories: administrative and professional or curatorial, clerical or general, and technical (see figure 4.1). The chief curator or director of the collection usually handles both administrative and professional/curatorial duties. Assistant or associate curators devote most of their time to professional/curatorial duties such as collection development, reference, research, and cataloging. Clerical/general employees handle the major volume of typing and/or data entry, circulation activities, slide and photographic mounting or sleeving, and filing, while the technical services staff handles photographic, audiovisual, and computer services.

```
┌─────────────────────────────┐  ┌──────────────────────────┐  ┌──────────────────────┐
│            I.               │  │           II.            │  │         III.         │
│      Administrative &       │  │    Technical Category    │  │   Clerical / General │
│  Professional / Curatorial  │  │                          │  │       Category       │
│          Category           │  │  A. Photographic Services│  │                      │
│                             │  │  B. Audiovisual Services │  │                      │
│  A. General Administrative &│  │  C. Computer Services    │  │                      │
│     Management Duties       │  └──────────────────────────┘  └──────────────────────┘
│  B. General Professional /  │
│     Curatorial duties       │
└─────────────────────────────┘
```

Figure 4.1. Staffing categories for visual resources collections.

In a small collection, one or two individuals may perform duties related to all categories; as the size and services of the collection expand in numbers and complexity, increasing staff specialization occurs. In planning for staffing, it is important to establish the activities required to operate the visual resources collection and to distinguish between those that are considered professional and those that are not. This is a useful method for informing administrators of the qualities, knowledge, and experience necessary for positions in different categories of visual resources collection work.

Administrative and Professional/ Curatorial Category

According to Neal Harlow, "professional responsibility is broad in scope, inherently intellectual, resting on a general body of knowledge, attitude and skills, and including integrity, competence, objectivity, initiative, and service."[2] Most visual resources curators would agree that this accurately describes what is expected of them.

The administrative and professional duties are generally those which involve the ability to exercise independent judgment, based on understanding of the techniques and procedures of visual resources collections management as well as the principles of the sponsoring administrative unit. Although these techniques can be taught to a nonprofessional, the adequate performance of the full range of professional duties requires professional judgment and a thorough understanding of the principles and objectives of each duty and its function in relation to the overall purpose of the collection. Professional duties carry a lot of pure administration and management, but professional knowledge of and experience in visual resources collections and the subject matter collected are essential in making wise decisions. The amount of experience required depends upon the size and type of the collection, and the specific needs of its users.

The assignment of duties can have a bearing on how satisfied staff (particularly curatorial and professional) are with their work. A widespread complaint is that too much time must be spent on duties they feel are below their ability level. Professional/curatorial staff should have adequate support staff to avoid this problem.

Staffing recommendations must be based on careful job evaluations. Following are the functions common to visual resources collections, categorized according to administrative and general professional/ curatorial.

GENERAL ADMINISTRATIVE DUTIES

To oversee and direct all aspects of the visual resources collection.

To interpret and clarify aims and objectives: this includes communication with users, participation in meetings such as a visual resources policy committee, and conferences with administrators.

To formulate policies and procedures: this involves translating objectives into plans and policies; developing new activities; planning priorities for new media formats, cost considerations, and space development; planning budgets; producing records, reports, statistics, and policies for circulation and other services such as photographic and audiovisual, computers, etc.

To expedite policy, organization, and management: this entails dividing activities to take advantage of staff specialties; supervising services such as computer, audiovisual, and photography; planning and organizing collection storage, user, and staff areas; and selecting supplies, furnishings, and equipment.

To manage personnel: this requires defining, describing, and reviewing jobs within the collection; determining duties, special knowledge, and skills required; recruiting; interviewing, and selecting staff from field of applicants; overseeing training and development; maintaining personnel records, doing performance evaluations; determining standards expected; handling disciplinary actions; producing staff manuals; holding staff meetings; assigning work; communicating administrative decisions to staff; supervising staff schedules and assessing work loads; and approving requests for leaves and vacations.

To promote public relations: this involves composing, designing, and editing miscellaneous printed materials such as collection policies and procedures; participating in professional activities nationally; conducting orientations and tours of the collection; and promoting communication.

To engage in self-development: this covers research and publication in the field, maintenance of memberships in professional organizations, and attendance at professional meetings and continuing education seminars and workshops.

GENERAL PROFESSIONAL/ CURATORIAL DUTIES

To develop the collection: this includes selecting new visual materials and weeding the old in a continuous control of quality and range in the collection; developing knowledge of subjects covered, current publications, and sources; receiving and reviewing suggestions from users regarding their needs; formulating policies for selection; communicating availability to users; accepting donations and gifts; and maintaining reference materials, desiderata files, and checklists of items required for teaching.

To facilitate accessibility to the collection: through classification, cataloging, and indexing, this involves developing the formal descriptive cataloging to be done for each item; developing added entries and cross-references (based on knowledge of users' needs and good judgment); formulating cataloging procedures for special materials; revising cataloging for sections of collection as needed (major projects requiring detailed organization and extensive time periods); expanding and developing classification and cataloging schemes; providing for subject access; determining policy regarding physical forms for catalogs, shelflists, and bibliographies; establishing procedures and overseeing filing and withdrawal of items and entries; supervising physical upkeep of storage files; maintaining a classification and cataloging manual for the collection; and developing necessary authority lists.

To direct production, preparation, conservation, housing, and handling of material: this requires determining methods and routines; overseeing conservation practices and procedures; establishing policies concerning binding, mounting, sleeving, and repairs; and security.

To manage circulation functions: this includes planning and supervising circulation operation; enforcing and interpreting circulation policies; selecting and designing records and forms, overseeing collection of statistical data; attending to overdues; handling complaints; and planning and supervising filing operations and shelf (or file) reading and maintenance procedures.

To provide information and assistance to users: this involves establishing policies for providing services to users, explaining arrangement and scope of collection, assisting users in locating and selecting slides, answering inquiries, informing users of information and material relevant to their special interests, participating in the development of visual materials for new courses, providing information on sources, and participating in planning for special lectures or productions.

Technical Category

Duties that require specialized training in photography, audiovisual production and equipment, and computer programming operations are included in the technical category. Although in a small operation, some of these services may be performed by the curator; if the collection services include all three of these special areas, it is advised that specialists be employed.

PHOTOGRAPHIC SERVICES

To produce materials for the collection: this involves copy photography, slide duplication, on-site photography, photograph processing and printing, managing and maintaining darkroom equipment and supplies inventories; and recommending needed darkroom and other photographic equipment.

AUDIOVISUAL SERVICES

To manage and maintain all audiovisual equipment: this includes scheduling, orienting users, maintaining equipment and supplies inventories, recommending needed equipment, and providing projectionist services.

COMPUTER SERVICES

To develop and maintain computer programs that meet the needs of the collection: this entails training staff and other users in data entry, access, and other computer operations; maintaining and developing the collection's database; developing computer programs as necessary for records, reports, and other related activities; maintaining computer supplies inventory; and recommending needed hardware and software.

Clerical/General Category

To perform clerical functions and general secretarial activities: this covers record keeping; ordering and payments; compiling statistics; maintaining office files; supplies; inventory; typing and/or routine data entry and printing; photocopying; assisting with shelf reading; issuing, reserving, and returning materials; maintaining circulation records; and explaining collection policies.

To perform tasks related to the processing of slides and photographs into the collection: this includes slide binding, photograph mounting or sleeving, and index and label preparation; performing simple descriptive cataloging; performing routine index and file maaintenance; filing of new material into the collection and refiling of circulated items; and maintaining indexes and storage files.

To manage clerical functions involved with recruitment and training of temporary, nonprofessional staff: this involves preparing timesheets; maintaining personnel records; processing payrolls; maintaining employee records; and orienting new part-time staff.

This internal division by duties is a natural way of separating and describing the jobs to be performed. The disadvantage to this can be the numbers of staff it seems to require; however, in most situations, staff members perform work in several categories. In delegating responsibility, important factors are the personal characteristics and interests of the individual staff members and their deployment where they are happiest, most efficient, and useful. For example, in collections with a large staff, several members may be classed as curatorial. It is often the practice to divide these curatorial responsibilities by historical periods covered in the collection, or Western and non-Western or Oriental. In many collections, the chief curator must be a generalist, able to perform any legitimate task in the collection. This is practical in emergencies and also provides vital insight into training methods.

STAFF SIZE

The size of the staff should be proportional to the required and/or desired functions and responsibilities of the collection. It is important to define the minimum number of staff positions required to perform the activities required or expected of the collection. The maintenance of accurate statistics is very important in providing information regarding the balance between demands and available staff. More will be said about this in chapter 5, "Reports and Statistics." Standards for staffing have been recommended in the Art Libraries Society of North America (ARLIS/NA) publication *Standards for Art Libraries and Fine Arts Slide Collections*.[3]

Since every collection is unique, the following guidelines should be adapted to suit the specific needs and requirements of each collection. Their application to a particular situation must depend upon a combination of relevant factors including the nature of the collection and its materials, its size and annual growth rate, the number of collection users, the degree of complexity of its cataloging system, its circulation rate, etc. The guidelines are to be understood as ideals rather than rigid requirements.

A collection of 15,000 to approximately 50,000 items should have a full-time person responsible, if its yearly circulation is under 20,000 and its growth rate is more than 1,000-5,000 per year. Collections of between 50,000 and 100,000 units with moderate yearly growth rates (5,000-10,000) and average circulation (20,000 to 40,000) should have a full-time professional chief curator, an assistant curator with full-time clerical assistance, and part-time help for slide mounting, refiling, etc. Collections of between 100,000 and 200,000 units with at least 8,000-10,000 per year growth rate and circulation rates of up to 60,000 slides should have at least one full-time professional chief curator, at least two full-time assistant or associate curators, a full-time clerical/general staff member, and several part-time clerical workers. Major collections which maintain large annual growth (10,000-12,000) and circulation (60,000-80,000) rates per year should have at least three professional curators and around 120 hours per week of full-time equivalent clerical help. The technical staff requirements should be based upon the nature and extent of the technical services performed, as described earlier in this chapter. Certainly any collection producing 3,000 slides or more per year in-house needs the services of a full-time photographer. Figure 4.2, p. 40, reflects these figures in graph form.

Student assistant help can be extremely effective in carrying out many of the routine clerical duties in an academic visual resources collection. However, collections should not rely entirely on this category of staffing. Student assistants require careful and patient training if they are to be valuable workers, and they make excellent employees, when they remain with the collection over an extended period of time. However, a major disadvantage with student help is that generally there is an imbalance between the length of time required for training and the average length of time students remain with the collection.

Collection Size	Circulation Rate	Annual Growth Rate	Number of Full-time Equivalents
15,000 - 50,000	- 20,000	+ 1,000 - 5,000	1 professional
50,000 - 100,000	20,000 - 40,000	5,000 - 10,000	1 professional, 1 asst. curator
100,000 - 200,000	up to 60,000	8,000 - 10,000	1 professional, 2 assts., 1 full-time clerical
200,000 +	60,000 - 80,000	10,000 - 12,000	3 professionals, +200 hrs./wk. full-time equiv. clerical help

Figure 4.2. Staffing size relative to collection size, circulation, and growth rates. From Art Libraries Society of North America, *Standards for Art Libraries and Fine Arts Slide Collections*, Occasional Paper No. 2 (Tucson, AZ: ARLIS/NA, 1983), 28-29.

JOB DESCRIPTIONS

A job description is a broad statement of a job's purpose, scope, duties, and responsibilities, produced by an analysis or evaluation that identifies the component parts of the job and the context in which it is performed. The analysis should also include education, experience, supervisory responsibilities, supervision received, work complexity, reports required, amount of specialized knowledge required, supervision given, range of relationships within and without the unit which the person needs to build and maintain, and impact of decisions that must be made. Job descriptions need to be continuously updated to avoid becoming outdated and ignored. The job description should be used not only in recruitment but also in employee appraisals. Sample job descriptions arranged by categories are found in appendix B.

It is not unusual for visual resources curators to be expected to provide an analysis and job description for their own jobs. One of the complications in this field is the variety in titles and job descriptions for the curator. The profession is relatively new, and administrators and personnel specialists are not aware of what is involved in the management and administration of this type of facility or resource. It is to the advantage of the curator to undertake this description; past experience has shown that when left to those who do not comprehend the scope and nature of the job, the analogies drawn with other fields are fallacious and usually of a nonprofessional nature. If possible, confer with a job classification specialist at the sponsoring institution to determine the institution's method of classifying jobs. The job categories described in the first part of this chapter, combined with the general duty descriptions specific to the situation, should provide a starting point for creating job descriptions.

It is not possible to produce a set of generic job descriptions for the visual resource curator and related staff. There are too many different specific characteristics from one collection to another; tasks and responsibilities are grouped differently and given different titles. However, it is recommended that each job in the operation be given a specific title and job description; a written statement describing each individual job and the involved duties, responsibilities, work to be performed, and equipment utilized. Periodic reviews of job descriptions will produce improved organization and comprehension by classifying responsibilities. This helps in the selection of persons for the requirements of the job and also helps with performance evaluations.

A job description should include the job title; to whom the incumbent reports and whom that person supervises; the job summary (general scope and function); the qualifications, knowledge, skills, experience, and abilities, both required and preferred; the general responsibilities; authorities; complexities and duties; supervision given and received; the services offered and their impact; the length of contract (if applicable); and the salary. It is important to have a description that provides for some upward mobility. This kind of descriptive information will enable the personnel expert to assign a value to the job in order to establish appropriate salary ranges. (See figure 4.3.)

Position title:

Reports to:

Supervises:

Basic description:

Qualifications:
- knowledge, skills, and abilities:
- education and training:
- experience:

Primary duties and responsibilities:
- list in descending order of importance
- list percent time for each

Actions and decisions made:
- independent of supervision:
- with supervisor's approval:

Information regarding salary and other benefits:

Figure 4.3. Example format for a job description.

RECRUITING AND INTERVIEWING

Due to the temporary nature of part-time or student personnel, the visual resources curator can expect to experience frequent opportunities to recruit and hire new personnel. Effective recruitment and subsequent hiring and training make the difference between poor and superior service and performance. A job opening, whether created by a new position or by a resignation, should be approached as an important opportunity to improve overall efficiency. The first step is a review of the current description and to make necessary revisions, as discussed above. It is also good management practice to attempt to anticipate vacancies well in advance and to begin the process of review and approval in order to recruit and hire as far in advance of the vacancy as possible.

Strategies will differ somewhat between the recruitment of permanent, professional/curatorial positions, permanent support staff, and part-time or temporary ones. For part-time positions for students (if the collection is academic), it is important to use the campus office of student financial aid as one source for job seekers. The federally funded College Work Study Program (CWSP) provides many academic visual resources collections throughout the United States with part-time help. In some areas CWSP students are recruited to work in other nonprofit institutions as well, such as as art museums and libraries, or other municipal departments. Personal contact with a staff member in the financial aid office who actually interviews prospective employees can be very valuable in drawing attention to your staffing needs as well as learning opportunities for students. Another effective recruitment method is to post notices in student gathering places in your building and other locations on campus. Contacts with student employees or collection users can often result in leads for students interested in part-time employment, as well.

In visual resources collections, usually a considerable proportion of the staff budget is expended for student assistants, yet administrators are often lax in the methods of selection, training, and supervision of this level of staff. In order to obtain the optimum value from the salaries paid and to provide the students with good job experiences, they should be subject to the same administrative demands for high and efficient performance as the permanent staff members.

The use of the institution's office of personnel services or employment will likely be mandatory for the listing of positions for permanent support staff. Many institutions require that all nonacademic staff be funneled through such channels. However, this does not mean that the curator cannot recruit informally among colleagues, not only within the parent institution, but even perhaps at other institutions in the surrounding area.

Although professional positions may also have to be handled through the office of personnel services or employment, a national listing is frequently used as well. Through such professional organizations as the College Art Association, Visual Resources Association, and Art Libraries Society of North America,[4] many visual resources collection positions are listed each year. It is important to recognize when the position warrants this type of a search and what exactly is involved. Once again, informal communication among colleagues can also produce some fine candidates. Recruiting nationally for professional/curatorial positions opens the door to opportunities for growth, development, and improvement of the visual resources collection and the development of a staff with diverse experience and ideas.

This is not to say that professional and curatorial staff vacancies should not be posted internally as well. These along with support staff positions should definitely be circulated in-house in order to give currently employed staff members promotional opportunities. However, it is important to restrict interviews to only those internal candidates whose qualifications meet job requirements.

In order to promote participation and representation of views and opinions of staff as well as others concerned with the selection, a search committee may be formed to interview and recommend candidates for permanent positions.

Interviewing

The purpose of the interview in staff recruitment is fourfold. The first objective is to determine if the applicant's experience and training are suitable to the specific requirements of the job posted. The second objective of the interview is to evaluate the applicant's personality and motivation in the context of the job. The third purpose is to assess the candidate's intellectual abilities. Last, but equally important, is to allow the applicant to learn about the job and to assess the employer.

The preparation for each interview should occur in advance. If possible, the candidate's resume and/or application form should be obtained prior to the interview and reviewed. A careful review of the requirements for the job should also be done in advance. It is helpful to organize an outline of what is to be covered and to write out several specific questions to be asked, as well as to review topics that should *not* be covered.

In order to make an intelligent decision, it is important to gain the most meaningful information possible in the time allotted. In order to keep the interview on the subject, and to eliminate the applicant's tendency to interrupt the discussion with questions about the job, the institution, or similar matters, the interviewer should describe how the interview will be conducted. As soon as the basic social pleasantries and introductions are completed, the interviewer should initiate the first topic to be discussed (see figure 4.4).

   I. Brief introduction and description of how the interview will be structured.

  II. Knowledge and experience. This part of the interview would involve questions relative to:
      A. work experiences and/or college and other studies
      B. present or recent activities
      C. goals and objectives
      D. self-assessment
      E. reactions to this job

      These questions should be broad and allow for discussion by the candidate. The interviewer should listen and not interrupt; ask questions that encourage self-appraisal.

 III. Ask motivational questions. Find out the candidate's interests and aspirations; what types of work he or she finds stimulating (e.g., problem solving, intellectual activities, ability to think under pressure)

  IV. Lead into discussion of how all this relates to the job; how well his or her capabilities could be applied. Discuss the candidate's strengths and limitations.

Figure 4.4. Suggested interview outline.

The specific questions in figure 4.5 regarding a candidate's qualifications can aid the interviewer in finding a visual resources curator, assistant, or with modifications, even part-time temporary help.

What is your academic background as it pertains to art and art history?
    degrees (B.A., M.A., M.F.A., Ph.D., etc.)
    number of hours in art historys or other relevant fields, if degree is less than M.A.
    areas of concentration or specialization in art and art history
    coursework in areas related to study of art history (e.g., anthropology, history, classics, architecture, film studies, etc.)

What has been the extent and nature of experience in:
    slide and/or photograph collections
    personal image collection
    use of slides in teaching situations
    copy photography
    general use of 35mm cameras

What has been the extent and nature of administrative/management experience:
    supervisory
    procedural
    formal coursework/training in supervisory management

Foreign-language skills:
    dictionary working knowledge
    reading knowledge
    fluency
    degrees

What is extent and nature of library work?
    cataloging and classification
    shelving and/or filing
    public service/reference
    bibliographic searching

Academic background in library and information science:
    degrees
    number of hours in library science, if less than M.L.S.
    areas of concentration or specialization related to visual resources collections

Computer experience:
    academic or workshop coursework
    applications in a job

Figure 4.5. Interview questions. From Eileen Fry and Nancy Schuller, "Visual Resources Job Information," *MA-CAA Newsletter* 4, no. 1 (1977): 4.

44 / 4—STAFFING

It is possible when interviewing staff to devise a numeric rating for the qualifications desired for specific positions. The numeric rating can be based on numbers 1-3, with the highest number indicating advanced ability, etc. For example, if the job to be filled requires data entry skills, then the number 3 would be assigned to the applicant with the best computer skills. Figure 4.6 is a sample of such a chart.

Names of Applicants	Qualifications								
	Academic background (including library & informational science)	Experience in visual resources collection work	Language expertise	Management / Administrative experience	Experience with audiovisual equipment	Experience in library work	Typing and other office skills	Computer experience	Other

Figure 4.6. Visual resources job applicant rating chart.

DISCRIMINATION IN INTERVIEWS

It is very important that the interviewer be familiar with the institution's policies regarding discrimination in hiring. If interviews have not been conducted frequently or recently, a call to a personnel representative for an update on information is advisable. It is potentially discriminatory to ask the following:

- the applicant's race, birth place, or religious affiliation
- date of birth or age unless needed under special minimum age requirements
- applicant's nationality or citizenship (However, it may be acceptable to ask if applicant is in the United States on a visa that forbids work here.)
- applicant's parents' or spouse's nationality
- applicant's native language, language commonly used at home, or how applicant acquired ability to read, write, or speak a foreign language (However, it is acceptable to ask the language the applicant speaks and/or writes fluently.)
- names and/or addresses of any relatives of applicant

Sexual discrimination is another important issue in interviewing. Women applicants must not be denied employment because of any "assumed qualities." Therefore, certain questions must be avoided:

plans for a family

birth control practices

number and ages of children

daycare arrangements

spouse's occupation

In an innocent effort to put a nervous applicant at ease, it is tempting to ask questions relative to the applicant's family or home. However, this must not be done and is another reason for preplanning each interview carefully. Should an applicant volunteer information relative to any of the above, the interviewer should simply say, "we're not allowed to discuss this in our interview." If your employer does not have information regarding fair employment practices and interviewing, contact a local chapter of the National Organization for Women (NOW) and/or the Equal Employment Opportunities Commission (EEOC).

At the close of the interview, the candidate should be informed of how the selection process will proceed: if a second interview is planned and if so, when this might take place. Immediately after a candidate has been selected and has accepted the offer, the unsuccessful applicants should be notified. A sample letter for these applicants is included in figure 4.7.

                                      Date

Dear _____,

    It was a pleasure to meet you last week and discuss the opening we have for an _____ in our visual resources collection.

    It has been a difficult task to select from a number of highly qualified individuals who have applied for this job. Your qualifications were reviewed against our current needs and I have decided to make an offer to another person whose background and experiences more closely match our needs.

    I sincerely appreciate your interest in our position and wish you much success in your career plans.

                        Sincerely,

Figure 4.7. Sample letter to unsuccessful candidates.

STAFF TRAINING

In order to ensure service of uniformly high quality, professional standards must be maintained and the staff must be well trained. Following staff selection, the curator must see that effective training is conducted in which staff members are taught everything necessary to do the job correctly and well. This training will combine a variety of methods. A written description of what is expected, the responsibilities, and standards of performance is essential. Often too much reliance is placed on oral communication for training. Audio-visual material, flowcharts, instructional material such as handbooks, and procedures for peer training are all very useful as well.

Training is a vital part of management and it is important to take seriously the development of formalized training procedures for each activity in the visual resources collection. Experienced staff should assist with training, but they should not be made entirely responsible for this activity. Investigation of jobs that are being performed poorly will often reveal areas where training has been weak. Particular activities have their own training needs; separate strategies should be developed for each. Each group of workers (i.e., filers, binders, circulation desk workers, data entry personnel) might be requested to report on what they perceive to be training needs in their areas. Interviews with staff who are leaving, called "exit interviews," can uncover training weaknesses as well.

Staff Appraisals

Staff appraisals should be viewed as a function of staff training and development. All staff members need feedback. In an ideal situation, there would be constant feedback, communication between management and staff about work being done. But since few of us exist in ideal situations, there is need for a formal performance appraisal at stated intervals. It is also important that the appraisal interview be completely separate from the "reward review" or "salary review." When these are done simultaneously, the employee remembers only the discussion of salary. The evaluation should be done with utmost candor and respect and should be a frank discussion of what is *really* expected. The overall objective, of course, is employee development and improvement. The evaluation interview is just one part of a continuous process that began with the job description, the interviewing and selecting of individuals, and their training in the capacity for which they were hired.

Although the employee should be encouraged to do the talking, the supervisor should set the specific objectives and limitations for the evaluation. The employee should be informed in advance of the form to be used and what will be covered. It is advantageous to have both parties review the form separately in advance and then meet together to complete it, discussing the individual points. Discussions that occur when completing the form together may develop further job performance issues for discussion. In advance of the actual interview, be sure that employees understand what is expected of them; decide on one or two primary objectives you wish to accomplish in the interview and develop a strategy for proceeding with and controlling the interview.

The job description that was used when the employee was hired may be too abstract or general to function for a performance evaluation. It is important to focus on what is specifically expected of an employee. In some instances an administrator will ask the employee to write a job description. However, this can result in a definition that describes what the employee is doing or would like to be doing, rather than what the unit needs that employee to do. It is considerate to consult with the employee, but the person conducting the interview should be responsible for this description. The work that has to be accomplished, the training, skills and knowledge required, what is *really* expected of the employee should make up the description. Only the most important aspects should be listed and ranked.

In many visual resources collection situations there is a problem of maintaining a good employee's motivation when there is no chance for promotion or a pay increase. A well-conducted appraisal will provide feedback to the employee; allow for greater challenges and a say in decisions; and simply listening can yield positive feedback. A sample performance evaluation for staff is included in appendix D.

When criticisms or reprimands must be made, they must be done diplomatically. Such discussions should take place in private and should begin with a question rather than an accusation. Listen as the person answers and explains, then make constructive, specific suggestions or recommendations. Avoid reprimands made in anger; don't interrupt the person's story, and do not get involved in an argument. Concentrate the discussion on the problem, not the personality. Try not to jump to conclusions.

VOLUNTEERS

When funds for staff positions are not sufficient to provide the services required or desired, the use of volunteers may be considered. In many communities there are individuals and organizations looking for interesting places where volunteer services are needed. Volunteers donate thousands of hours each year in libraries, museums, and historical societies. Visual resources collections, specializing in the history of art and architecture, are concerned with the subjects which many volunteers find interesting and enjoyable.

If utilization of volunteers is to be successful, there are techniques in selection, use, and motivation that can be helpful. It is important to know where to find volunteers and how to make the work attractive. Just as with salaried staff, it is important to know how to interview and select volunteers (and how to reject them, as well, if it appears they are not right for the job), and how to place them in the collection where they will be best used and derive the most from the experience.

To begin with, the curator must determine where the volunteers will be assigned and who will supervise them. If there are to be several volunteers, either the curator or a designated member of the staff should be the volunteer coordinator. This person should also be the liaison with the source organizations. Some likely sources are service organizations, civic associations, student groups, and associations of retired persons. A possible recruiting tactic might be to give slide lectures to several groups to create interest in visual resources work, or write letters describing the need to officers of key service organizations in the area.

Prospective volunteers should be interviewed, and these interviews may be as carefully structured and the jobs for which they are interviewing be as fully described as those for paid staff. In addition to evaluating the volunteers' skills, it is equally important to pay attention to personalities and how these people would relate to the other staff. The objective of the interview is to determine what skills volunteers have that would be valuable to the visual resources collection, as well as their motivation, dependability, and ability to work with others, accept direction, and responsibility.

Volunteers want to feel that they are needed, appreciated, and are accomplishing something. If a menial job must be assigned to a volunteer, this individual must be made to feel that it is an important part of the overall work and that everyone shares in it. There should be a conscious effort to provide praise, encouragement, and opportunities for recognition. Although volunteers require special management techniques, judging from the many highly successful programs in existence throughout the country, they are a very promising source for staffing for visual resources collections.

COMMUNICATION

A very important element in staff management in any situation is effective two-way communication. The communication may take several different forms, but the curator must be prepared to encourage this by being approachable and willing to listen to other points of view. The most important characteristic of a good communicator is the ability to listen. No matter how small the staff, staff meetings are good forums for communication. These will be most successful if they are well organized, with an agenda that is circulated in advance for the purpose of allowing staff to make additions. A suggested schedule is one staff meeting biweekly with professional and curatorial staff and one each semester which includes clerical and technical services staff as well.

The effectiveness of the visual resources collection depends to a certain degree on the image it presents to its users and potential users. Printed materials designed to show how the collection functions and the services are provided, as well as oral orientations, are an important communication tool. Official communications in written form should include the circulation policy and other policies regarding collection development, slide production, copyright, training instructions, standards of performance, and other sections of the official policies and procedures manual. These written instructions should be read and evaluated for their effectiveness before distribution to prevent misunderstandings.

Newsletters can be an effective method of communicating information regarding the visual resources collection. Items regarding collection development, staff additions and achievements, and statistics can be included. Although a chore, a once or twice per semester publication can be valuable in keeping both staff and users informed of interesting and valuable information. Use of effective methods of communication will help achieve a cohesive, self-reliant, self-confident, and committed staff who will require less supervision.

FINAL THOUGHTS ON STAFFING

A major issue among curators is the goal for professional recognition within their institutions. One indication of the ambiguous status which characterizes the position of the curator or director of the visual resources collection is to be found in the variety of the official job titles used and the job descriptions that accompany them. The professional status surveys that have been conducted during the past decade illustrate the variety of position titles for the person in charge of the visual resources collections: "Library Research Assistant," "Media Room Specialist," "Cataloger," "Slide Curator," "Slide Librarian," "Curator of Visual Resources," and "Director." Just as the job descriptions must be tailored to meet criteria for each individual collection, so too must the titles for the jobs described and their specific contexts be tailored.

In conclusion, there appear to be some important personal qualities which suit people to visual resources work and have little relation to academic qualifications and background. These include patience and a willingness to do thorough, precise work, a sense of order and organization, and attention to details. These qualities are as necessary for the clerical worker as for the chief curator, and when these qualities are present, they contribute greatly to the harmonious and effective functioning of the collection.

NOTES

[1] Nancy Kirkpatrick, "Staffing," in *Guide for Management of Visual Resources Collections* (Albuquerque, NM: Mid-America College Art Association, 1978), 48.

[2] Neal Harlow, "Misused Librarians," *Ontario Library Review* 49 (November 1965): 170-72.

[3] Art Libraries Society of North America, *Standards for Art Libraries and Fine Arts Slide Collections*, Occasional Paper No. 2 (Tucson, AZ: ARLIS/NA, 1983).

[4] College Art Association, 275 Seventh Ave., New York, NY 10001; Visual Resources Association, Joy Alexander, ed., Department of the History of Art, Tappan Hall, University of Michigan, Ann Arbor, MI 48109; ARLIS/NA, Pam Parry, ed., *Update*, 3900 E. Timrod St., Tucson, AZ 85711.

5
Reports and Statistics

The *annual report* works in conjunction with the budget proposal and budget report to present a complete record of the annual activities of the visual resources collection. Libraries use established methods for reporting their activities and expenditures for the purpose of communicating information within the profession. Although many visual resources curators have determined on an in-house basis how best to organize and present the annual report, the profession has yet to adopt a systematic framework for reporting its functions locally that can also be used for comparison among collections nationally. It is the purpose of this chapter to suggest methods that can ultimately result in a standard for accomplishing this comparison.

METHODOLOGY AND TERMINOLOGY

Periodic reports are effective means for communicating the importance of the visual resources collection. Such information can be an expedient method for evaluating the efficiency of the collection, a means of reporting to upper administration, informing users of activities, justifying budget needs, and developing and communicating long and short-term goals. This reporting process is truly an essential element in effective management. Even though there are many items which are particular to individual collections, numerous commonalities exist among collections that can be reported, and can serve as a basis for comparisons. Some examples are circulation figures, collection holdings (formats and numbers), numbers of users or borrowers, annual acquisitions, hours open for service, staff make-up and size, and physical facilities.

The most effective approach for *collecting information* for the annual report is to be actively assembling it throughout each year. Establishing a method for documenting each activity to be included in the report is imperative. For activities not easily quantifiable, one may set up file folders and drop notes or other pertinent information into the appropriate folder each time there is information for the annual report relative to that activity. For example, to report on staff activities, keep a record (a published notice, a conference program) of awards received, articles or papers published, talks delivered, etc., and add it to the file. Such activities are often difficult to recall when the report is actually being compiled.

Monthly reports covering the quantitative functions in the visual resources collection are a handy method for maintaining information for the annual report. These monthly totals, when viewed over a period of time, reveal the patterns of activity, the "peaks and valleys" for such activities as circulation, equipment use, photographic services, slide and photograph mounting, acquisitions, etc. For example, comparisons of several years of circulation figures on a monthly basis will help the curator to see the established use patterns, and provide a basis for planning for those months during which additional filing staff is needed. If staff funding must be reduced, such records, established over a period of time, will indicate when a maximum number of staff members are required and when it is possible to operate with fewer people. Even when funding is not the issue, this information graphically describes when part-time

50 / 5 – REPORTS AND STATISTICS

help is needed for filing and when these personnel can be used for other projects. Figure 5.1 shows a year's filing statistics collected at The University of Texas at Austin, Art Department, Slide and Photograph Collection. Forms and procedures for collecting activity statistics for filing or circulation, binding, equipment use, photographic production, acquisitions, etc., appear in appendix D.

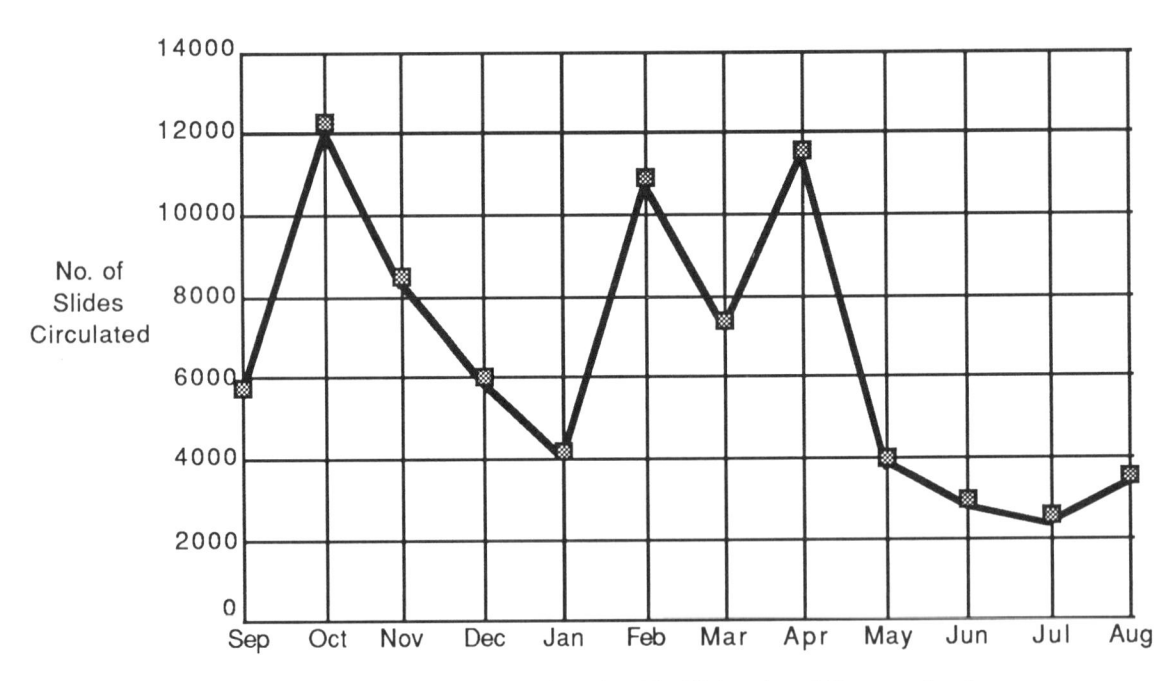

Figure 5.1. Example of one year's filing statistics collected at The University of Texas at Austin.

It is important before outlining the contents of the annual report to establish a *standard for the terminology* used to describe these categories. When staff members are required to report quantities of work done and time expended in doing it, it is necessary for everyone to be counting the same way. In binding slides, if the cover glass must be cleaned, that time must be factored into the hours spent binding. Distinction also should be made between special mounting or binding methods[1] and routine methods (which are less tedious); between slides that must be extensively masked (to conceal unnecessary parts of the transparency) and those which require no masking at all. When circulation figures are reported, do they include only items that are officially checked out, or *all* items refiled? The glossary of terms included in appendix C is an initial attempt to standardize term usage to make the data collection process more accurate and consistent. The use of standardized terminology will produce more accurate comparisons of collection activities from year to year, but also make comparisons between collections possible. Some of the terms defined are standard library terminology while others are limited to visual resources curatorship developed through consultation with other curators. It must be understood that this glossary is limited; it is an initial effort at a list that will be expanded and revised in the process of use.

It is suggested that the standard for types of visual resources collections be those categories established in the Art Libraries Society of North America's (ARLIS/NA) *Standards for Fine Arts Libraries and Visual Resources Collections.*[2] The American National Standards Institute's (ANSI) *American National Standard for Library Statistics* is intended to help librarians to collect, organize, and interpret library-related statistics.[3] Although visual resources collections are not included in this document, the methodology presented applies in a general way. It establishes standard terminology definitions, divides types of libraries, then describes the contents of an annual report. It is directed at public libraries with numerous branches and state library systems, and therefore is far more detailed than needed for visual resources collections. However, there are items that can apply to visual resources collections.

Following is an *outline of the major elements for a visual resources collection annual report*. Each section will be discussed as well as methods for gathering the data. The overall format divides the report into quantitative (the first five) and nonquantitative sections.

The quantitative section, more than any other, contains elements that are common to visual resources collections in general and, if reported in a standard fashion, will have the potential of producing data that can be compared with past performances, or matched with the same activity in other visual resources collections. After a period of time, this kind of information will have research value to the profession. The quantitative section isolates those aspects of a visual resources collection which are measurable (i.e., can be expressed in numeric terms) and that are common to most collections. These sections are expenditures and income, staffing, acquisitions, circulation, audiovisual equipment use and services, and photographic production services.

The nonquantitative section will vary more from collection to collection and will be used to report facts and functions that are not suitable to numeric reporting. However, this section is no less important than the other, for it contains information about staff development and professional pursuits, special projects, collection strengths and weaknesses, and short- and long-range goals.

Figure 5.2 is a suggested outline for developing the annual report. Following it is a fuller description of each section.

I. Identification of the collection/type of collection

II. Income

III. Expenditures
  A. Commercial purchases (subdivide by format)
  B. In-house production (subdivide by format)
  C. Supplies and equipment for maintenance of the collection
    1. Clerical supplies
    2. Slide binding, photo mounting supplies
    3. Reference material
    4. Audiovisual supplies (lamps, cords, trays, etc.)
    5. Printing/copying
  D. Capital expenditures
    1. Audiovisual equipment
    2. Collection furniture (slide/photo files, slide sorters, light tables, etc.)
    3. Computer hardware
    4. Typewriters
  E. Service and repairs
    1. Maintenance agreements
    2. Audiovisual equipment
    3. Photographic equipment
  F. Professional development/travel
  G. Wages/personnel (subdivide by categories)
  H. Total expenditures

IV. Circulation
  A. Slides
  B. Other formats
  C. Audiovisual equipment
  D. Numbers of users/borrowers, categories/types (if applicable)
  E. Copy stand users

(Figure 5.2 continues on p. 52.)

V. Acquisitions (subdivide by formats and audiovisual equipment)

Include figures on classification and cataloging, subject areas acquired, slide and photograph mounting or sleeving, and numbers of items withdrawn from the collection.

VI. Staff make-up and size

VII. Staff development and professional pursuits

VIII. Special projects accomplished and special projects planned

IX. Collection strengths and weaknesses, urgent needs

X. Short- and long-range goals

Figure 5.2. The annual report.

ANNUAL REPORT: QUANTITATIVE PORTION

Identification of the Collection/ Type of Collection

This should be a brief descriptive statement which characterizes the collection in terms of the ARLIS/NA *Standards for Art Libraries and Fine Arts Slide Collections* types, e.g., the size category and type.[4] When comparing visual resources collections nationally, this preliminary distinction of size and type of collection helps to make adequate comparisons among similar collections rather than comparing all collections with one or two ideal ones, the latter usually being large, well-financed, and well-managed collections.

Income

A complete listing of all income should appear in the annual report. There should be a standard report format for the budget which distinguishes regular budget allocation, grants, gifts, and any other special income procured during the year. This can follow the same line item form as described in the budgeting chapter (chapter 3), which would facilitate comparisons with previous years as well as with other collections which report in the same way.

Expenditures

The line item budget format described in chapter 3 is the most expedient format for reporting expenditures. Items purchased will vary from collection to collection, but slide or other acquisition purchases, supplies for photographic production, clerical supplies, binding and photo mounting and sleeving supplies, audiovisual expendable supplies, and services and repairs are common to most.

The expenditures for *acquisitions*, both those purchased and those produced in-house, will disclose the collection's practice of balancing the acquisition of top quality original images with images produced through in-house copy photography. It also indicates the benefits derived from a staff photographer. The in-house production expenditures should itemize expenditures for film, processing, chemicals and paper for photographic printing, copy stand and enlarger lamps, and other miscellaneous expendable supplies.

Numerous miscellaneous expenditures are grouped in the *supplies and equipment for maintenance* section. The divisions for clerical supplies, binding supplies, reference material, and audiovisual supplies are fairly general and can be subdivided if necessary. Expenses for clerical supplies includes not only the usual pads, pens, and pencils, but also typewriter and computer ribbons, paper clips, glue, floppy disks and commercial software, notebooks, looseleaf binders, etc. Listed under slide binding are slide mounting frames, signal dots, labels, film cleaner, denatured alcohol, wipes, cotton tipped applicators, matte knives and blades, and scissors—everything needed to glass mount slides. A second subdivision of this section is for the same type of supplies required for dry-mounting or sleeving photographs and cuts, or for maintenance and care of other formats collected.

Reference material is an expense that will be considered with acquisitions if the collection is also a reference center, such as in a number of architecture school collections. However, in most visual resources collections there are reference items that are used so frequently that they should be purchased rather than borrowed from the library.[5] Purchases of computer software program references would be reported in this section as well.

Audiovisual supplies expenditures include all those items that accompany the use of audiovisual equipment. Projector lamps, remote control cords, power extension cords, carousel (or other) slide trays, and containers used for transporting slides, are all reported in this section. An interesting result from the reporting of this data is the recognition that art history courses require expensive, expendable supplies just as their studio art counterparts do.

Printing and duplicating may not be expenses incurred in all visual resources collections, but if circulation forms, slide and photograph request forms, circulation policies, etc., are used in large numbers, it may be necessary to have them produced at a printing/copying service rather than on the departmental copy machine. Such expenses should be reported in this section.

The practice of prorating *capital expenditures* over a period of years was discussed in chapter 3, "Budgeting." However, if this practice is unsuitable to the situation, these expenditures should simply be reported in the year in which they are incurred. This includes audiovisual equipment, furniture and other equipment such as slide and photograph storage files or cabinets; slide sorters; light tables; and other nonexpendable equipment such as typewriters, computers, printers, and photographic and darkroom equipment.

Any operation that involves the use of equipment also requires an allocation for *service and repairs*. As the use of audiovisual equipment increases, so do the repair bills. Keeping track of such expenses helps chart the service record for specific pieces of equipment and indicates when items need to be replaced. There will be annual fees or service contracts for computers, printers, and typewriters that should also be reported. Repairs for cameras and other darkroom equipment should also be itemized in this section. Annual preventive maintenance on all projectors is a good investment and costs less on a systematic basis than major repair bills. Even if such expenses are not charged directly to the visual resources operation, the curator should attempt to ascertain the costs, for they are part of the operational needs of the collection.

Professional development/memberships/travel are administrative expenditures that may not be included in the visual resources budget. They are listed here, however, for they should be factored into the annual budget somewhere, and since the collection benefits from this form of staff development, it belongs here rather than in what is left over from the faculty or administrative travel budget. The outlay doesn't have to be large, and including it emphasizes its significance. This item should include some, if not all, funds for travel to professional conferences, seminars, or meetings; memberships in professional organizations; and subscriptions to professional journals.

Personnel wages and salaries complete the picture for overall costs for operating the visual resources collection. This category is most logically divided between permanent staff and part-time or temporary staff, and then further subdivided by professional and curatorial, clerical, and technical. Chapter 4, "Staffing," describes categories for staff.

Circulation

Determine and qualify at the outset how the count is to be done (slides refiled or slides actually checked out). If the objective is to support staffing needs, then use the numbers of refiled slides and photographs, for this establishes the work load. Counting what is checked-out describes user patterns; however, the counting of filed items is more useful for visual resources collections since most have a fairly restricted and identifiable body of users. Both categories can be reported if the figures are gathered.

Through the use of coded circulation drop cards (as described in chapter 7, "Circulation and Control") and individual return bailers or boxes, it is possible for the filers to keep track of refiled slides by user and therefore report figures for individual users as well as totals refiled. Users should be instructed to return slides removed from the files to their respective bailers or boxes. A sample form for recording refiled slides is in appendix D. Circulation figures can yield a variety of useful information when kept on a weekly basis throughout the year.

Identification of user groups is important for the collection. Information about use by individuals from specific groups can help bring attention to the level of service provided by the collection, help direct collection development policy, and indicate on whose behalf the efforts of the staff are being directed.

Use of audiovisual equipment should also be reported as a category of circulation, as should use of any photographic equipment that is available, such as a camera, copy stand, etc. With an established list of audiovisual equipment, a monthly and later an annual record can be kept of either individual items or groups of like equipment that are used. (See appendix E for a sample form.) Over a period of time use patterns can be identified. It can be seen how items are utilized; which ones might be retired, traded, or sold to other departments; and which items are so heavily used that additional purchases are warranted.

An accurate circulation accounting includes the numbers of users. Were sixty thousand slides circulated to forty-five individuals or to just five? Was the movie projector used fifteen times by one person or by seven? If the collection is open to the public, a user profile will be important for supplying their needs and perhaps for obtaining additional funding.

Acquisitions and Holdings

Report numbers of items (slides, photographs, etc.) held at the beginning of the fiscal year, the numbers added, the numbers withdrawn, and the numbers at the end of the year. In addition, itemize acquisitions each year by subject area (e.g., pre-historic, pre-Columbian, Egyptian, Greek, Roman, medieval, Renaissance, etc.), by teaching area (e.g., art history faculty, studio faculty, etc.), and by source (commercial, copy photography, duplication, donations, etc.). These figures can be either actual figures or percentages of the total. (See accessions log in appendix D.)

This is also the appropriate place to list figures for new slides classified and cataloged into the collection, numbers reclassified, and cataloging corrections made. Since newly acquired slides usually must be mounted in glass, the numbers of slides bound becomes a part of the total acquisitions and collection development picture, as does the rebinding and repair of old slides. New photographs are usually mounted or sleeved and these figures should be included as well.

Equipment acquisitions covers items acquired, as replacements or as new items. This category should include audiovisual and photographic equipment as well as major furniture purchases such as storage files and slide sorters and viewers, typewriters, and computer equipment. If appropriate, totals for categories of equipment can be listed.

Staff Make-up and Size

This section reports the quantitative aspect of the staff and can be set up in a chart, as described in figure 5.3.

Category	Appointment
Professional and Curatorial	
Administrative	1 FT (9 mo.)
Curatorial	2 FT (12 mo.)
Volunteer	1 PT (9 mo. at 12 hrs./wk.)
Technical	
Computer	1 half-time (12 mo.)
Audiovisual	1 half-time (9 mo.)
Photographer	1 FT (12 mo.)
Volunteer	0
Clerical Total:	7 at 203 hrs./wk.
Filing	2 at 20 hrs./wk. (12 mo.)
Binding	3 at 45 hrs./wk. (12 mo.)
Data Entry	1 at 20 hrs./wk. (12 mo.)
Volunteer	1 at 8 hrs./wk. (9 mo.)
% CWSP	40% of above.

Note: This is a hypothetical example and not intended as a standard.

Figure 5.3. Example of chart to describe a visual resources collection staff.

Rather than listing staff by name (that comes in the nonquantitative section on staffing) in this section, they are grouped by the categories of professional and curatorial, technical, and clerical (as discussed in the staffing chapter). For each, establish the numbers of full-time staff and their general areas of responsibility. The numbers of hours per week worked by hourly or part-time staff should be reported as well as the percent of funding through the College Work Study Program (CWSP). Since the latter are usually involved with filing of circulated materials and the mounting of slides and sleeving photographs, these figures correlate with the totals for circulation and slide and photo mounting. Over a several-year period, these figures create useful staffing patterns.

Additionally, volunteer hours per week should also be reported. It is important that the administration realize the results of volunteer efforts, not only because it reflects resourcefulness on the part of the curator, but also because this calls attention to the total effort required to maintain the level of production or work demanded by use.

ANNUAL REPORT: NONQUANTITATIVE PORTION

Staff Development and Professional Pursuits

In this section, the activities of staff who have been active professionally, received awards, delivered papers, or been involved in some other professional activity should be described. This is an opportunity to bring the achievements of staff members to the attention of people who may not be involved in reviewing annual staff evaluations.

Special Projects: Accomplished and Planned

Special projects, purchases, or works completed during the year are described in this section. An example would be a project to recatalog the slides of the work of a particular artist as well as to develop and weed the holdings of the works represented by that artist in the collection. Another might be the development of a totally new classification scheme for a specific body of work contained in the collection, such as slides of pre-historic art, medieval metalwork, or maps. Perhaps funds were provided to purchase a large number of slides of a particular subject which required extensive research and revision of the existing classification and cataloging system. These would be reported as special projects. The development of a computer database or automated circulation system would be suitable to this portion of the report. Special projects need not be restricted to the holdings, but could also include the development of a policies and procedures manual, the revision of certain policies, the implementation of an automated system, the production of a classification and cataloging manual, etc. Plans for future projects can be enumerated in this section as well. These descriptions formally announce plans for the collection and invite input from the readers of the report.

Collection Strengths and Weaknesses

It may seem that the report of the strengths of a collection would be about the same each year. However, as the weaknesses are continuously reduced, the strengths will be broadened. It is also important to remember that individuals who have not read previous annual reports will not be aware of the strengths and weaknesses of the collection, so it is important for this section to be included each year. The strengths and weaknesses can be described for collection holdings and development policy, the photographic services, the circulation procedures, the services, and the staff—in other words, almost any aspect of the collection. In reviewing the weaknesses each year, a survey of past years' reports should show that they are diminishing.

Short- and Long-Range Goals

In the first chapter of this publication, the importance of planning and goal setting to the administration and management of a collection is stressed. Goals, both long-range and immediate, are not static; they should be revised and rethought continually. The annual report is the vehicle used to record these objectives and aspirations. Reading past reports can reveal to the administration the development of goals as well as their achievement. This is also a forum for the description of urgent needs and recommendations for administrative support.

COLLECTION AND USE OF STATISTICS

The basis of rational management is information. Reports with reliable and thorough statistics should improve the quality of information available to management. The first requirement for the gathering and comparison of statistics is an agreement on the terms and their definitions. The glossary in appendix C is an initial step for this standardization in visual resources collections. In management, statistics perform special functions: they form a common vocabulary for description of programs and activities; they show relationships more directly and clearly than words; and they are a neutral, totally objective method for communication. The daily accumulation of information and statistics relative to the activities involved in the operation of the visual resources collection is an integral part of the effective management of the collection.

The methodology for the gathering process is to first isolate and describe those aspects of visual resources collection functions which are quantifiable. Some of these have been described in the first part of this chapter under the quantitative section of the annual report. The details involved in each function should be defined to prevent confusion over what is being counted. The glossary of terms is intended to help with this. Once the factors become agreed upon for units or isolated activities that can be measured quantitatively, there are comparable units or activities that can be compared with previous years, or with other collections. Surveys can be based on these comparable units. These statistical units should be broad enough to have wide applicability, yet specific enough to remain meaningful.

Numerous types of visual resources activity units have enough basic similarities to permit description and evaluation. Figure 5.4 lists some of these activity units.

Activity Units:	Visual Resource Collection Type			
	Art School	Academic Institution	Museum	Other
Acquisitions				

Slides
   # at beginning of year
   # added
   # withdrawn
   # at end of year
Other formats collected
   Same analysis as above
Circulation: (suggested categories)
   In-house
   Other
	Art history ____
	Studio ____
	Art educ. ____
	Other dept ____
	Students ____
			Curators ____
			Director ____
			"Friends" ____
			Public ____	

Personnel				

# full-time 	
   # part-time
   # professional / curatorial
   # technical
   # clerical				

Physical facilities				

total sq. ft.
   seating capacity
   viewing capacity
   storage capacity				

Slide mounting / photograph mounting or sleeving				

# new slide / photo 	
   # remounts slide / photo
   avg./hr. slide / photo				

Acquisitions				

# commercial sources 	
   # donations
   # in-house production
      # slide duplication
      # copywork
      # on-site photography
      # photographic prints
      other				

Financial				
income expenditures				

Figure 5.4. Form to collect statistics for various types of visual resources collections by activity unit.

The chart describes units that, taken singly or used in conjunction with other data, tell something about the activities of a particular visual resources collection and make possible comparisons among specific types of collections. Most of these activities are already recognized as common among visual resources collections, needing only a uniform reporting system.

In reporting holdings, the concepts of quality and quantity cannot be overlooked. If a visual resources collection contains forty thousand slides, the statistics do not reveal that 20 percent of them are pink, black-and-white, poor-quality copy work, or duplicate slides. Therefore, reporting numbers per se means little unless some factor of quality is included. To report accurately the quality of any one visual resources collection would require complex statistical sampling procedures. (Curators as well as users often disagree on quality!) Also, strengths and biases of the holdings are not necessarily a sign of poor acquisition decisions, but more a reflection of the needs of the local users. To evaluate general collection holdings, some form of checklist must be formulated. This is complicated by the use of diverse classification systems in visual resources collections nationally. For some collections, to report quantities of holdings in each medium would be difficult because their primary divisions are by periods rather than media.

Counting the Collection

Library standards suggest that as a minimum, at least one-fourth of the collection should be counted each year, and that a continuous inventory should be made on a cycle of two to four years. (Public book librarians average a 1 percent loss per year.)[6] It seems reasonable to suggest a similar counting system for visual resources collections. Each collection could count its total holdings in its main classes to arrive at a total. Annual loses are not so easily determined for several reasons; for example, many collections lack shelflists. Also, the practice of combining privately owned slides with collection slides for convenience often results in collection slides being missing for a year or so and then reappearing.

The number of items added each year can be derived easily through an access procedure. Each slide should be assigned a unique accession number consisting of a prefix which indicates the year acquired, followed by a hyphen, and then numbered serially—88-00,001, 88-00,002, etc.—or a unique consecutive number. An example of an accessions record page is in appendix D. Records should be kept for slides withdrawn, with an indication of whether or not a replacement was obtained. These three items will result in total numbers at the end of the fiscal year. The same procedure can be set up for other formats collected.

The procedures for maintaining *circulation* records are covered in chapter 7, "Circulation and Control."

A method for reporting on *personnel* or staff is important, but because staffing patterns and job catagories and descriptions vary greatly, such reports can be misleading. Most book libraries report according to professional and nonprofessional staff, which is confusing for visual resources collections because not all curators have professional status. A partial solution to this might be to include in the category of professional staff the description for staff who have decision making responsibility in the collection. Since a great deal of work in a visual resources collection is clerical in nature, such personnel should be reported as well, for if there is no staff to do the clerical work, it becomes the work of the curator!

Also, a word on using the term *full-time equivalent* (FTE) in the report for part-time clerical staff. Since much of the clerical work in the collection is done by part-time student workers under the supervision of the curator or other full-time curatorial staff, it is more descriptive to indicate the number of individuals and the average number of hours per week for a given period of time or a total of weekly hours worked. There is a big difference to a supervisor between 2.25 full-time equivalents and 8 part-time students working approximately twelve hours per week each.

Staff salaries, though a frequent topic of discussion within the profession, are not easily compared because of the differences in pay scales as related to costs of living in various parts of the country as well as the different responsibilities assigned or required of the incumbents. Perhaps salary ranges (differences between highest and lowest salaries) for visual resources curators and various staff positions would be more useful if reported by collection types as well as geographic regions.

Statistics on *physical facilities* should include (1) number of square feet of space for the total operation (include office, work areas, darkroom space, housing of other formats if under the supervision of the collection); (2) numbers of viewing and sorting stations for users to assemble lectures; (3) number of square feet occupied by slide storage cabinets or files (include space for users to pull out racks or drawers) and size of holdings; (4) square footage break down (if possible) for the individual sections or areas such as photographs, darkroom or copy stand space, circulation area, curator's office, and other staff areas; and (5) other spaces.

The importance of the general total gross square feet is that it reflects potential growth restrictions and the general service capabilities to the users. The numbers of viewing stations indicate potential on-site use, which also promotes collection control. It is useful to examine spaces allocated to storage files, slide and photograph study and sorting space, and circulation at a number of different collections. Once these data are assembled, they could help establish a standard for basic space needs for collections with specific numbers of users, collection size, circulation totals, etc.

Slide and/or photo mounting or sleeving figures can be maintained on a weekly basis by the staff involved with this process. In appendix D is a sample form for collecting slide mounting or photograph mounting or sleeving statistics. It is important that the staff member supervising the mounting make clear how the hours and totals are to be gathered and counted.

Acquisition statistics can be collected through a combination of information gleaned from the purchase records, which will indicate sources, quantities acquired, and prices, and the acquisitions record, which can be structured to provide the subject orientation and the requestor. There should also be a record of donations in connection with the letters of acceptance sent to donors as well as reflected in the acquisitions log. If the collection is building a computer database for collection holdings, the data entry format (see chapter 8, "Microcomputer Applications") can be designed with a field or fields to record this information, which can be calculated and reported annually.

The photographer should submit a weekly or monthly report by category of *in-house photographic services*. Appendix D contains a form for reporting these figures.

Financial reporting used for national comparisons should include only a minimum of items, such as total income, total expenditures, and total expenditures for acquisitions and production. This uniformity would make possible comparisons in visual resources programs, leading also to the potential of developing standards.

The daily gathering of information and statistics relative to the activities involved in the operation of the visual resources collection is an integral part of the effective management of the collection. In order for the information to be reliable and accurate, it must be gathered systematically and consistently. Once a system for collecting information and reporting it is set up, each monthly and annual report should be easy to prepare. The use of the same reporting format each year makes comparisons more effective as well.

The value of annual statistical reporting is not fully realized if no action is taken beyond producing it. Statistics alone cannot describe fully a visual resources program. Collected accurately and consistently, and used properly, they can serve the individual curator as well as the profession as a whole. Statistics can help the profession to look at itself objectively and to learn what is happening, rather than what is thought to be happening.

NOTES

[1] Christine L. Sundt, "Moisture Control through Slide Mounting," *International Bulletin for Photographic Documentation of the Visual Arts* 8, nos. 3 and 4 (Fall/Winter 1981): 8-9, 8-11.

[2] Art Libraries Society of North America, *Standards for Art Libraries and Fine Arts Slide Collections*, Occasional Paper No. 2 (Tucson, AZ: ARLIS/NA, 1983), 28-29.

[3] American National Standards Institute, *American Standard for Library Statistics* (New York: ANSI, 1969).

[4] Art Libraries Society of North America, *Standards for Art Libraries and Fine Arts Slide Collections*, 19-30.

[5]Christine Bunting, *Reference Tools for Fine Arts Visual Resources Collections*, Occasional Paper No. 4 (Tucson, AZ: Art Libraries Society of North America, 1984).

[6]Kenneth E. Beasley, *A Statistical Reporting System for Local Public Libraries*, Monograph No. 3 (Philadelphia: Pennsylvania State Library, 1964), 19.

6
Policies and Procedures Manuals

A policies and procedures manual is both a policy statement for users and a training manual for staff. The access to recorded information regarding regulations and procedures is a vital component in collection management and control. Contacts with visual resources collections experiencing problems of various kinds have revealed one common characteristic: few of these collections had written documentation outlining basic policies and procedures governing users and staff. It is a frequent practice among such collections to follow practices and policies formulated in an ad hoc manner, sporadically enforced, handed down to new staff and users by word of mouth. These practices result in inconsistencies in the handling of materials as well as uneven treatment of users.

The type of collection will govern the kinds of policies and procedures established, as well as the extent of the written documentation. However, whatever the type of collection, the official manual should contain information specific to the general resources of the collection, the users and their access, circulation, staffing services offered, administrative functions, as well as acquisitions and collection development procedures and policies (see figure 6.1).

I. GENERAL INFORMATION: description of the type of collection, its resources and services.

II. USER INFORMATION
   A. Circulation: access to collection formats and audiovisual equipment.
   B. Services provided.
   C. Summary of classification scheme for formats in collection.

III. COLLECTION DEVELOPMENT AND MAINTENANCE
   A. Acquisitions and development policy; copyright statement.
   B. Routine for processing new acquisitions.
   C. Data processing.
   D. Conservation and maintenance procedures.

IV. ADMINISTRATIVE FUNCTIONS
   A. Annual activities; timeline checklist.
   B. Staffing: organizational chart and job descriptions.
   C. Records and reports: correspondence.
   D. Sources for supplies, equipment, and services.

Figure 6.1. Suggested outline for policies and procedures manual.

GENERAL INFORMATION

Description of the Resources of the Collection

The introduction should describe the type of collection and its scope (what is collected), the role of the collection in relation to other units (department, library, museum, college, etc.), and the specific administrative structure. This section can further provide a listing of what will be described more completely in the individual sections of the manual. It can give an overview of the purpose and description of the collection, its holdings, its services, equipment, and facilities.

USER INFORMATION

Circulation and Access to the Collection and Audiovisual Equipment

Who may use the visual resources collection, for what purposes, when it is open, and how the collection is arranged are covered in this section of the manual. Included are circulation policies for all the formats collected (including audiovisual equipment) as well as information regarding the categories of borrowers eligible to use the collection, hours open, dates closed (holidays and vacation times), the loan periods, reserves and renewals, replacement fines for lost or overdue items, and sorting and filing procedures. A copy of the current printed circulation policy should also be included. If an automated circulation system is in use, it should be described and copies of the circulation forms (user records) provided. A general outline of how the collection is classified and a description of any additional means of access (catalogs, searchable database, etc.) are helpful for staff new to the collection and also as a guide for orienting new users. (This outline might double as a handout for new collection users.)

Services Provided

Here, services offered, to whom they are available, and necessary procedures may be described. In-house photographic services, use of copy stand and camera equipment, reservation and use of audiovisual equipment, projectionists, procedures allowing students to review slides and photographs from classes, and special orientations for users are items to be included here.

COLLECTION DEVELOPMENT AND MAINTENANCE

A collection development statement describing what is collected and policies regarding donations, withdrawals, and duplication of materials can be listed within this subheading. Who may request images and for what purposes, the curator's role in requesting items, time requirements, and quantity and quality restrictions should be covered.[1] Accepted practices for deaccessioning and replacing items from the collection should be included in the policy as well as a statement regarding copyright. This may be a brief statement, or it may be a lengthy, inclusive document covering a multitude of situations, depending upon which is best suited to the needs of the collection and its users.

Following the policy should be an outline describing the routine of processing new acquisitions, including assigning accession numbers, identification of images, mounting in glass for slides and mounting or sleeving for photographs, classification and cataloging, and labeling and filing new images in the collection. This should be a step-by-step description of each activity from the time the item is ordered until it is filed in

Collection Development and Maintenance / 63

its place in the collection. Include copies of official forms that are used in any of these steps. An example of such a chart for processing slides is given in figure 6.2, pp. 64-65.

Information should be included on all aspects of accessioning and date entry, database additions, corrections, deletions, classification and cataloging, proofing, updating, and printing. Complete accession records are an essential part of the acquisition process. Certainly for replacement purposes, but also for other cross checks, records of the sources for all collection items should be maintained. Such records can be in log or card form, or both. An example accession log page appears in appendix D. When in card form this also serves as the data collection or accession card.

The computer database functions should be thoroughly documented and will require a separate manual. This is an important aspect of computer automation and is addressed in chapter 8, "Microcomputer Applications."

Included also should be a description of how reclassifications and corrections are handled. Having an established procedure ensures that each correction is dealt with in a standard way, correctly and completely.

Conservation procedures for the various formats included in the collection is a function of maintenance. The harmful effects of heat, light, and moisture on photographic images and the balance required between use and careful handling and maintenance methods should be described. Information about long-term storage conditions, the care necessary in projecting, exhibiting slides and photographs, and binding slides in glass mounts, or sleeving or mounting photographs can be covered. Specific step-by-step instructions for slide or photograph mounting, specific to the materials used, should be included as well.[2]

Complete instructions for both filing of new acquisitions in the collection and refiling of circulated material should be covered. This can comprise an explanation of the alphanumeric filing codes (if used); methods for removing circulation (or out) cards (if used); maintenance of filing statistics; and procedures for easing out the slide storage drawers or racks, handling of interfiled shelf cards (if used),[3] and adding guide cards. All procedures for storage file maintenance should be described. If there are specific printed instructions for training filers, a copy of these should be included as well.

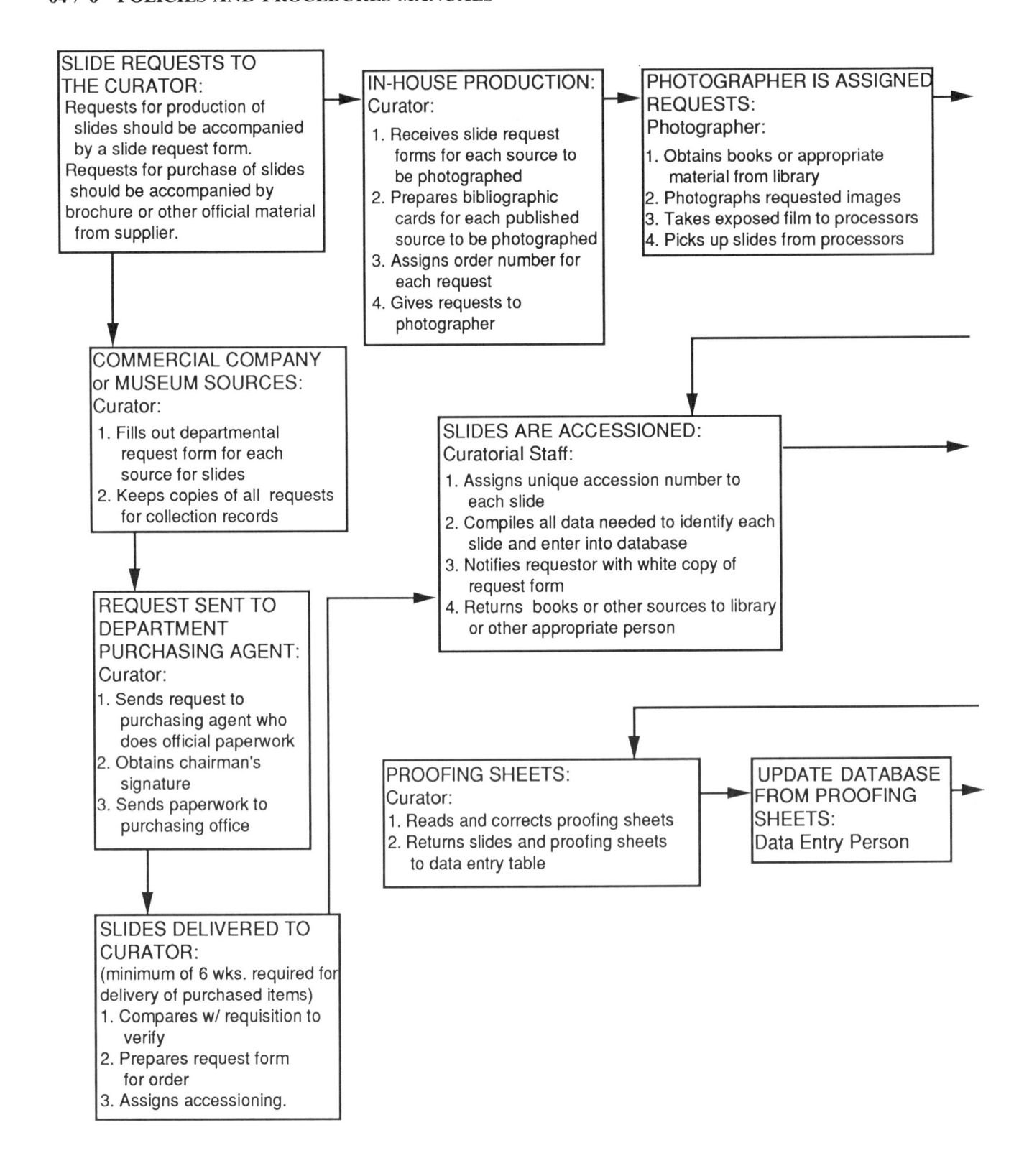

SLIDE REQUESTS TO THE CURATOR:
Requests for production of slides should be accompanied by a slide request form. Requests for purchase of slides should be accompanied by brochure or other official material from supplier.

IN-HOUSE PRODUCTION:
Curator:
1. Receives slide request forms for each source to be photographed
2. Prepares bibliographic cards for each published source to be photographed
3. Assigns order number for each request
4. Gives requests to photographer

PHOTOGRAPHER IS ASSIGNED REQUESTS:
Photographer:
1. Obtains books or appropriate material from library
2. Photographs requested images
3. Takes exposed film to processors
4. Picks up slides from processors

COMMERCIAL COMPANY or MUSEUM SOURCES:
Curator:
1. Fills out departmental request form for each source for slides
2. Keeps copies of all requests for collection records

SLIDES ARE ACCESSIONED:
Curatorial Staff:
1. Assigns unique accession number to each slide
2. Compiles all data needed to identify each slide and enter into database
3. Notifies requestor with white copy of request form
4. Returns books or other sources to library or other appropriate person

REQUEST SENT TO DEPARTMENT PURCHASING AGENT:
Curator:
1. Sends request to purchasing agent who does official paperwork
2. Obtains chairman's signature
3. Sends paperwork to purchasing office

PROOFING SHEETS:
Curator:
1. Reads and corrects proofing sheets
2. Returns slides and proofing sheets to data entry table

UPDATE DATABASE FROM PROOFING SHEETS:
Data Entry Person

SLIDES DELIVERED TO CURATOR:
(minimum of 6 wks. required for delivery of purchased items)
1. Compares w/ requisition to verify
2. Prepares request form for order
3. Assigns accessioning.

Collection Development and Maintenance / 65

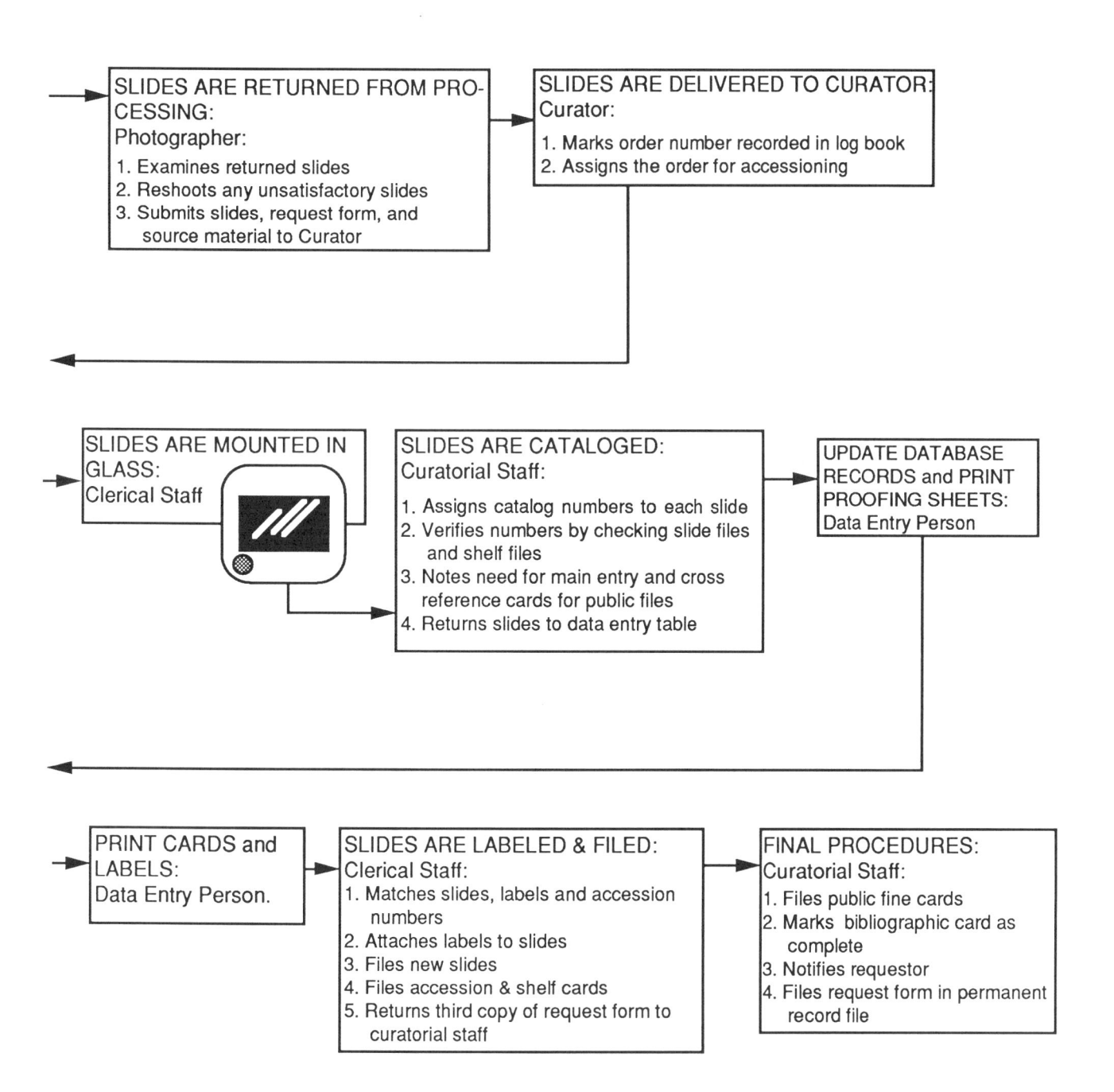

SLIDES ARE RETURNED FROM PROCESSING:
Photographer:
1. Examines returned slides
2. Reshoots any unsatisfactory slides
3. Submits slides, request form, and source material to Curator

SLIDES ARE DELIVERED TO CURATOR:
Curator:
1. Marks order number recorded in log book
2. Assigns the order for accessioning

SLIDES ARE MOUNTED IN GLASS:
Clerical Staff

SLIDES ARE CATALOGED:
Curatorial Staff:
1. Assigns catalog numbers to each slide
2. Verifies numbers by checking slide files and shelf files
3. Notes need for main entry and cross reference cards for public files
4. Returns slides to data entry table

UPDATE DATABASE RECORDS and PRINT PROOFING SHEETS:
Data Entry Person

PRINT CARDS and LABELS:
Data Entry Person.

SLIDES ARE LABELED & FILED:
Clerical Staff:
1. Matches slides, labels and accession numbers
2. Attaches labels to slides
3. Files new slides
4. Files accession & shelf cards
5. Returns third copy of request form to curatorial staff

FINAL PROCEDURES:
Curatorial Staff:
1. Files public fine cards
2. Marks bibliographic card as complete
3. Notifies requestor
4. Files request form in permanent record file

Figure 6.2. Acquisition of slides: Routine procedures.

ADMINISTRATIVE FUNCTIONS

Although the administrative and management duties increase as visual resources collections grow, there are numerous administrative functions that should be performed in collections, regardless of size. The procedures and policies should outline the administrative requirements for the collection.

A chart tracing *annual activities* is a valuable resource, both for instruction and as a reminder of the administrative activities that need to be accomplished each month. For a large collection this chart can also include the staff members responsible for each function. This chart can be organized monthly, as shown in figure 6.3, by quarter or semester, or by whatever division best suits the needs of the collection. This serves not only as a reminder, but also as a visual representation of the fluctuation of routine activities, enabling the curator to see when best to schedule special projects that require additional staff time. This chart can help a new curator comprehend the full range of annual activities, and should even be useful in staff recruiting.

AUGUST

Room / equipment schedule: fall
New library proxy cards for staff
Submit proposals: wages & MO&E.
Send job requests to CWSP office
Work schedules: part-time help
Memo to new faculty
Schedule new user orientations
Memo re: student users
Assign trays, circulation cards, work and storage areas.
Begin to interview and hire part-time help
August and summer statistics
Annual statistics
Prioritize work in progress

SEPTEMBER

Work on annual report
Continue to interview and hire part-time help
Orientations for new faculty, TAs, student teachers and graduate students
Slide and photo collection committee meeting
September statistics

OCTOBER

Special equipment requests
Annual report due
Staff evaluations
October statistics

FEBRUARY

Annual inventory: furniture and equipment
February statistics

MARCH

Slide and photo collection committee meeting
March statistics

APRIL

Recruit part-time help: summer and fall
Correspond with new faculty hired for next year re: slide needs
Room / equipment schedule for spring exams
Memo re: slide needs for next year
Memo re: return of all slides for inventory / shelf reading
April statistics

NOVEMBER

Recruit part-time help for spring
Memo: spring semester slide requests
November statistics

DECEMBER

Room / equipment schedule for fall exams
Memo: return of slides from fall
Refile all slides
Reclaim uncataloged slides used during fall
Recall slide trays and equipment keys
Statistics for December and fall semester
Projection equipment: annual maintenance
Submit wages proposal for spring semester

JANUARY

Room / equipment schedule: spring
Prioritize work in progress
Interview / hire part-time help
Submit list of part-time help
Work schedules for part-time help
Memo re: collection services to new faculty
Memo re: use of collection by students
Assign slide trays, circulation cards and work spaces for spring
Review budget
January statistics

MAY

Reclaim uncataloged slides used during spring
Refile all slides following exams
May and spring statistics
Recall slide trays and equipment keys
Conduct annual inventory / shelf reading

Interview / hire part-time help for summer
Submit list of part-time help for summer
Work schedules for part-time help for summer
Room / equipment schedule for summer
Assign slide trays, circulation cards, work and storage spaces for summer
Prioritize work in progress

JUNE

Submit orders for unencumbered annual budget
Submit "special" requests outside annual budget
June statistics

JULY / AUGUST

Plan for budget requests for coming year
Early orders for supplies and equipment for fall
July statistics

Draft annual report
User petitions for coming year
Refile all slides from summer
Reclaim uncataloged slides used during summer
Recall slide trays and equipment keys
Begin to compile data for annual report

Figure 6.3. Annual activities: Monthly activities.

Staffing

Well-documented policies, procedures, and instructions presented in an organized format are a valuable training aid for the entire staff. An organizational chart including both full-time and part-time staff, followed by job descriptions and lists of duties for each position, should be a part of the staffing section of the manual. An example of an organizational chart appears in figure 6.4. Included in this section also should be copies of application forms and any other forms used by or for the staff: evaluations, work schedules, timesheets, descriptions of benefits, holidays, and the like. Certainly any rules or regulations established by the collection related to staff should be included here. (See appendix D for sample part-time staff application forms, weekly work schedules, and weekly timesheets.)

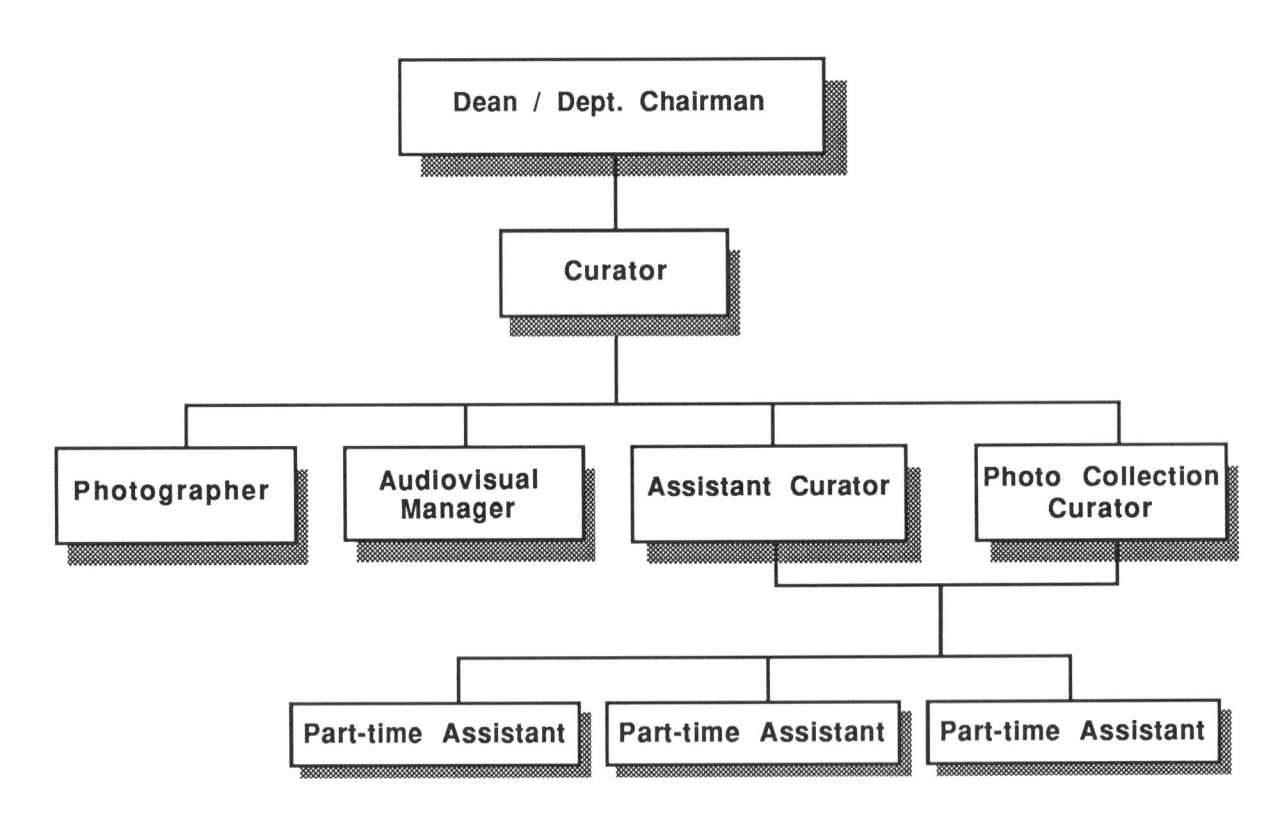

Figure 6.4. Sample staff organizational chart.

RECORDS AND REPORTS

The manual should include a description of reports and records useful in the administration of the visual resources collection. These become less burdensome to produce when standard formats for the recording of the information contained in them are established. The timeline chart of activities described earlier includes the production of records and reports and when each is due. This section of the manual should include examples of these report formats as well as reference to how the information contained in them is compiled. (See chapter 5, "Reports and Statistics," for descriptions for formats for various reports and forms for the collecting and recording of statistics which become part of these reports.) Including examples of memos and letters that are issued regularly, such as information sent to new users, overdue notices, reminders about return of equipment and visual materials, schedules for orientations, and reminders to submit requests for new material for upcoming lectures and/or classes, will facilitate distribution of these standard items, once again saving the curator's time and promoting equal treatment of users.

SUPPLIES, EQUIPMENT, AND SERVICES

Certain supplies and services constitute standard annual purchases for the visual resources collection. The manual should contain a list of these items, specifications required for ordering, a source or supplier, and the quantities regularly purchased. It is also valuable to list services regularly required by the collection and reliable vendors. This directory of supplies and services is useful not only for the collection staff but also as a quick reference for outside requests for information.

It can be expedient to list supplies by activity, such as slide binding, photograph sleeving or mounting, audiovisual equipment, or in-house photography. Figure 6.5 is an example of what might appear in the section for slide bindings supplies.

Suppliers	Supplies	Annual Quantity
Best Camera Co. Box A Somewhere, CA.	Parrag Lightweight Mounts w/ Anti-Newton Ring Glass 100/bx. Cat # 19,833	7,500
Same as above	Proloc Precision Fastener Stainless steel Cat. no. 19,878	2
The Tape Store 2222 So. Ave. Downtown, NY.	No. 425 Ultra Thin Metalized Polyester Tape. 48 gauge polyester, metalized on both sides, .0007 in. thick; tensile strength: 12 lbs. 120% adhesion to polyester. 24 oz./in. color: bright aluminum, both sides. 1/4" x 100' rolls.	12 rolls

Figure 6.5. Activity-oriented supplies record.

It is helpful if the policies and procedures manual can be produced on a word processor and stored on disk so that it can be easily revised and expanded. Practically every section of the manual is subject to changes, and if it is to function effectively, it must be continuously revised and updated. A current and easy-to-use manual is a vital instrument in the daily operation of the visual resources collection, for both staff and patrons.

NOTES

[1] Helen H. Wykle, "Collection Development Policies for Academic Visual Resources Collections," *Art Documentation* 7, no. 1 (1988): 22-25.

[2] Gillian Scott, ed., *Guide to Equipment for Slide Maintenance and Viewing* (Albuquerque, NM: Mid-America College Art Association, 1978), 4-9. For additional information on slide mounting see Eastman

Kodak, *Mounting Slides in Glass*, AE-36 (Rochester, NY: Eastman Kodak, 1971); Christine L. Sundt, "Mounting Slide Film between Glass—For Preservation or Destruction?" *Visual Resources* 2, nos. 1-3 (1981-1982): 35-62; A. G. Tull, "Hazards of Mounting Slides," *Photographic Journal* 114 (1974): 184-85, 232-35; A. G. Tull, "Film Transparencies between Glass," *British Journal of Photography* 125 (1978): 322-23, 349-51, 353.

[3]A shelflist is a complete record of the holdings of a collection (or library) arranged in file (or shelf) order. See chapter 7, "Circulation and Control," for further discussion.

7
Circulation and Control

Most visual resources collections differ from libraries in that their primary purpose is to support teaching activities rather than research. Although research may be conducted in visual resources collections as well, these collections rarely contain what is considered primary visual material (exceptions being such collections as the Warburg and Courtauld Institute, the Witt Library, etc.). Not all visual resources collections circulate materials in the same way that library books circulate, and those that do have a relatively limited group of borrowers. To whatever extent circulation is conducted, the organization of this activity, the associated implementation of policies and procedures, and planning for and training of staff and users is the responsibility of the visual resources curator.

Control of visual resources material involves more than checking materials in and out. Just as do book libraries, visual resources collections maintain control over the materials contained in them. Control is promoted through such elements as a well-located circulation counter or desk, carefully thought-out and understood circulation policies and procedures, well-organized and easily accessible storage for images, a carefully maintained collection with an ongoing maintenance and development plan, skilled filers, shelflists for inventory control, carefully oriented users, and access security.

The extent to which these controls are utilized will vary from collection to collection. The type of collection is the factor in determining the circulation policies and controls required. As in other sections of this book, the types of collections defined in the *ARLIS/NA Standards for Art Libraries and Fine Arts Slide Collections* provide a useful definition of three general types:

1. Academic Fine Arts Slide Collections
    library administrated
    dept./school administrated

2. Museum Fine Arts Slide Collections
    limited to curatorial staff
    open to public

3. Public Library Fine Arts Slide Collection[1]

POLICIES

Controls begin with procedures and policies for circulation and the physical means by which it is conducted and regulated. Regulation and control are necessary to promote and at the same time protect access to the visual resources. Because of the variety of types of collections and their individual requirements, no one circulation control system can be universally acceptable. The nature of the formats collected, the needs of the users, and what the staff can realistically handle must influence these policies. It is advisable for the curator to involve a committee which includes users in the formulation of these policies. Clearly defined, written, and widely understood circulation policies are a necessity. A concise printed handout saves the curator repeated explanations and defending of policies. The more "official" the document looks, the more effective it will be.

The circulation policies should include a brief statement of purpose or mission of the collection and its administrative position; a description of the circulation function and the materials that circulate; categories of authorized borrowers (if several types are provided for); procedure for borrower registration; the loan periods; user orientation requirements; procedures for access to files and removal of images; sign-out procedures; reserves; procedures for overdue, lost, or damaged materials; renewals; and loans over vacations, breaks, or summer. These written regulations should be available at the circulation desk, they should be distributed at user orientations, and they should be included in staff policy and procedures manuals.

CIRCULATION SYSTEMS

"The objectives of a good circulation system are to: save borrowers' time, to speed up the routines of checking material in and out, to reduce costs, and to relieve librarians for more professional work."[2] The circulation activity can be divided into six areas:

1. registration/identification of borrowers
2. identification of items being checked out
3. identification of items being checked in
4. reserves and recalls
5. overdue notices
6. circulation statistics

The particular methods employed must be simple and efficient, both for users and staff, and minimize excessive delay or waiting at the circulation desk. They should be economical and adaptable for all types of formats collected, including audiovisual equipment, and if necessary allow varying loan periods.

In a collection serving numerous borrowers, some method for identifying qualified borrowers is important. This may be an alphabetical card file or user authorization cards issued to borrowers. The purpose of these records is to provide information that enables the visual resources collection staff to recover items not returned in a timely manner.

The actual charging system identifies the items taken out with the name of the borrower. This can be done either with an automated or a manual system, listing what is removed (preferably a unique number for each item, such as an accession number or bar code number) as well as the name and other pertinent information about the borrower. Other necessary information includes the date the materials are checked out, the date due, if they have been placed on reserve for use at a later date, and name or initials of the staff member handling the transaction.

Manual Systems

The most common system currently used in visual resources collections is what is known in libraries as the "transaction" or "absence" system. This refers to material that is absent from the collection. In a transaction recording system, the user and the items borrowed are recorded and kept in the "out" file for the duration of the loan only. The cancelled charge sheets provide information for circulation statistics.

The charge sheet used in the visual resources collection is often 8½-by-11 inches in size, is convenient for storage and consultation, and is sufficient to record data for the numbers of slides borrowed by a user at any given time. Examples of various charge sheets are included in appendix E.

This form of circulation system promotes borrower participation in the charging operation by having the individual simply list what is being checked out. Such a method is functional for many collections which comprise limited subjects and are used by a small number of patrons at any given period of time. There are, however, some disadvantages: first, for the borrower, the time-consuming task of listing each item being borrowed; second, the chance of inaccuracies in compiling this list; and third, the awkward process for the staff to locate the borrower for specific items that are removed from the files.

The only solution to the first problem is to reduce the information on the charge sheet to the minimum necessary to identify the borrower and the items being taken out. The unique accession number for each item and the artist's name or other pertinent descriptive information about the image is the minimum necessary for the staff to be able to locate an item checked out, or in the case of a damaged or lost item, the accession number will provide information necessary for replacement. The only remedy for the problem of locating borrowers for specific items missing from the files would be a subject index of slides signed out at any given time. However, this is not feasible with a manual circulation system. Another solution is the use of in-file circulation (or drop) cards.

Circulation for frequent and regular borrowers can be more efficiently handled with the use of assigned coded circulation cards (2-by-2 inches in size) inserted wherever a slide or slides are removed. This practice is common among academic visual resources collections for use in slide files and has had some measure of success. Despite some drawbacks to this method, the positive aspects promote its continuation.

One method for dealing with both the problems of inaccuracy in signed out items as well as amount of time required to sign them out is to photocopy the label information on the slides. Though expensive, particularly if equipment must be purchased or rented, this procedure saves time for the borrowers and is a more reliable accounting of items removed from the collection. However, though borrowers' time is saved with this method, staff time may be increased because of having to position slides on the machine for copying. And, if 8½-by-11-inch paper is used, only twenty slides can be recorded at a time. Therefore, if fifty slides are checked out by a user, the circulation staff will have to position slides on the copier surface three times. This method produces more paper than other charge sheet methods, and the problem of locating the borrower of missing material remains the same.

So long as the number of borrowers is small, the charge sheet system, coupled with some form of in-file indication of what is removed, is a sufficient circulation system for most visual resources collections. This method for circulation issued at The University of Texas at Austin Art Department with very few problems, with an average annual circulation of 75,000 slides during the last five years. There is no doubt, however, that such a system would be less effective with hundreds of users.

Automated Systems

Automated systems should provide the same information as the manual systems described, be more efficient, and provide improved service to the borrower. Only with the microcomputer has it become possible for visual resources collections to consider the automation of their circulation systems at a reasonable cost. Automating circulation allows the visual resources collection to reduce borrowers' time spent in the circulation process, thus providing better service, reducing inaccuracies, gaining improved control over the collection, and facilitating the search by artist or subject for items already checked out. Automation of circulation does not have to be on a major scale to function efficiently. If the individual situation is carefully analyzed, even a simple system can be successful. How sophisticated the automated loan system will be depends upon how much time and money can be spent and the extent of information desired about borrowed items.

Planning for automated circulation should begin with a list of the desired tasks to be performed, both for the present and the future. Decide if a "transaction" (absence) system, as described under manual systems, is desired, or if an "inventory control" system is what is needed. The absence circulation system database contains only the items currently on loan and requires only enough storage for what is checked out. With this system, records are deleted when items are returned; all subsequent loans of these same items must be entirely reentered.

If an inventory control system, the entire circulating collection is recorded in a database. Inventory databases represent an enormous investment in time and require sufficient computer storage for the entire collection. The database may contain some or all of the information in the collection's main database, such as accession number, the artist's name, title, date, source, subject headings, call number, and unique number such as a bar code number or the accession number.

MAINTENANCE AND CONTROL

The primary goal of circulation is to make material in the visual resources collection accessible through logical physical arrangement and effective management. This is usually taken for granted until a user has difficulty locating an item. Effective management of the storage files or racks is an integral part of the overall circulation operations. If there is open access to the storage files, disturbances to the file order are likely. Policies regulating the circulation of slides and photographs and how they are signed out are just one phase of control for the collection. Other controls include user orientations; the circulation desk and its location; shelf or inventory lists and their use; sorting and refiling procedures and staff training; collection weeding, replacements, and collection development; file arrangement and other access such as cross-references; overdue notices and fines; and collection security.

User Orientations

In most visual resources collections, it is usually not possible for a totally untrained person to make use of the collection effectively. The curator and staff must provide training for users. Either individual or collective instruction can be useful. Of course, the individual orientation is usually best because it is possible to address specific needs or interests of the borrower. In group sessions, the instruction tends to be more general, but this can still be a practical way to introduce users to the arrangement of the holdings, what is available, how to prepare for using the collection, and the policies and procedures that govern its use. Careful training of users promotes more successful access to images needed and therefore more satisfied users. In addition, simple hints about searching in the files help maintain shelf order and control.

Circulation Desk

A centralized location for the circulation desk, near the entrance to the collection and convenient to the staff, where circulation and user records are kept and all items are signed in and out, as well as a single entry and exit for the facility are important elements in circulation control. The centralized circulation desk gives the users a specific point where information may be acquired. It need be nothing more than a well-located desk which all users pass. This location facilitates differentiation of regular patrons from the newcomers, the latter of whom can be oriented to collection use immediately. This desk should be the responsibility of a member of the full-time staff, but can be staffed by a part-time assistant. The overall supervision of circulation, overdues, recalls, filing, and training is a professional activity and should be handled by the curator or a permanent member of the curatorial staff.

Shelflists

A shelflist is a record of items as they appear in file (or shelf) order. As the official record of collection holdings, it is useful for locating materials and for verifying source information. It can take several forms. If there is a complete database of the collection, the shelflist may be a computer printout of the records in file order. It more commonly exists in card catalog format, housed in a safe place, often separate from the actual items. An interfiled slide shelflist consists of squares of approximately 2-by-2-inch card stock, one for each slide in the collection, which contains duplicate label information for the slide it accompanies and is filed either immediately in front of or behind its slide.

The separate shelflist can be produced on 3-by-5-inch cards or in a printed list and contains specific information about the item. It is filed, or listed, in shelf order (i.e., the order in which the slides, photographs, or other formats are filed). This form or shelflist is not so handy for the users as the interfiled version. However, being housed separately, it is more often used by the collection staff and is not so subject to loss or mutilation through use as the interfiled version; it also does not consume valuable space in the slide storage files.

The interfiled slide shelflist is popular with users because it constitutes an easily accessible permanent record of specific slides in the collection. The interfiled shelflist card can be produced simply by duplicating the slide labels. Considering its advantages, it is interesting to note that this is not a widely practiced procedure. This is an indication that it has disadvantages as well. One such problem already noted is the valuable space that the interfiled shelflist occupies. Another disadvantage is that the interfiled shelf cards, unless secured with a rod in the bottom of the slide file drawers, will often become misplaced or lost.[3] Additionally, the constant handling of the shelf cards by slide users (and filers) causes wear and tear and need for replacement, unless they are enclosed in a protective covering.

Automated database management systems such as the Santa Cruz *Universal Slide Classification System*[4] will provide a shelflist, if programmed to produce such a report. This list can be updated at intervals with new additions and various modifications.

Inventory and Shelf Reading

Another form of control that utilizes the shelflist (whatever its form) is the periodic shelf reading or inventory. The purpose of this is to compare shelflist records with items in the collection. Over a period of time lost items, replacements, withdrawals, and changes in cataloging contribute to inaccuracies between the holdings and the records. It is extremely important for the shelf file records to reflect what is really in the collection and to ascertain that the collection is in proper order. Another function of the inventory or shelf reading process is to establish what is lost in order to determine what should be replaced, if possible, as well as the needs for or successes of various security and control procedures. An analysis of the collection strengths and weaknesses can be accomplished through shelf reading as well.

One helpful procedure for missing slides is to insert a 2-by-2-inch card where the slide should file containing the call number, date, and accession number and the word *missing*, thereby notifying users that an item is lost. If after a predetermined length of time the slide is not returned, it can either be replaced or officially withdrawn.

Collections should be inventoried at a specific time, at least once a year if possible. The inventory should be at a time when user demands are lowest and loans are at a minimum. The curator can either recall all slides in circulation for this procedure, or rely on circulation records to account for slides on loan. Large collections unable to inventory the entire collection annually can inventory selected sections until the entire collection has been "read." The sections can be chosen either because missing items have been reported in the area, because they have received heavy use, or simply because they have not been verified in a long time.

Whatever the size of the collection, shelf reading or inventory can be a monumental task. It has to be one of the most monotonous jobs performed in a visual resources collection and should not be done for long periods of time without interruption. It requires a well-trained staff and should be closely supervised. However, the information generated from this procedure is of great value in informing the curator of the state of the collection. It identifies missing items, indicates problems relating to either use or filing, and points out where special attention is needed for replacement or multiple copies.

Sorting and Filing Procedures

A necessary part of circulation and control is the careful supervision of filing and other related tasks. Filing is a function that often utilizes part-time help. Because variations occur in the filing workload during different times of the day and throughout the year, these workers may need to be trained to do a variety of other tasks. Overseeing circulation requires the training filers to be sympathetic to the overall service aspect of the job. In order to file accurately, they must know and understand the classification scheme used in order to increase their overall understanding of the logic behind the system. Training can be done with a set of photocopies of labels from the collection which are to be sorted in file sequence. The filers should also be trained to understand the use of the shelflist as a tool in verifying call numbers and shelf order.

After initial training, new filers should be closely supervised. In a drawer system, for example, all newly filed slides can be turned on edge diagonally for verification by the supervisor. When filing photographs, they can be left up, slightly above others, being careful not to damage the edges when closing the drawers. Once the new filer has demonstrated the ability to file in proper order and location, such close checking and supervision can cease. Filers should be instructed to call to their supervisor's attention to any items in need of repair, rebinding, relabeling, recataloging, or replacement due to damage. Coordination between the circulation filers and the repairers is imperative to avoid items removed for repair being out of circulation for extended periods. When an item is removed for maintenance, a marker should be left in its place in the file with the date and a brief explanation. Filers should also be trained to look for misfiles and to refile them correctly, to straighten and shift the contents of the files to ease crowding, and to add guide cards and revise drawer labels where needed. One practice is to assign filers maintenance duty over specific sections. This encourages a sort of "pride of responsibility," thus promoting better maintenance of the files. Misfiled items and crowded drawers lead to user dissatisfaction.

The refiling of circulated materials is a priority activity in any visual resources collection utilized for teaching and should be done as rapidly and accurately as possible. The filers should follow an established procedure, which might include selection of items to be filed, inspection and cleaning each item, sorting and counting, proper removal of circulation cards (if used) from the files, and accurate recording of statistics. Even though the filers may have little direct interchange with collection users, the accuracy of their work and the dispatch with which it is executed will have maximum impact on the way that the visual resources collection and its services are perceived by the users.

Weeding, Replacement, and Collection Development

A component of file maintenance and management is the continuous process of assessing its strengths and weaknesses, its gaps and gluts, and weeding or deaccessioning damaged or excess items from the collection. The benefits of this practice manifest themselves in space gained in the files. Users' time is also saved by reducing the number of poor-quality or redundant images that must be browsed through in order to find what is needed. Weeding provides a continuous check on the need for repairs and relabeling and provides feedback on the strengths and weaknesses of the collection. Policies or guidelines for weeding and evaluation should be established to govern this practice as part of the general collection development policy. An example of such a policy follows:

> Slides (or other formats) which no longer meet the objectives of the collection, either in quality or content, or for which acceptable additional copies exist will be withdrawn from the storage files. Disposal of such material is at the discretion of the curator, contingent upon any provisions the administrative unit or institution may have regarding such actions.

Evaluation and weeding should be the responsibility of a staff member who is involved with the selection process and knows the users' needs, someone who can view the collection holdings from a long-range perspective developed through working with and planning for the collection.

Determine the areas of the collection most in need of analysis and evaluation and set priorities for the order in which this will be done. This work is best done during low use periods. The first step in this process is to establish correct file order and to identify any missing items. A useful signal in a slide file is a 2-by-2-inch card marked "missing" with the call number or description of the item and the date. Review the items carefully, one item at a time, judging the quality of each image; comparing it with newer, better quality images; assessing accuracy of identification and cataloging information; and determining its relevance to borrower needs.

For the materials to be withdrawn without replacement, remove the item and all file cards and references to the item (including any computer data entries). For those items to be withdrawn only after being replaced, mark records, but leave the item in the file until the replacement is received. It is helpful to mark the labels of items to be replaced with the letter *R*, for example, so that users will know that replacement is in process. Obtain replacements as promptly as possible.

When good-quality nonessential or surplus slides or photographs are discovered during the evaluation process, a valuable option after withdrawing them is to offer them for exchange (if your institution allows) with another collection for something you do not have, but could use. Notices for slide exchanges are run in issues of the *International Bulletin for Photographic Documentation of the Visual Arts*.

If sufficient operating space is a problem in the main facility, the visual resources curator may consider relocating little used items, or sections of the collection into a separate or remote "closed stack" storage area, thus opening space in files for more frequently used images. Caution should be taken to ensure that environmental conditions are safe wherever the materials are stored. One method for tracking a slide's use is to mark a slide with a special color dot to signal that it has been used at least once during the year. The next year, if it is used, it will receive another dot (a different color) when it first circulates. After several years using this system, it is possible to determine which slides are being used and which ones are not. Figure 7.1 illustrates this marking system.

This process of collection evaluation, done routinely throughout the year, will enable the curator to expand his or her knowledge of the collection holdings and make informed selection of new images based on actual strengths, weaknesses, and use of the collection. Weeding provides better service, improved access, and more reliable and efficient use.

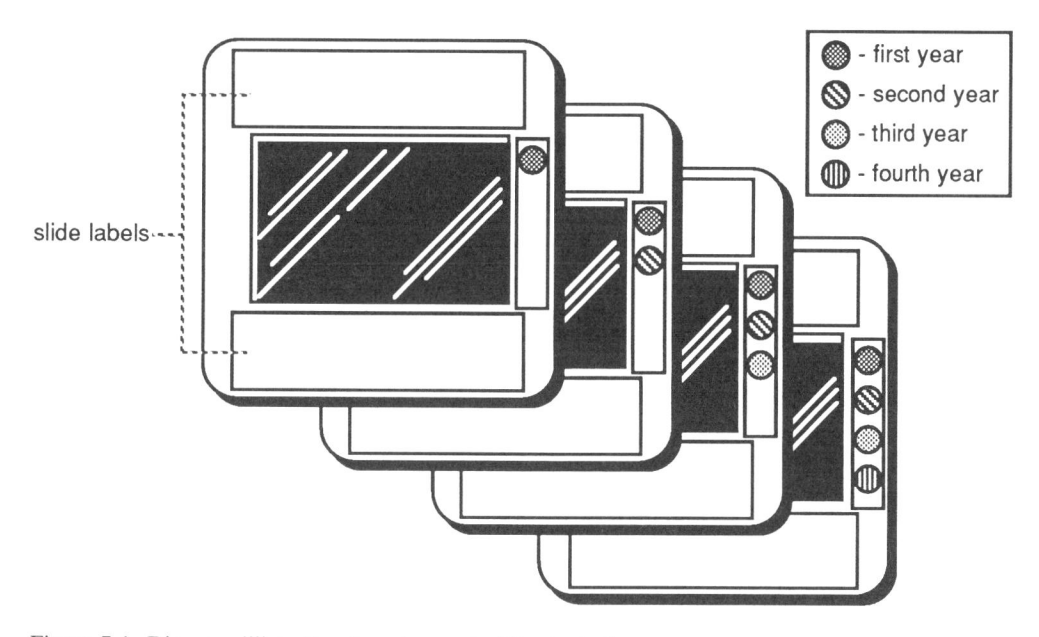

Figure 7.1. Diagram illistrating how to mark slides to indicate usage.

File Arrangement and Other Access

Since efficient and ready access to slides is part of circulation, the physical arrangement of the storage units is important. Most visual resources collections emphasize a self-help policy in access and circulation, and therefore communication to the users about how the files are arranged and the overall "logic" of this arrangement is very important. The arrangement is important in providing access to the items.

There are several possibilities for determining file arrangement: whether to arrange by classification order or some alternative system, whether providing for maximum space efficiency is the primary consideration, or whether promoting ease in browsing is the top priority. If the first consideration is the primary goal, determine whether and/or how much the collection can be subdivided and whether users locate their own material or rely on staff to locate and pull requested items.

Shelf or file order can be varied to modify the physical arrangement of an existing classification system; for example, pulling all images that illustrate printing techniques out of their various places in the classified order and putting them together in a special printmaking section. The location of groups or classes stored or filed out of the classified sequence can be indicated with directional signs. Such special collections of images developed by removing individual items are more precise in focus and probably more valuable to users, but designation of these individual items requires the additional effort of developing indexes or catalogs, either separate or interfiled, indicating to the user where the image of the work sought can be located. An example of this latter disposition might be a special group of images documenting a particular textbook housed separately from the main collection.

The configuration or arrangement of the storage files can promote accessibility and control in several ways. Like items or classes can be grouped together or separated to reduce congestion caused by crowding of users in one area. The arrangement of the files in the facility will also determine how well the files can be monitored by staff during use.

Most image collections are designed for browsing and easy access. While advantageous to the user, this arrangement increases the labor required for refiling, shelf reading, searching for misplaced slides, and the needs of collection security.

Security

Security is an important factor in collection control. In many collections, especially those associated with academic programs, access to the collection after regular hours is common. By providing keys or passes, or making arrangements with building security personnel, the curator may offer after hours access to special patrons. With a clear understanding on everyone's part regarding policies for collection use after hours and a thorough orientation by the curator for these special users, this arrangement can be successful. Policies for after hours, unsupervised usage should be developed with and endorsed by the departmental chairperson, museum director, or school dean, to ensure that any liabilities that may result from special access to the collection after hours are covered by the institution.

Fees, Overdue Notices, and Fines

The return of borrowed library materials has been a problem in libraries ever since materials began to circulate. Tardiness in return of material is a common problem among visual resources collections. Procedures for handling overdue and/or lost items and a schedule of fines and other penalties should be clearly given within the circulation procedures. From the circulation records one should be able to determine when and to whom overdue or recall notices need to be sent. The loan periods should be clearly defined and stated. Users should be advised when materials are due at the time they are checked out. Telephone calls, letters, reminders, and even a bill for overdue fines are methods for inducing users to return materials and equipment. Collecting fines can be a very time-consuming process. Cost effectiveness should be calculated when establishing a fee schedule and billing policy for overdue materials. However, a collection experiencing marked loss of materials by users may wish to collect replacement costs. For slides this figure is somewhat difficult to determine since the purchase price of a slide is only a small portion of its actual replacement costs. Added costs include the mount, labels, and, of course, labor. Unit cost records are useful when losses occur. In many instances, overdue or missing items are best recovered through peer pressure, from one colleague requiring material being held by another.

Control for the visual resources collection resides in a combination of procedures and policies, consistent yet flexible, that facilitate efficient use of the items contained within the collection by all the intended users.

NOTES

[1] Art Libraries Society of North America, *Standards for Art Libraries and Fine Arts Slide Collections*, Occasional Paper No. 2 (Tucson, AZ: ARLIS/NA, 1983).

[2] Nevada Wallis Thomason, *Circulation Systems for School Library Media Centers* (Littleton, CO: Libraries Unlimited, 1985), 4.

[3] An example of this type of interfiled slide shelflist card can be found in Betty Jo Irvine, *Slide Libraries*, 2nd ed. (Littleton, CO: Libraries Unlimited, 1979), 128.

[4] Wendell Simons, and Lurene Tansey, *Universal Slide Classification System* (Santa Cruz, CA: The University Library, University of California, 1967).

8
Microcomputer Applications

The purpose of this chapter is to introduce to the visual resources curator the possible uses of microcomputers in the visual resources collection for managerial functions. Rather than providing specifications on how to set up a system, some of the fundamental decisions involved when computer automation is undertaken are discussed. Benefits that can be derived from automated systems are also presented.

Computer technology can be applied to various functions and services in a visual resources collection. These functions include acquisitions and collection development, classification, index or catalog production, search and retrieval, circulation, label and index production, statistics gathering and analysis, and other reports.

Since the goal of automation is to do something less expensively, more accurately, and more rapidly, and to replace inefficient manual procedures, the visual resources collection is a highly suitable candidate for computer automation. Anyone associated with such an operation for even a short time is aware of the labor-intensive, time-consuming character of every detail of its operation and use. Each step in preparing an image for use is characterized by tedium and repetition, and is replete with occasions for errors. Much effective work has been done manually, but today, due to high-volume demands, the high cost of labor, recent technological advancements, and more computer literate users, the manual approach has become less desirable. As we see increasing interest in the collection of and subsequent access to all types of visual images and related information, the effective management of this material becomes imperative.

In the operations of visual resources collections basically two types of control are involved: physical and intellectual. The functions and services that are associated with the *physical control* of the collection are acquisition; production of labels, cards, and other catalogs; and circulation. *Intellectual control* involves not only the developing of complete image descriptions that accompany each slide or photograph, but also the creation of added access paths to the visual images by means other than the usual divisions of art medium, form, chronology or culture, and geographic designations. Providing such control for visual images is possible with computer automation; however, it requires not only broad subject expertise on the part of the staff and authority list of acceptable terms or a subject thesaurus,[1] but also an additional, time-consuming step in the cataloging process.

Improvements in access to images through more effective physical and intellectual control is possible with computer automation. Automating the most repetitious tasks should certainly be reason enough to proceed with plans to automate. Indeed, since many tasks are interrelated, automation of one often implements another.

HISTORICAL BACKGROUND

The earliest attempts at computer automation in visual resources collections occurred in the 1960s and 1970s with mainframe computers. Especially in university settings, where equipment already existed and its use was fostered among the academic departments by low cost time and available terminals, such projects were encouraged. For the most part, they developed in isolation, each institution going its own chosen direction, and resulted in the duplication of efforts and development of redundant but incompatible systems. Nevertheless, several of these programs are still functioning, expanding, and in a few cases, being adopted at other collections. Others, for a variety of reasons, were abandoned. A general description of some of these projects can be found in Richardson and Hannah's *Guide to Automation in Visual Resources Collections* and Markey's "Visual Arts Resources and Computers."[3]

The primary focus in these early mainframe projects was one of intellectual control: indexing and information retrieval for a specific class of images. But even these efforts proceeded slowly. The absence of a national standard indexing vocabulary required each project to develop its own. There was often less than enthusiastic support on the part of users, who saw no real advantage in these indexing and retrieval schemes for their routine use. They were already able to locate needed images and were more interested in a solution to alleviate the slow and tedious procedures involved in processing new images into the collection. Another drawback to these early endeavors was the fact that the mainframe required a programmer to modify or develop new routines; its use was limited to how it was already set up. Furthermore, programming languages were difficult to use, and there was usually no direct access to a printer.

MICROCOMPUTERS

In the late 1970s, when microcomputers became commercially popular, automation found its way into visual resources collections quite rapidly. Descriptions or reports of successful projects began appearing in the *International Bulletin for Photographic Documentation of the Visual Arts* and Art Libraries Society of North America's *Art Documentation*.[3]

The microcomputer's main asset is the elimination of most of the problems mentioned regarding mainframes. With its ease of operation, relatively low cost, ever-increasing variety of powerful software programs, and increased storage capacity, the microcomputer soon became the solution to more efficient transactions of many visual resources functions. The programmer can be eliminated because of the relatively simple-to-learn programming languages, and original programming is not required if an appropriate standard software program is acquired to meet the needs of the collection.

In spite of all the benefits associated with computer automation in visual resources collections, the lack of standardization, both within individual collections and among collections, remains a major problem. The lack of uniform procedures for classification, cataloging, indexing and descriptive language, circulation, and administrative functions means that an automated system developed for one facility cannot be easily adapted by another.

This lack of standardized procedures has also prevented development of a strong market for commercially available application software specifically designed for visual resources collections. The desire to automate may be the factor that will motivate collections to begin to develop and adopt standards. One of the great advantages of automation is the potential for shared information (networking). Standardization is necessary for this to be possible. This subject of standards is receiving increasing attention within the profession.

The past reluctance of users and administrators to support computer automation may be more easily overcome than the reluctance to accept nationally approved standards. In analyzing the visual resources collection user needs, it is apparent that users are generally able to locate the images they routinely need for teaching. In the past, the indexing and retrieval capabilities addressed in many of the mainframe projects simply did not present any real or immediate advantage to these routine users. Considering the time and money required to initiate such projects, it would seem that the benefits to the routine users should be far greater. Most image collections have operated for decades without extensive indexing. In fact, in many collections, the only indexing is the self-indexing character of the classification system, which promotes browsing. Extensive subject access undoubtedly increases the usefulness of the collection, particularly to nonsubject specialists. The top priority of most routine users, however, generally is to have the images in the files in a timely manner, accurately labeled, where they can be found easily. Thus a sound benefit to the regular user would be for the computer to speed and improve the process of preparing the slides and photographs for use, facilitating the production of labels as well as shelflists, accession records, and indexes. A natural by-product of this physical control is a searchable database of the entire collection which may be adapted for use as a circulation system.

Through the use of a database management system,[4] complete image identification data can be entered, and then through specific routines, labels for images can be produced with label text being entered once, proofread, and printed, thus eliminating errors and repetitious typing of labels and various index cards. If desired, a second copy of the label can be produced to serve as an interfiled shelflist for slides. A unique number such as an accession number or a bar code can be utilized for circulation, as described in chapter 7, "Circulation and Control." Reports on overdues, what has circulated, who has borrowed images, etc., can also be produced.

The data, entered once, can be searched according to predetermined parameters. Various indexes, catalogs, and lists such as artist/architect authority files; comprehensive lists of artist's or architect's works in the collection; inventory lists of work in the collection from a single museum; and records of all portraits of a single subject, are exemplary of what may be created.

NEEDS ASSESSMENT

Any plan to automate should focus first on those functions and services that will benefit the routine users most. This may help secure funding and overcome any initial resistance from administrators or users to the time and money required. In order to provide accurate input for the assessment, the curator or a designated staff member must become fully familiar with the capabilities of the automated system. The needs assessment is an analysis of current manual procedures and services to determine the purpose and necessity of each. Since the primary purpose of automation is to improve existing procedures and services, it is necessary to examine current practices with the goal of combining or eliminating steps and reducing time involved. This appraisal encourages the elimination of procedures that may be redundant, underused, ineffective, or completely unnecessary. It will also identify those functions and services that are most suitable for some type of computer operation, most easily automated, and that might most benefit the majority of collection users. Such evaluations can also strengthen and improve existing functions.

Identifying the objectives of computer automation, such as increased productivity, job satisfaction, improved services, decreased operational costs, reduced staff, and increased staffing grade levels, is part of the process. Equally important is the computer's possible effect on the work flow and the determination of initial and future requirements. It is helpful to receive input from all levels of staff in this process.

By first examining the functions in this way, the priorities can more easily be established for what should be automated first, and identification of services and functions where automation of one might implement another can be determined. Priorities that reflect the need for automation as well as the ease of implementation should be established.

Figure 8.1 shows a sample planning worksheet that can be used to analyze the services or functions of a visual resources collection. The worksheet lists only general activities, and must be modified to meet the needs of the individual collection. Each activity can be assigned a priority, keeping in mind the rational work flow within the collection as a whole. It is most important to approach computer automation from the point of view of how the quality of service to users can be improved.

The planning worksheet helps to visualize repetition in handling or production of a single body of information. For example, the repetitive process of writing down identification for items circulated can be eliminated with an automated circulation system. Of primary importance in planning is the identification of activities that are routine, repetitious, and would require the least complex automated solutions. However, the assumption that just because it is feasible to automate an activity, it is therefore desirable and beneficial to do so, can be erroneous. There are situations where a manual procedure is better, cheaper, and faster.

In examining collection functions and establishing priorities, it is useful to categorize them as either intellectual management or physical control management. Functions in both areas can be suitable for computer automation. For the most part the activities associated with physical control are more easily automated, and may affect frequent users more due to speeding the preparation of images for use. Automation of label production (physical control) can produce a side benefit of automating another function, a searchable database (intellectual control).

There are advantages in beginning with those functions that are most easily computerized, thereby manifesting an immediate return on the investment. Once it can be demonstrated that results can be achieved through the use of computers, it is more likely that support for continuance and development of the program will be achieved.

Activities/Functions	Priority to Automate rate: 1-5 (low)	Type of function		Appropriate software			Retain manual method
		Intellectual control	Physical control	DBMS	WP	Spreadsheet	
Acquisitions	2		X	X			
Binding	n.a.	n.a.	X				X
Classification & Cataloging (including subject access)	2	X		X			
Circulation and Control	4		X	X			
Label and index card production	1		X	X	X		
Photographic services	5		X				
Audiovisual equipment management	3		X		X		
General administration	2		X	X	X		

Figure 8.1. A planning sheet for automating a visual resources collection.

The establishment of broad, effective intellectual control over visual resources collections is undoubtedly the most complex task facing visual resources curators. Why then begin the complicated and time-consuming task of computer automation of manual systems with the most demanding aspect of the project? Search and retrieval of visual images requires insightful planning in order to design the kinds of searches that are needed and a standard authority list or thesaurus. In several existing projects curators have developed their own indexing terms. Completion of the AAT,[5] currently under development and sponsored by the Getty Foundation, and/or the Library of Congress Subject Headings for Prints and Photographs[6] may eliminate the need to do this. More is said on subject thesauri later in this chapter.

ESTABLISHING PRIORITIES

Priorities that outline what will be automated first, second, and so on should be established. These plans should project expansion of system capabilities for future user needs, projects, and growth. Hardware and software can be requested according to this master plan, and thereby the expense as well as complexities of the project can be distributed over a period of time.

SELECTION

This planning provides the necessary information for making software and hardware selections. With microcomputers, a combination of the features of the database management system or other software, the speed of the central processing unit, and the system's storage capacity (i.e., how much data it can hold) will set the limits on what can actually be accomplished with the computer. Any computerized function must operate within these restraints. It is preferable, if not limited to a specific brand of hardware, to select the software program that will best perform the required jobs and then purchase the hardware that will operate that program. Software packages within a generic category (e.g., database management systems, word processing systems, spreadsheet programs) differ more from one another in their operations than hardware does, and the differences in functions of software programs have much more effect on what is to be accomplished. The characteristics of software programs available, together with the capacity requirements or volume of records to be produced, determine the selection of the software package.

When considering hardware, first ascertain if the parent institution has special arrangements with a computer manufacturer for discounts. While such arrangements will limit choices, they can mean a considerable reduction in costs. It is also important to consider the future possibilities for expansion or enhancement of the proposed system. This expansion can be in terms of added terminals, added functions, additional storage, new applications, software upgrades, vendor stability, and levels of ongoing vendor support. Microcomputers are a rapidly evolving technology. No system bought today can be viewed as the final solution; it will either be expanded or replaced by another system, which will, of course, allow for importing the previously established database.

PURCHASE VS. IN-HOUSE DEVELOPMENT OF SOFTWARE

The decision for software should be based on considerations of the commercially available software packages, the purchase of a basic software package which might be customized in-house, and the development of a system locally or in-house. When considering commercially available programs, communication with other curators currently using such programs is an absolute necessity. Having established the need for the collection to be automated, it is possible to inquire if all of the requirements can be met by the programs. Software programs will all look and sound good in the promotional material, but it is necessary to read reviews in the professional journals and to communicate directly with users in order to establish their true applicability to the specific requirements. A resource for information regarding programs in use by collections is the "Directory of Microcomputer Users" published in the *International Bulletin for Photographic Documentation of the Visual Arts*.[7]

Customizing a basic software program or developing an entire system locally requires a commitment of personnel. (If the development is to be done by a curent staff member, then that person's responsibilities may have to be assigned to someone else.) The curator and the person doing the development must prepare detailed specifications of what the system is to achieve. There is an element of chance involved in the venture: it will probably take longer than planned; there is no guarantee that the program will do all that is required; and the development may never end, i.e., there will be endless enhancements, corrections, and expansions. In addition, thorough system documentation is an absolute must to ensure continuation of the project should there be a staff turnover as well as for routine utilization of the system.

Commercially available software eliminates some of these risks, but perhaps at the expense of committing to a system that does not perform all that is desired or that limits later expansion. Therefore, one of the most important considerations in committing to an off-the-shelf program is the ability to export the collection database once established to another system should a change become necessary or desirable.

IMPLEMENTATION: STANDARDS FOR DATA ENTRY

Once the system is purchased and installed, the integration of automated systems into the routine collection work flow, the development of input procedures and record formats, and staff and user instruction begin. The collection's well-established manual procedures will have to be adapted to the automated system. Unstructured activities will need to be altered in order to conform to a structured routine. This involves the creation and enforcement of routines and procedures for the handling of data in a standardized manner and the establishment of an authority list that defines acceptable terms to be utilized in routine data entry.

The first step in data entry is the analysis of the existing manual system to design a standard structure or form for the collection of the data. Information must be entered into a systematic format to store, manipulate, and retrieve records. This format is the standard record structure or format. For examples of several standard record formats developed at visual resources collections, see appendix F.

The manual procedures for organizing descriptive image information to be utilized on labels have varied considerably in visual resources collections. However, the result (i.e., the label) is fairly standard: the basic factual data identifying the individual image, usually arranged hierarchically. In a manual system, the typist is responsible for assembling the data provided in the required order and format on the label.

With an automated system, it is necessary to develop a format (standard record format) comprising carefully defined individual data fields into which the information is entered. Defining the data to be entered into each field involves deciding the purpose of each field, the format, and the size (maximum characters that can be entered). The individual fields in the record format do not need to be arranged in the order in which they will appear on the labels. It is preferable to consider an arrangement that reflects the natural order in which information is received with the images and one that makes efficient use of the space on the computer screen.

The size and structure of database records for images require close analysis based on the current and perceived future use of these records. Most database management systems have fixed fields, i.e., a specified fixed amount of information that can be entered and stored in each field. Variable fields, available with some database management systems, have the advantage that entire titles can be accommodated, but with short titles, no blank spaces will be stored. However, the advantages of fixed fields are that it is possible to determine the amount of space that will be required to store a specific number of records for the entire database and the ability to produce reports that fit into fixed lengths, such as the confined spaces of a slide label.

As each field of the record format is being developed on the computer, most database management systems will require the designer to specify if each specific field is to be mandatory. This means the computer will not allow data for the record being entered to be stored unless information is entered in the mandatory field. The advantage to having certain fields so designated is to prevent the storage of records without such important information as titles or accession numbers.

Indexed fields or access points in a record format refer to fields that facilitate fast searches because the data are presorted and then stored in the presorted order. This arrangement can vary from a single indexed field to all fields, based on how the information contained in the record is to be used. As usual with computers, there are tradeoffs. Indexed fields require more storage space than nonindexed fields. The larger the record and the more fields indexed, the more storage space is required. It is also important to know if punctuation marks are indexed, since they affect how information is retrieved. Keyword searching is also a feature of some database management systems that receives a lot of attention. Keyword searching makes it possible to search and retrieve records containing specific words predesignated at the time the record is entered in any field. The main disadvantage to this type of searching is the large amount of memory required to index keywords.

Currently most visual resources collections involved in database development create their own standard record formats, or use ones prescribed on commercially available software; however, it is important to be aware of the foremost example of standard data collection formats utilized in the library field: the MARC standard record format ("MAchine Readable Cataloging"), which was created in the 1960s. MARC, though first designed for books, has since undergone many revisions adapting it for use with other media such as serials, maps, manuscripts, and other visual materials. An expanded MARC format (MARC-VIM) is being applied in numerous visual collections, such as the Smithsonian Institution's National Museum of American Art for its Inventory of American Sculpture,[8] the National Gallery of Art's Photographic Archives,[9] the Special Collections Photo Archive of the General Library of the University of New Mexico at Albuquerque,[10] and the Photo Archive of the Getty Center for the History of Art and the Humanities.[11] Including MARC in this chapter does not imply its recommendation for all visual resources collections. Most curators would probably find it more detailed than necessary. However, its current application in a number of collections gives it a national exposure that may ultimately result in an accepted standard.

Once the data entry format is established, actual data entry can begin. In the early stages, it is useful to enter information on a variety of images to "test" the effectiveness of the format. It will still be possible to modify the format, adding or deleting fields, or changing their size. Most collections begin their computer databases with either all new acquisitions or a selected section of the collection. In collections having many old slides and photographs with inconsistent information and cataloging, it may be expedient to concentrate on entering new acquisitions and begin data entry of the older material at a later date when the automation procedures are well established, the staff is more confident, and the older materials have been weeded.

The second component in the establishment of data standards and the order for information in the fields is to determine content standards, i.e., the acceptable terms and abbreviations to be entered in the data fields. While the record or data collection format is usually designed by the visual resources staff, possibly with a computer consultant, the development of standards for terms and abbreviations utilized in a collection for data descriptors are best developed in consultation with collection users and staff. Such terminology as that used to describe art media, for example, the use of "pottery" or "ceramics," "textiles" or "fabrics" and abbreviations for such descriptions ("ptg." or "pntg." for painting, or "sculpt." or "sculp." for sculpture) must be consistent in order to simplify both the entering (and retrieval) of data.

In-house data standards or authorities are also needed for artists' names; museum, city, country, and state names; and subject descriptors if used, and should include standard abbreviation forms when necessary. Many of these standards can be developed in-house, although, the standards adopted for artists' names; museums; and city, county, and state names should be derived from some published authority, if possible. Some suggestions for sources to provide artist name authority standards are the *Encyclopedia of World Art*, Thieme-Becker, *Kunstler-Lexikon*, Vollmer, *Lexikon der Bildenden Kunstler des XX Jahrhunderts*, and *Art Bibliographies Modern*. An effective method for establishing an artist authority list is described by Donna Rogers in an article in the *International Bulletin for Photographic Documentation of the Visual Arts*.[12]

A standard abbreviations list for data descriptions used in visual resources collections has been published by the Visual Resources Association.[13] The motive of its publication and distribution is to assist collections in developing an in-house authority for abbreviations. This list can form a starting point from which the curator can add standard abbreviations for terms specific to the needs of the individual collection. The Visual Resources Association Standards Committee is currently working on standard abbreviations for locations of art works and museum and city names.

Subject Thesauri

The principal obstacle to subject access to images of works of art is the lack of an established workable standard for description. The Art and Architecture Thesaurus and the Library of Congress Terms for Graphic Materials, standards mentioned earlier in this chapter, are still in the development stages. When completed these will expand greatly the potential for access to images both in image collections and in bibliographic formats. However, even with the benefit of a standard thesaurus, complete or even partial subject analysis will add substantial amounts of time required to catalog images as well as to the training time required for the cataloger. Perhaps it is more appropriate and efficient for subject analysis of works of art to be done in museums by the curators who are responsible for the art collections themselves and who are actively engaged in the research and documentation of these items. In many cases, visual resources collections are secondary repositories of images for the support of generalized teaching. They lack the expert staff needed to conduct extensive subject analysis of comprehensive collections of images of works of art. Perhaps a solution to subject indexing might be for suitable subject headings to be included with the routine descriptive data that accompany images of works of art when they are sold to collections by museums or commercial vendors.

SYSTEM DOCUMENTATION

Documentation is packaged with all commercial software. The quality of computer documentation has improved greatly in the past few years and there are independent publications available on some of the more well known and popular software programs as well. This is useful and important reference material for the user. However, another kind of documentation is also important: the in-house system documentation for locally produced programs, routines, and procedures developed for the collection's automation project.

System documentation, as noted earlier in the chapter, is a vital aspect of an efficient automation environment. Such records provide all the instructions, directions, and restrictions required by the staff when working on the system. They aid in training new staff, although the best training must include utilization of the system. The more hours spent at the terminal, the more proficient one becomes in the use of the system; therefore, if there are several staff members it is good to coordinate work assignments in order to distribute time at the computer evenly among those who need to learn its use, and to maximize use of the equipment as well.

FUTURE TRENDS

The long-range direction of computerized systems for visual resources collections will most likely be interactive programs for visual and textual access. A computer linked with an optical videodisk player that is capable of displaying both images and text indexed and cross indexed according to an extremely broad range of criteria, in any order, or in various combinations, would be ideal. The retrieval system utilizes a large jukebox, housing many disks containing thousands of images. Already numerous videodisk projects related to art and architecture are being developed, including ARTSearch at the University of Wisconsin, Helen L. Allen textile collection; University of Iowa, School of Art and Art History; Library of Congress Prints and Photographs Division; and M.I.T. School of Architecture.[14] The development of PICASSO-FILE by the Architecture Machine Group at M.I.T. demonstrates how this technology can be used to deal with the works of art of a single artist. Since both computer-generated search instructions and videodisk transmissions can travel over a communications network, a researcher can receive the visual information on a system at a distant location. The computer-linked videodisk is a powerful tool capable of handling enormous amounts of information—both image and text—in combinations and at a speed never before possible. This development has the potential to revolutionize image collections.

SUMMARY

A successful visual resources collection computer project requires commitment from the administration and precise articulation by the curator of the needs and goals for the collection. For the administration, the project must offer advantages to the routine users of the collection. Many of the indexing and iconographical retrieval features of the earlier mainframe projects were interesting, but did not offer a substantial enough advantage to the routine users who were familiar with this material. So, deciding what the computer is to do is the first step and then, if there is not a hardware restriction imposed by the institution, the choice of the most suitable software package is next in importance. Software is the most vital element in the program's success.

One last consideration is data entry. "Entering a collection of 20,000 items at a fast rate of two minutes per item will take close to 200 hours."[15] That would be inputting clear, correct, consistent information. No matter what the software used, the quality of the input governs the quality of the output. Many old, large image collections, because they require weeding, review of label information, classifications for accuracy and consistency, updating of country names, and other measures for bringing the collection into flawless, consistent order, are not yet ready to be entered into databases. These steps, once accomplished, will greatly facilitate the efficiency of the data entry process.

Computer automation offers a substantial advantage to visual resources collection management. And visual resources collections should not wait indefinitely for the "right" program to be developed: "The perfect system will always be a myth."[16]

NOTES

[1]"An authority list *per se* normally consists in its root form of nothing but the terms that you are authorized to use in indexing; it is just a straight alphabetical list of what is allowed. When you begin to show linkages among the terms, listing some that cannot be used and telling what to use instead (i.e., See Reference), or if you begin to put "See Also" references into three kinds—broader generally, narrower generally, or related in some way—then you have a *thesaurus*." Philip Leslie, quoted in Kevin Roddy, "The Belmont Conference in Subject Access," *Visual Resources* 2, nos. 1-3 (1981-1982): 103.

[2]Zelda Richardson and Sheila Hannah, eds., *Introduction to Visual Resources Library Automation* (Albuquerque, NM: Mid-America College Art Association, 1980); Karen Markey, "Visual Arts Resources and Computers," *Annual Review of Information Science and Technology* 19 (1984): 271-309.

[3]Quarterly publication by the Visual Resources Association at the University of Michigan, History of Art Department, Ann Arbor, MI. Quarterly publication by Art Libraries Society of North America, Tucson, AZ.

[4]A database management system is a computer program that accomplishes the tasks of creating, accessing, and maintaining a database.

[5]Toni Peterson, "The Role of the Art and Architecture Thesaurus in Automated Data Retrieval," *Automatic Processing of Art History Data and Documents*, Vol. 1 (Pisa: Scuola Normale Superiore; Los Angeles, CA: The J. Paul Getty Trust, 1984), 309-18.

[6]Elizabeth Parker-Betz, *Subject Headings Used in the Library of Congress Prints and Photographs Division* (Washington, DC: Library of Congress, 1980); Elizabeth Parker-Betz and Helena Zinkham, *Descriptive Terms for Graphic Materials: Genre and Physical Characteristics Headings* (Washington, DC: Library of Congress, 1986); Elizabeth Parker-Betz, *Graphic Materials: Rules for Describing Original Items and Historical Collections* (Washington, DC: Library of Congress, 1982).

[7]"Directory of Microcomputer Users," *International Bulletin for Photographic Documentation of the Visual Arts* 13, no. 3 (Fall 1986): 10-11.

[8]E. Fink and C. Hennessey, "A National Database for Information on Sculpture in Public and Private Collections throughout the US and Abroad," *Spectra* 15, no. 1 (1988).

[9]A. Gibbs and P. Stevens, "MARC and the Computerization of the National Gallery of Art Photographic Resources," *Visual Resources* 3, no. 3 (Autumn 1986): 185+.

[10]Stella DeSaRego and Richard Spector, "IMAGES," *International Bulletin for Photographic Documentation of the Visual Arts* 15, no. 1 (Spring 1988): 20-30.

[11]Bret Maddox, "To VIM with VIGOR," *International Bulletin for Photographic Documentation of the Visual Arts* 15, no. 3 (Fall 1988): 18-20.

[12]Donna Rogers and Jeffrey Hamm, "Compiling an Authority List on a PC," *International Bulletin for Photographic Documentation of the Visual Arts* 14, no. 3 (Fall 1987): 11-13.

[13]Nancy Schuller, *Standard Abbreviations for Image Descriptions Used in Visual Resources Collections*, Special Bulletin No. 2 (Ann Arbor, MI: Visual Resources Association, 1988).

[14]See "Microcomputers: Interactive Videodisk, Optical Disk Use" in the bibliography.

[15]Eric Anderson, "Seminar on Microcomputers in Libraries and Media Centers at Northern Illinois University," *International Bulletin for Photographic Documentation of the Visual Arts* 10, no. 2 (June 1983): 12.

[16]Nolan F. Pope, *Microcomputers for Library Circulation Control* (Indianapolis, IN: INCOLSA, March 1984), 10.

Appendix A
Sample Floor Plans

Small Visual Resources Collection

Capacity 40,000 slides
640 sq. ft.
1/8" = 1'0"

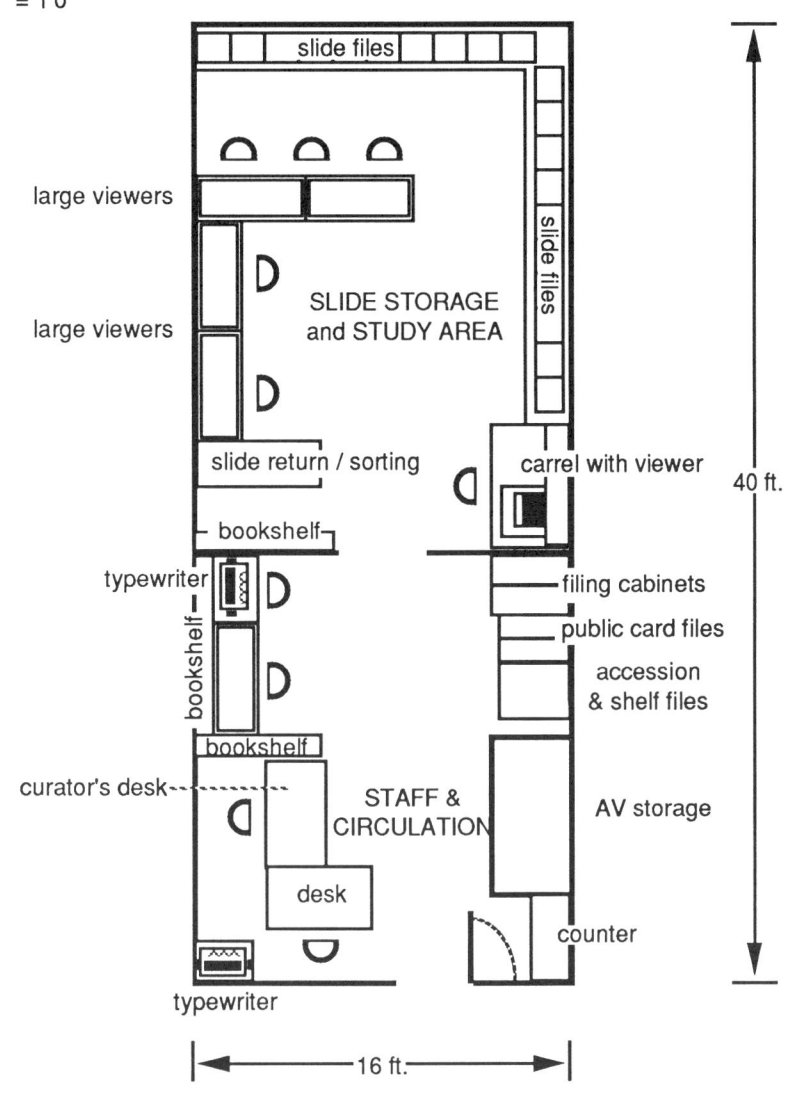

90 / APPENDIX A — SAMPLE FLOOR PLANS

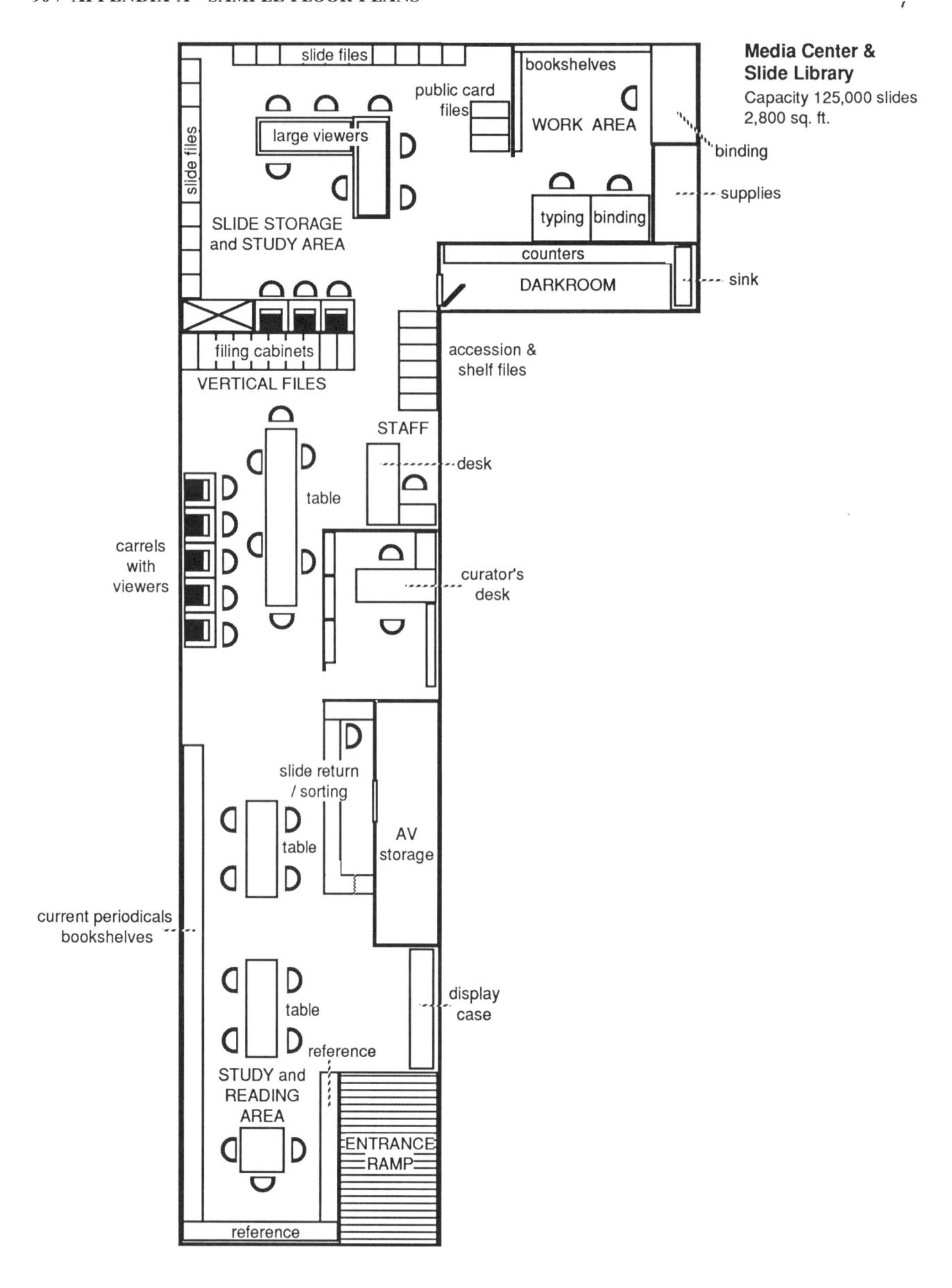

Media Center & Slide Library
Capacity 125,000 slides
2,800 sq. ft.

Appendix A – Sample Floor Plans / 91

Large Slide Library
Capacity 200,000 slides
2,240 sq. ft.
1/8" = 1'0"

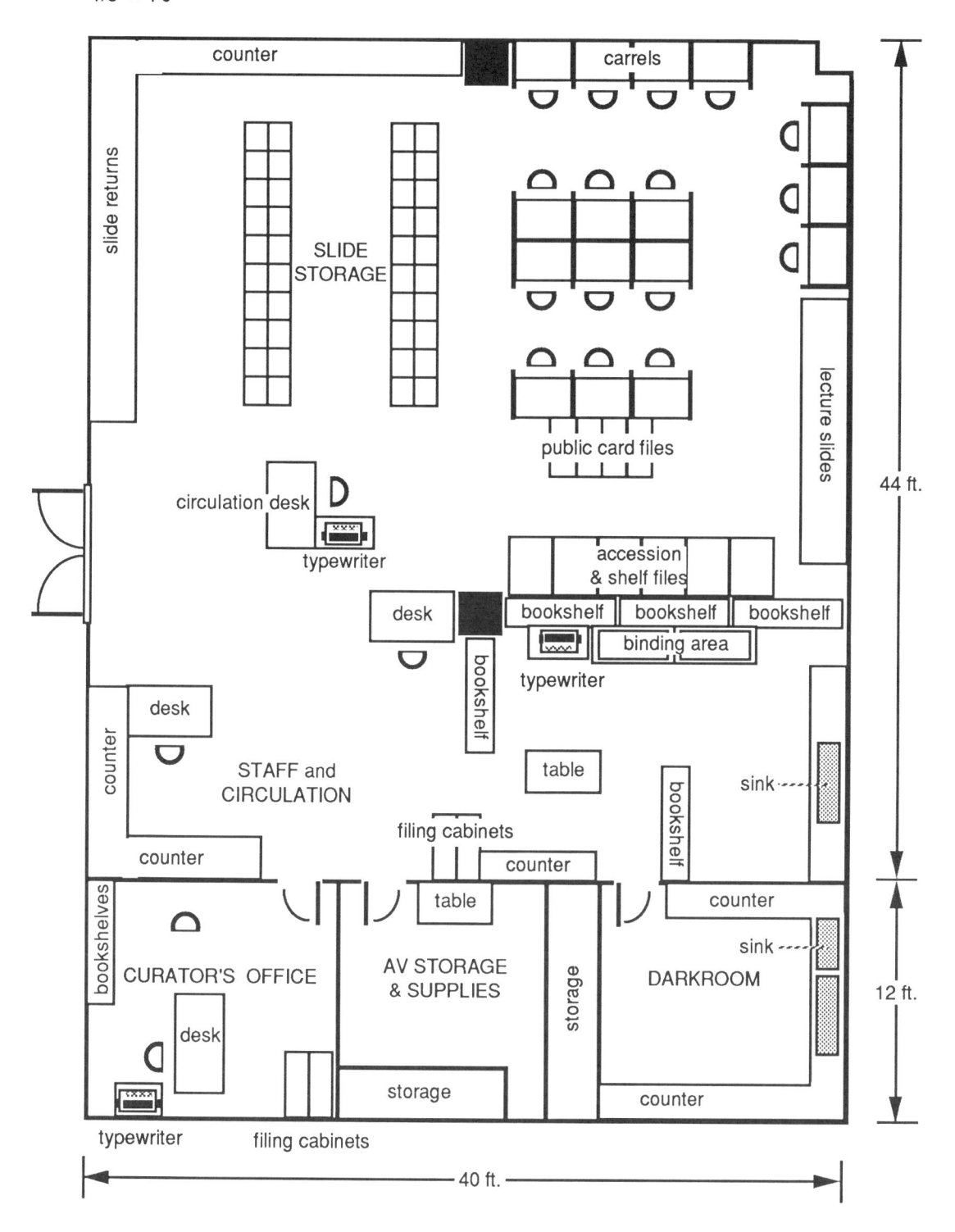

92 / APPENDIX A – SAMPLE FLOOR PLANS

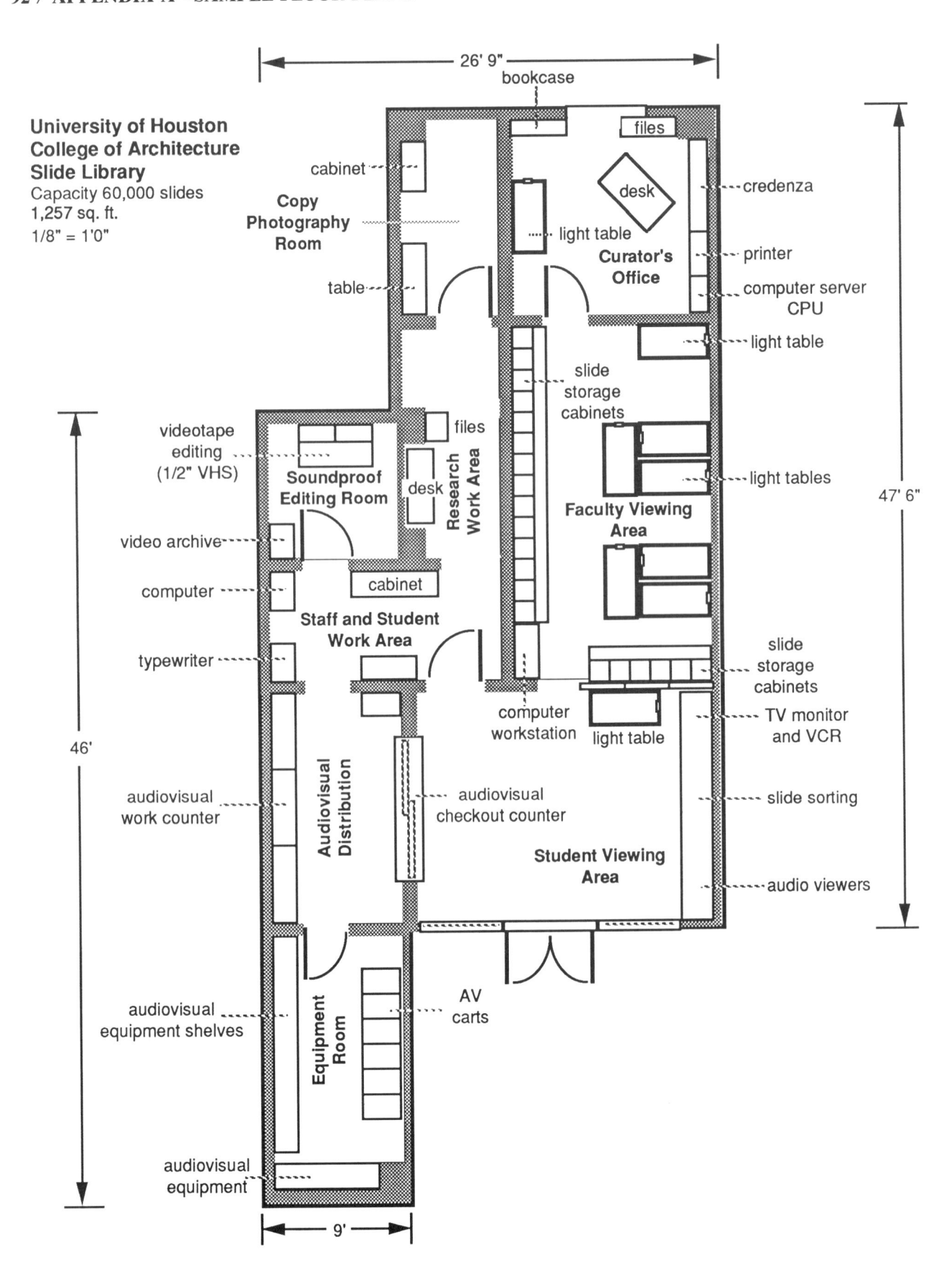

**University of Houston
College of Architecture
Slide Library**
Capacity 60,000 slides
1,257 sq. ft.
1/8" = 1'0"

26' 9"
47' 6"
46'
9'

- bookcase
- files
- cabinet
- desk
- credenza
- **Copy Photography Room**
- light table
- printer
- table
- **Curator's Office**
- computer server CPU
- light table
- videotape editing (1/2" VHS)
- files
- slide storage cabinets
- **Soundproof Editing Room**
- desk
- light tables
- video archive
- **Research Work Area**
- **Faculty Viewing Area**
- computer
- cabinet
- **Staff and Student Work Area**
- typewriter
- slide storage cabinets
- computer workstation
- TV monitor and VCR
- light table
- audiovisual work counter
- **Audiovisual Distribution**
- slide sorting
- audiovisual checkout counter
- **Student Viewing Area**
- audio viewers
- AV carts
- audiovisual equipment shelves
- **Equipment Room**
- audiovisual equipment

Appendix A — Sample Floor Plans / 93

**University of Missouri
at Kansas City Slide Library**
Capacity 98,000 slides
41,000 photographs
approx. 1,309.5 sq. ft.

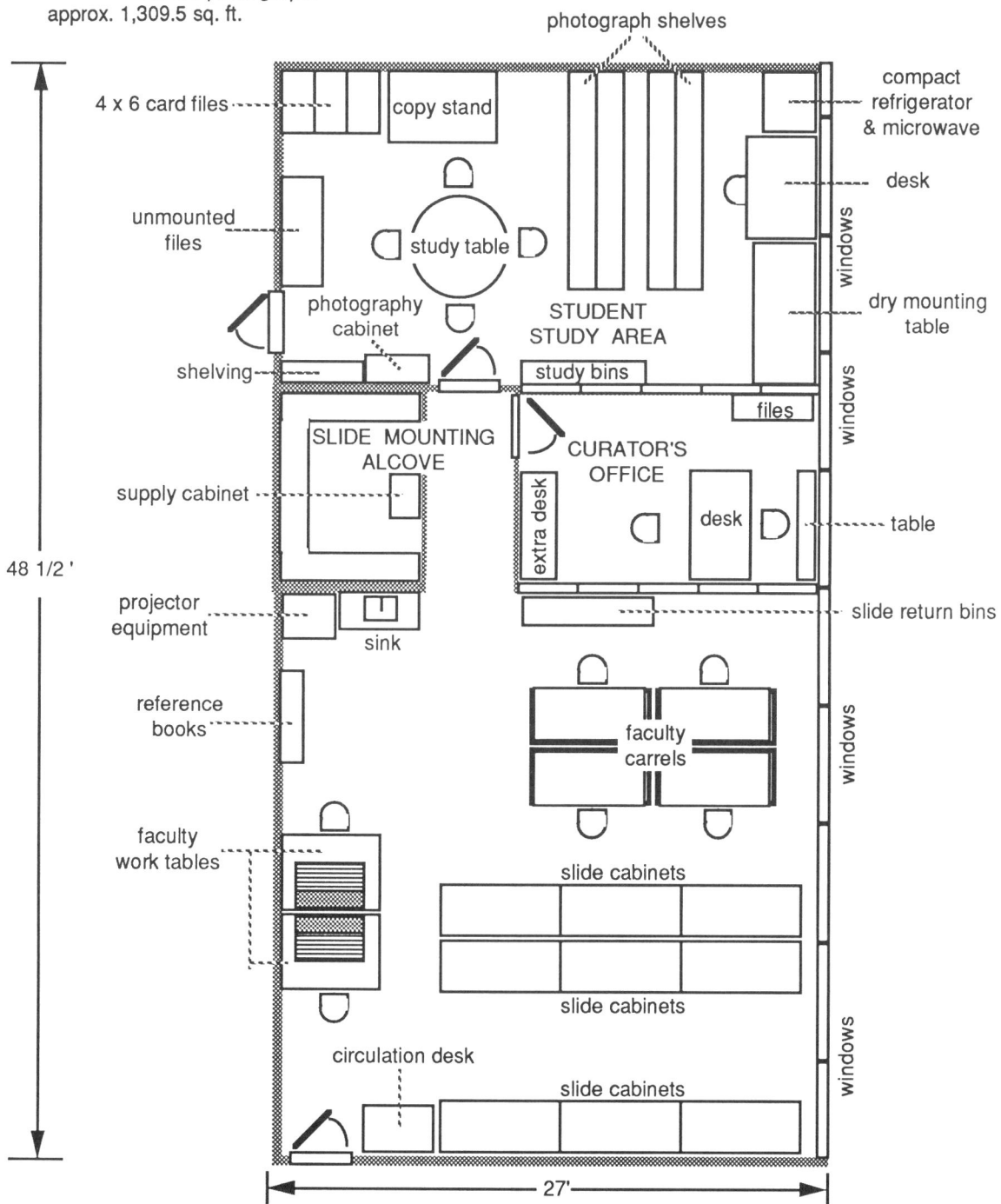

Note: The curator's office has glass windows on all three interior walls.

94 / APPENDIX A – SAMPLE FLOOR PLANS

California Polytechnic State University
School of Architecture and Environmental Design
Instructional Resource Center
Capacity 160,000 slides
approx. 2800 sq. ft.
Copy photography is in a separate lab.

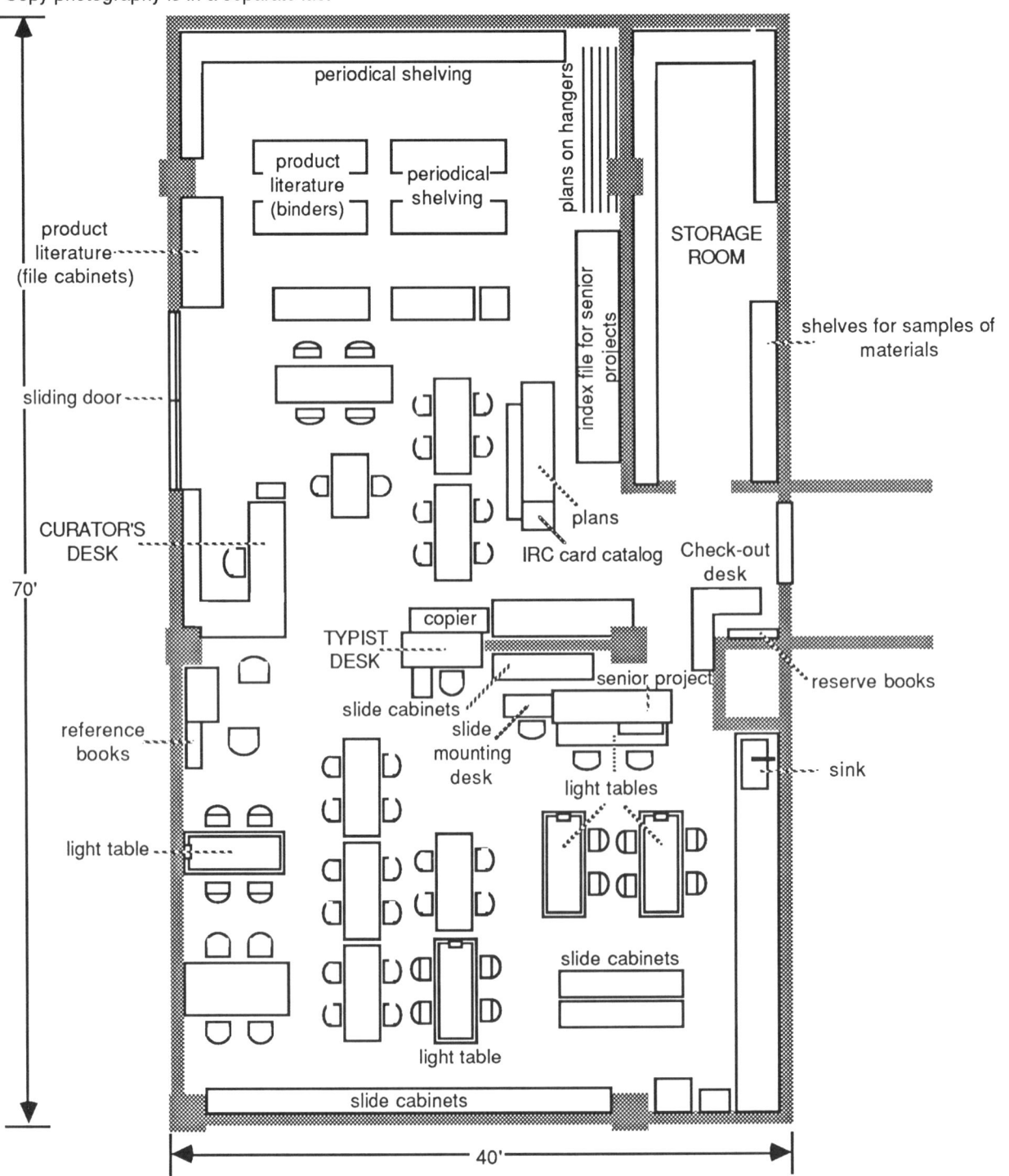

Appendix A – Sample Floor Plans / 95

Arizona State University
Art Slide Collection
Capacity 250,000 slides
5,000 photographs
approx. 1,146 sq. ft.

Curator's Office 126 sq.ft.
corridor
exterior doorway
shelves
file cabinet
refrigerator
wall mounted light board
desk
corridor
table
sink
closet

file cabinets
Assistant Curator's desk
2 computers & printer
typewriter
supply cabinet
check-out cart
copier
slide mounting
Graduate Asst. desk
table
Graduate Asst. desk
bookcases
slide cabinets
slide cabinets
light table
slide cabinets
faculty light tables (vertical)
light table
slide cabinets

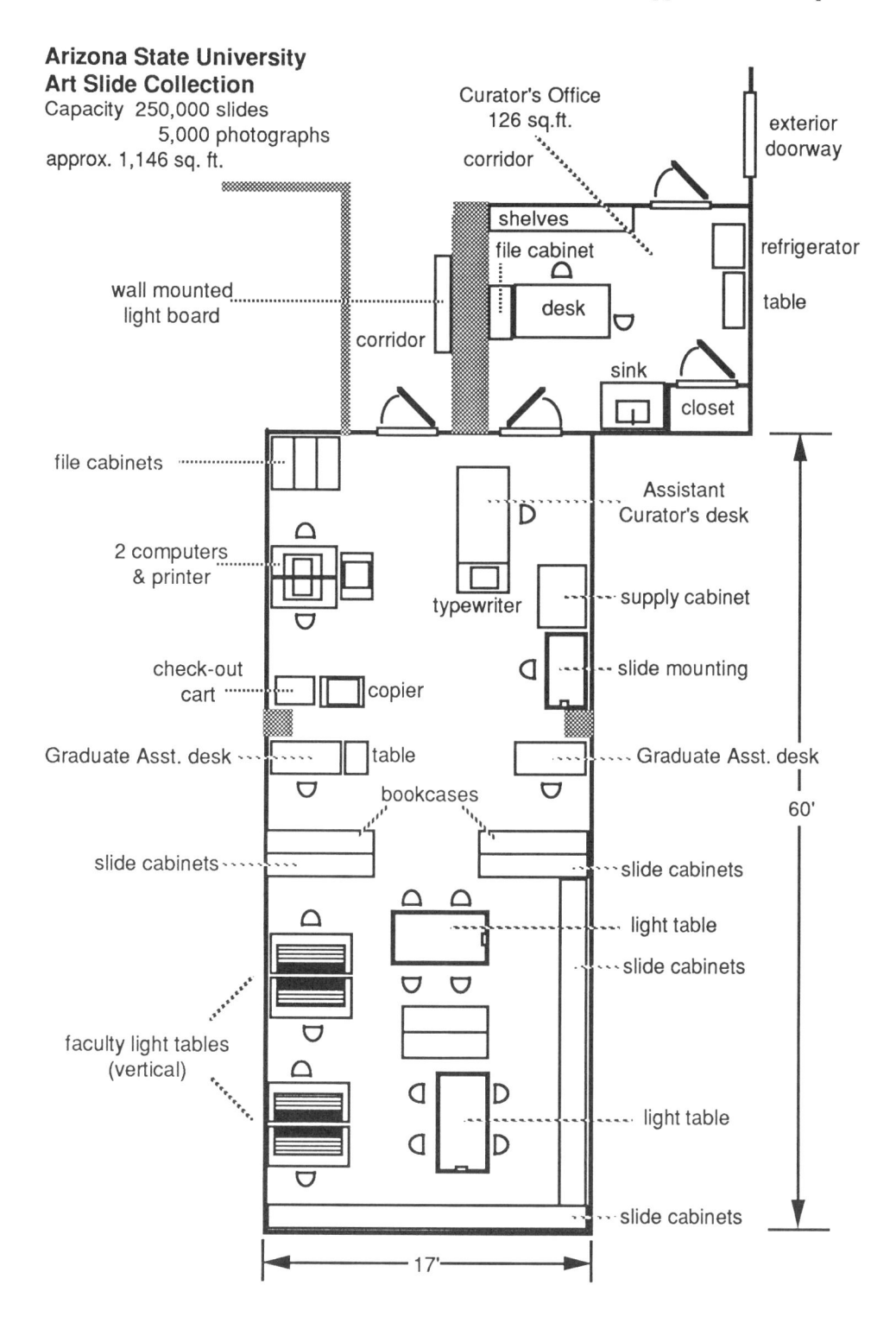

60'
17'

96 / APPENDIX A – SAMPLE FLOOR PLANS

The University of Texas at Austin Art Department Slide and Photo Collection

Capacity 500,000 slides and 30,000 photographs
approx. 3,575 sq. ft.
2 mm = approx. 1' 0"

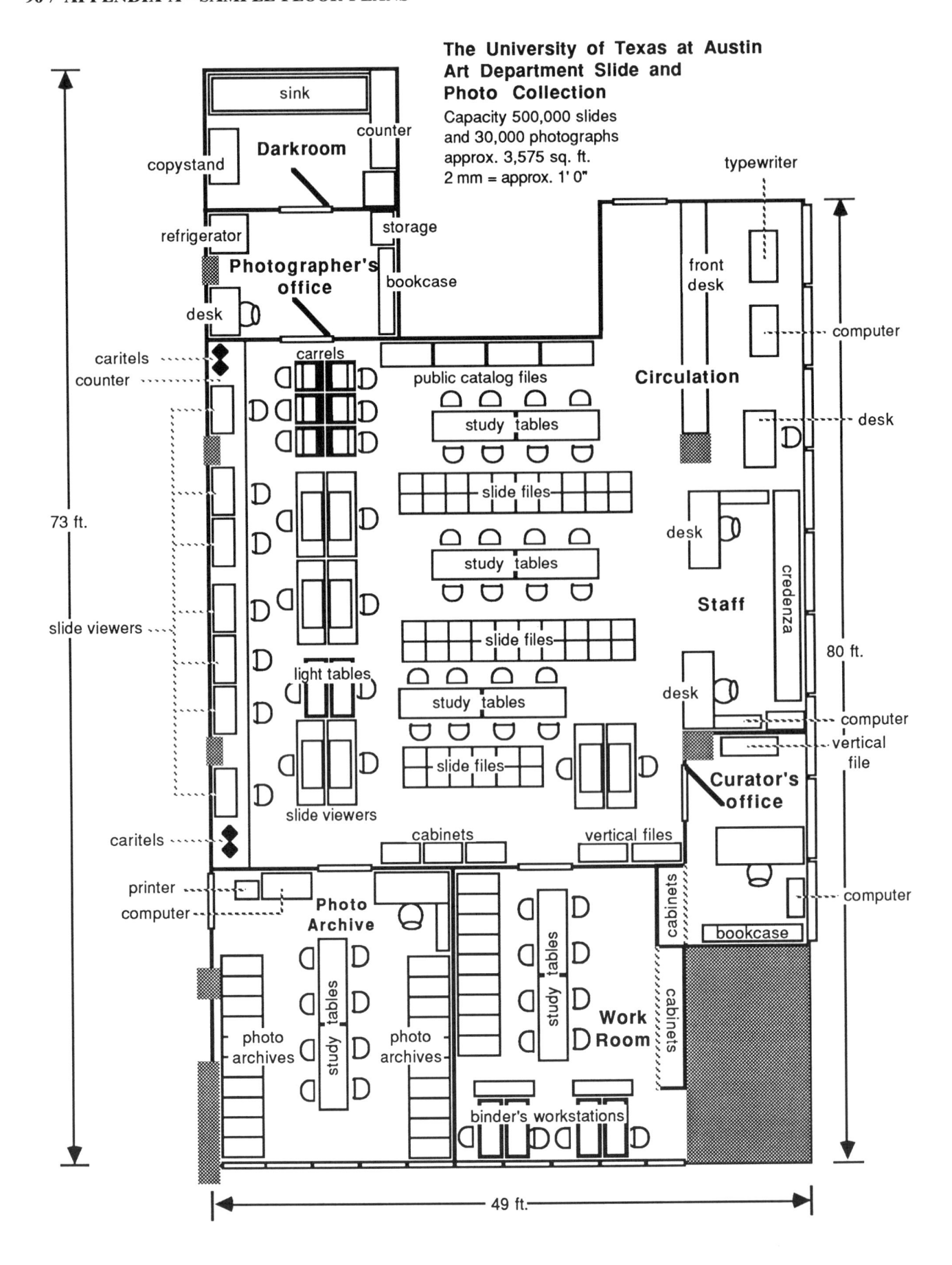

Appendix B
Sample Job Descriptions

The following job descriptions were collected from a number of sources and represent a sampling of the types of jobs most frequently found in visual resources collections.

ADMINISTRATIVE AND CURATORIAL EXAMPLES

EXAMPLE A

TITLE: Curator, Art Slide Collection

PRIME FUNCTION:
Performs work of considerable difficulty in developing and maintaining policies and procedures for the acquisition, preservation, storage, cataloging and retrieval of specialized photographs and/or related specialized collections.

EXAMPLES OF DUTIES AND RESPONSIBILITIES:
— Catalogs slides, photographs, other imagery, publications, books, monographs, and/or related materials.
— Establishes systems for document storage and retrieval.
— Directs and participates in difficult reference assignments.
— Prepares specialized detailed bibliographies and indexes.
— Utilizes computerized tools to aid in cataloging and related library assignments.
— Supervises personnel performing cataloging and related library assignments.
— Prepares and updates procedures manual.
— Assists in the operation of a computer-linked microfiche viewer.
— Develops and implements classification schemes for documents not classifiable under existing library systems.

KNOWLEDGE AND SKILLS:
— Considerable knowledge of the principles and practices of museum management.
— Considerable skill in supervisory principles, practices and techniques, research methods, written and oral communication.

98 / APPENDIX B—SAMPLE JOB DESCRIPTIONS

MINIMUM QUALIFICATIONS:
- Master's degree in art history or suitably related field.
- Seven years of museum curatorial or library experience; or,
- Any equivalent combination of experience, training and/or education approved by the personnel department.

EXAMPLE B

TITLE: Curator

QUALIFICATIONS: Must have a broad knowledge of all art historical areas dealt with and be able to handle material in the four to five foreign languages encountered on a daily basis. Knowledge in correlative areas such as history and literature is necessary. In addition, must be facile with bibliographic tools and research methods necessary to expedite cataloging of over 12,000 slides annually. Familiarity with the use of slide material in classroom teaching.

DUTIES:

30%   *Administration:* In consultation with department chairman supervises the curatorial, preparatory, and clerical work in a large fine arts related collection for teaching and research. Supervises and trains one Art Assistant II and one Laboratory Assistant II. Administers a collection of over 200,000 slides used by at least fourteen departments for teaching and research. Plans annual work schedule for entire collection and develops collection for new and visiting faculty independent of department chairman's supervision. Determines overall policies and priorities, both independently and in consultation with department faculty. Maintains internal budget control and has signature authority for all slide collection expenditures within the fiscal limitation set annually by the chairman. Seeks additional funding through proposals to department and extra-departmental sources; determines amount of assistance needed and plans distribution of general assistance funds. Hires, trains, and supervises individuals with special language and/or subject skills to work on projects on a temporary basis. Responsible for accuracy of technical aspects of slide production. Assesses quality of photographic work and initiates and evaluates new processes. Works with faculty in designing and operating teaching and study projects. Maintains liaison with other slide collections both nationally and internationally, in order to keep abreast of technological improvements, classification schemes, and new sources, as well as to develop organizations; follows new developments in the field via professional publications. Visits other collections and attends meetings of slide curators. Compiles comprehensive records of acquisitions by source, year, and accession number; maintains extensive source files for optimum use of available funds; develops sophisticated artist index authority file and manuscript shelf number and negative files for aid in retrieval of protean slide material.

30%   *Cataloging:* Does original cataloging of slides, requiring a thorough background in the history of art, facility in several foreign languages, and, expertise in the use of research tools.

10%   *Reference:* Aids faculty in slide retrieval via interpretation and clarification of classification scheme, use of auxiliary aids, and suggestion of appropriate material available in collection.

10%   *Acquisition:* Formulates acquisition policies, determines the need for new acquisitions, sets priorities for material, requiring familiarity with vast institutional and commercial sources, as well as a current knowledge of art historical literature. Negotiates and accepts gifts from private donors; negotiates exchanges and duplication of private collections.

10%   *Circulation:* Maintains circulation records and regulates lending. Sets priorities with regard to extra-departmental and institutional use of the collection. Maintains good public relations while assuring that departmental needs are given priority. Analyzes volume and patterns of use in order to determine how effectively the collection is functioning. Refiles circulated slides to assure accuracy in unnumbered collection.

Appendix B—Sample Job Descriptions / 99

10% *Photocopy:* The curator will supervise the departmental photocopy facility for the production of 6,000 slides annually.

EXAMPLE C

TITLE: Head of Slide Department, Museum Library

REPORTS TO: Executive Director of Museum Libraries

SUPERVISES: Assistant Slide Librarian
Two Slide Catalogers
Slide Circulation Assistant
Photographer
Part-time assistants (4 workers at 10 hrs./wk.), 1 FTE
College Work Study assistants (8 workers at 10 hrs./wk.)
Two FTE Volunteers (5 at 4 hrs./wk.)

BASIC FUNCTION:
Responsible for organization, planning, coordination, maintenance, and direction of all activities of the slide department of the library. Oversees all slide acquisitions and photography, slide cataloging, processing, filing and circulation, reference services, and collection policies and procedures. Staff responsibility includes recruitment, training, supervision, and evaluation of both professional and support staff.

PRIMARY DUTIES AND RESPONSIBILITIES:

1. Organizes, plans, and directs all slide department operations. Coordinates the activities of staff and oversees work flow from the time a slide is acquired through the processes of its accessioning research, cataloging, mounting, labeling, filing, and circulation.

2. Responsible for researching, developing, and refining classification systems for slides. Since national standards for the cataloging of images do not exist, other library classification principles and procedures must be adapted for use. Classification systems developed in-house must be interpreted to staff; staff work must be checked to ensure consistency and accuracy.

3. Supervises slide department staff. Responsibilities include recruitment, hiring and firing, job training, work planning and assignments, staff meetings, and personnel evaluations. In addition, interviews candidates for other senior library vacancies and makes recommendations for hiring to the executive director.

4. Responsible for short- and long-range planning of slide department services, equipment purchases, cataloging projects, and facilities planning. Evaluates departmental operations and researches, plans, and implements new systems and procedures.

5. Prepares and oversees slide department budget in conjunction with the Executive Director. Also administers funds for College Work Study students in conjunction with the student employment office.

6. Purchases slides, equipment for viewing, storing, labeling, monitoring, and photographing slides, as well as departmental supplies.

7. Develops slide collection based on knowledge of art history in response to the needs of faculty members and staff, by copy photography slide duplication and selected acquisitions.

8. Researches (foreign- and English-language publications) to catalog slides added to the collection.

100 / APPENDIX B—SAMPLE JOB DESCRIPTIONS

9. Communicates slide department policies and procedures to collection users and provides reference assistance.

10. Works with other museum departments (e.g., rights and reproductions, Department of Museum Photography) to supply slides of museum objects both in-house and to outside institutions. Advises curators and other department personnel on the photography of art, photo equipment needs, and copyright for the development of new slide sets.

11. Keeps in contact with slide suppliers, equipment vendors, and photographers regarding new products and slide offerings.

12. Manages production of slide sets for the marketing department's slide sales program. Monitors quality control and initiates new sets.

13. Monitors environment of slide department area (temperature and humidity) to ensure that slide conservation environment standards are met.

EXAMPLE D

TITLE: Learning Resources Specialist

WORKING TITLE: Art Slide Curator

IMMEDIATE SUPERVISOR: Department Head

ORGANIZATIONAL UNIT: Art Department

QUALIFICATIONS:

Knowledge, skills, and abilities: Organization, operational, and supervisory knowledge and abilities. Ability to deal effectively with various patrons. Knowledge and skills in typing, copy photography, computer usage, and operation of audiovisual equipment.

Education and training: Master's degree in art history required. Advanced studies in European languages also helpful.

Experience: Prior experience in a slide library.

CHIEF OBJECTIVE OF POSITION:

To administer and maintain the Visual Resources Facility in the art department, which involves policy making and implementation; development, maintenance, and supervision of the fine arts slide collection and all other visual material and equipment housed in the visual resources facility; budget management and record maintenance; training and supervision of student workers; and reference and user orientation.

DECISIONS AND ACTIONS:

With supervisor approval: Goals and objectives, annual budget requests, and changes in visual resources facility policy of operation.

Independent of supervisor approval: Fine arts slide collection development, maintenance, and supervision; slide and equipment acquisition; selection, training, and evaluation of student workers; reference service and user orientation; record keeping; budget management; and policy implementation.

WORK TASKS AND DUTIES (INCLUDING PERCENT TIME):

25% *Administrative:* Establishes policies, operations, and procedures for the visual resources facility and publishes these annually; formulates annual goals and objectives, develops strategies to achieve these; formulates supply and acquisition needs for annual budget; orders supplies and

Appendix B—Sample Job Descriptions / 101

monitors special needs; anticipates equipment needs providing information for departmental plan and updates; documents internal procedures, prepares annual report and requested planning documents; serves as departmental representative to audiovisual services and as publicity liaison to Public Information Office; serves on appropriate departmental committees, i.e., library, publicity, and recruitment; attends departmental staff meetings; maintains membership in appropriate professional organizations.

20% *Collection development:* Catalogs slides according to established system; researches and produces computer labels for slides using reference sources including those in foreign languages; enters catalog data into computer database; reviews mounting of slides done by student workers, corrects any errors, files new slides into collection; maintains departmental library acquisitions file, monitors budget, and processes orders for books.

15% *Acquisitions:* Acquires new slides and other visual material by two procedures: (1) makes selections from appropriate commercial slide companies based on the needs of the collection, prepares and receives the orders; (2) copy photographs from books and journals collected from art faculty and the curator on a schedule formulated and published by the curator, codes the film and mails for processing. Acquires rental visual resources material for faculty by processing requests, checking in and shipping out material, and monitoring rental budget.

15% *Collection maintenance and circulation:* Refiles slides returned by patrons on a daily basis after being counted and sorted by student workers; keeps circulation records for annual report; pulls slides which need cleaning, new labels, or mounts due to being damaged, need to be replaced, or are erroneously cataloged; maintains departmental audiovisual equipment, including use scheduling, bulb changing, repair, and maintenance scheduling.

15% *Supervision:* Selects student workers based on qualifications of neatness, accuracy, art history background, and photography skills; instructs workers in slide room maintenance tasks of mounting, attaching labels and signal dots, sorting for refiling, copy photography assistance; assigns tasks on a daily basis; periodically reviews tasks done for accuracy.

10% *Reference and user orientation:* Publishes and instructs patrons in the use of the visual resources facility, including how to use the slide collection; what the circulation policies are for faculty, staff, graduate and undergraduate students; other special requests; how to use and sign up for audiovisual equipment. Provides slide collection reference service both orally and with computer printouts. Performs other duties as assigned by department head.

Contacts within and without the organizational unit as a routine function of job.
(Does not include contacts with supervisors, co-workers, and subordinates.)

Persons or Organizations	Purpose	How Often	Inside/ Outside Unit
Audiovisual Services	Order films, schedule equipment, equipment maintenance.	daily	inside
Computer Services	Attend workshops, acquire information on microcomputer use, maintenance, and help with problems.	bimonthly	inside
VRA	Professional international organization for which elected officer, attend annual meeting, read and write for quarterly journal.	monthly	outside

EXAMPLE E

POSITION TITLE: Photographic Resources Manager/Archivist

IMMEDIATE SUPERVISOR: Manager, Art Services Division

QUALIFICATIONS:

Knowledge, skills, and abilities: Administrative skills necessary for the day-to-day operation of a service department; familiarity with photographic processes and conservation; firm background in library systems and operations; thorough knowledge of archival systems and procedures; solid background in art history; and up-to-date knowledge of issues pertaining to copyright policies and procedures.

Education and training: Master's degree in art history or related field.

RESPONSIBILITIES:

Development of visual resource archives: (1) Directs the development and maintenance of the visual resources archives (slides, large transparencies, black-and-white photographs, and negatives), including documentary photographs of the museum's galleries, operations, and programs; photography of the works of art in the museum's collections (the above includes more than 50,000 black-and-white negatives and several thousand color transparencies). (2) Develops long-range plans for storage, conservation, handling, and processing of photographic materials by performing research to obtain information or examples of storage and preservation solutions involving similar collections and/or materials. (3) Oversees organization and upkeep of an encyclopedic art history slide collection of over 75,000 slides by directing the Photographic Services Assistant, interns, and volunteers in tasks such as filing, labeling, masking and mounting slides, and assisting with copy stand work in the photography department. (4) Originates requests and coordinates requests from others for photography of the museum's collections and operations, acquires slides for the art history collection from commercial sources, and routes requests for slides to be made from books and journals.

Oversees arrangement and description of the photographic records acquired for permanent documentation and research use: (1) Organizes filing and retrieval systems for the various visual resource collections. This includes devising and implementing information systems through accessioning, cataloging and development of appropriate databases by supplying titles, dates, and checking attribution for images in the archives. Must have ability to analyze and classify photographic documents and to perform related research to identify and classify photographs of works of art and architecture from all periods and cultures of the world. (2) Identification and retrieval systems must be consistent with others (registration, collections, photography) used in the museum and must adhere to standard terminology of art historical classification.

Provides archival reference services and directs the preparation of responses to internal and external requests: (1) Provides archival reference services and directs the preparation of responses to the research needs of museum staff members and to inquiries received by mail or telephone from outside: other museums and art historians, researchers, publishers, state and local agencies, and the general public (on an international basis). (2) Informs the Director and curators about outside requests to publish photographs of objects in the museum's collections. Confers with the public affairs office and/or the Director whenever there is a question about commercial usage of museum images. (3) Coordinates preparation of orders for existing and new photography with the photography department. Manages the borrowing of slides from the slide collection. Oversees the sale of photographic materials; transparency rentals; and borrowing by lecturers, researchers, and publishers. (4) Drafts forms for applications and permissions for publication of museum photographs. Maintains records and statistics which relate to requests for permission to reproduce museum images. (5) Establishes and reviews reproduction fees and price lists for the sale and rental of photographic materials. (6) Participates in professional activities related to visual resources management.

Formulates, revises, and implements the museum's rights and reproductions policy: (1) Must keep abreast of legal aspects of copyright for works of art and must ensure that the museum's rights and reproduction policies and procedures conform to ethics and law. (2) Formulates policy revisions which pertain to rights and reproductions, consulting with the Director and Chief Curator before such revisions are made. Periodically informs the staff of current museum-related copyright matters and issues in the areaa of rights and reproductions. (3) Performs research to update or correct existing policy and maintains guidelines for the making of photographic reproductions of works of art from the collections of the museum.

Supervises the day-to-day operation of the office and the work of assistant and volunteer staff: (1) Supervises the day-to-day operation of the photographic services office. This includes supervision of the work of assistants, student interns, and volunteers in tasks such as mounting, labeling photographs on the word processor, and filing and maintaining the photographs and slide collections. Interviews and selects student interns based on art history background and photography experience. (2) Supervises the Photographic Services Assistant, whose foremost duties are the scheduling of photography assistants and establishing priorities in routing requests to photography department.

Routine contacts:

Contact	Nature of Business	Frequency
Other museums, universities, publishers, newspapers, magazines, scholars, curators, authors, lecturers	Requests for photographs, rights to publish reproductions, materials for lectures, etc.	daily
Library of Congress	Interpretations of Copyright Law.	as needed
Photograph conservators	Consultation about conservation of photographic materials.	as needed
Trustees, council members, friends of the museum	Requests for photographic services and materials.	occasional
Other museums and visual resources professionals	Clarification and comparison of policies, fees, information, storage and retrieval methods, etc.	as needed
Other libraries and archives	Interlibrary loans, slide exchanges, lending and borrowing of photographic materials for research purposes.	as needed
Vendors	Purchase of supplies, furnishings, slides and photographs, and photo processing.	as needed

CURATORIAL AND CURATORIAL ASSISTANTS

EXAMPLE A

TITLE: Assistant Slide Curator

REPORTS TO: Art Slide Curator

ORGANIZATIONAL UNIT: Art Department

104 / APPENDIX B—SAMPLE JOB DESCRIPTIONS

QUALIFICATIONS:

Knowledge, skills, and abilities: Knowledge of art history, history, and literature. Reading knowledge of at least two foreign languages, preferably French and German. Competency in specialized bibliographic searching skills. Familiarity with art history classroom teaching methods.

Education and training: A degree in art history.

BASIC FUNCTION:

Principal assistant to the Slide Curator and as such performs, with the exception of administration, all duties necessary to all functions of the art history slide collection.

PRIMARY DUTIES AND RESPONSIBILITIES:

45% *Cataloging:* Does original cataloging of slides.

20% *Circulation:* Maintains circulation records and regulates lending. Set priorities as to extra-departmental and institutional use of the collection and must maintain good public relations while assuring that departmental needs are given priority. Analyzes volume and patterns of use to determine effectiveness of circulation policies. Refiles circulated slides.

20% *Reference:* Aids faculty in slide retrieval via interpretation and clarification of classification scheme, use of auxiliary aids and suggestion of material available in the collection.

15% *Collection development:* In consultation with the curator, formulates acquisition policies and priorities for the development of the collection requiring familiarity with the institutional and commercial sources for sides, as well as art history literature. Responsible for ordering new slides and for judging quality and accuracy of the new acquisitions.

EXAMPLE B

TITLE: Assistant Slide Librarian I

REPORTS TO: Slide Librarian II

SUPERVISES: Part-time staff

BASIC FUNCTION:

Responsible for accessioning, researching, and cataloging slides. Assists department head in overseeing slide department operations, in supervising staff, and in developing slide classification system.

PRIMARY DUTIES AND RESPONSIBILITIES:

1. Catalogs new slides and recatalogs old material for the slide collection according to an in-house classification system. This includes researching (foreign- and English-language publications) classifying slides from all media and cultures, establishing and typing authority file and catalog cards.

2. Assists other slide catalogers and helpers in interpreting slide classification principles.

3. Assists the head of the slide department in researching and developing classification systems in specific areas for slide acquisitions.

4. Assists faculty, students, museum education, and curatorial staff in locating slides.

5. Oversees slide processing through a variety of stages (e.g., binding, typing, labeling) and helps direct work of part-time employees to ensure efficient use of time and smooth work flow.

Appendix B — Sample Job Descriptions / 105

6. Acts as a liaison between the department head and staff and brings problems to the attention of the department head.

7. Assists in the planning and implementation of new systems, procedures, and projects.

8. Acquires, organizes, and arranges slides of exhibition objects and related material for current museum exhibitions.

9. In absence of Department Head, assumes full responsibility for supervising four full-time employees and part-time student workers and overseeing the operations of the slide library.

EXAMPLE C

TITLE: Slide Library Assistant II

REPORTS TO: Slide Librarian IV

SUPERVISES: Student Slide Filers (6)

BASIC FUNCTION:
Coordinates slide circulation and maintains the slide files. Types slide department correspondence and handles office procedures.

PRIMARY DUTIES AND RESPONSIBILITIES:

1. Coordinates the circulation of slides in and out of the library.

2. Refiles returned slides and files new slides and checks the filing of all slides.

3. Provides assistance where necessary to new and current users of the library.

4. Maintains uncataloged slide files and helps users locate uncataloged slides.

5. Trains and supervises slide filers.

6. Handles all office procedures.

7. Does elementary cataloging and research as assigned. Recatalogs and corrects cataloging mistakes in current slide system.

8. Maintains slide circulation records and statistics. Enforces slide library loan policies and follows up overdue slide loans.

9. Provides daily maintenance of the photocopy machine, monitors supplies, and initiates reordering.

10. Assists patrons with slide orders and handles payment for slides.

EXAMPLE D

TITLE: Slide Collection Bibliographic Specialist

QUALIFICATIONS:

Education and training: Undergraduate major or MA in art history or related humanities discipline. Reading knowledge of at least two foreign languages. Knowledge of photography. Expertise or interest in Middle Eastern, Islamic, Indian, or Far Eastern art and architecture.

Knowledge, skills, and abilities: Ability to work under pressure and to remain flexible. Understanding of academic environment and ability to provide service in its context. Willingness to expand field of subject expertise.

Experience: Familiarity with library automation or computer programming. Experience in library technical processing.

BROAD FUNCTION OF POSITION:

One of two positions reporting to the Slide Librarian to assist in the operation of the slide and photograph collection, including cataloging of slides, patron assistance, and supervision of some processing operations.

SPECIFIC DUTIES:

1. Catalogs slides according to the Fogg classification system either manually or in on-line system using AACR2, LC Graphic Material rules, Art and Architecture Thesaurus, Library of Congress Subject Headings, or other applicable standards. This includes research needed to establish authorities and other basic facts needed for classification.

2. Assists patrons with reference questions, routine policy information, and circulation in the absence of circulation staff.

3. Supervises the checking in of developed film and other aspects of processing for classified slides. Enforces quality control.

4. Makes guide cards or labels for collection.

5. Makes monthly invoices for personal orders, fines, and replacements.

6. May need to handle any of the other duties of the slide collection operations in order to meet patron needs.

7. Assists in making decisions about revisions of classification schemes and other aspects of the unit's operations.

8. May train student workers for specific tasks.

9. May oversee the work of photographer.

10. May assume comparable duties as required.

EXAMPLE E

TITLE: Library Assistant III

REPORTS TO: Slide Curator

SUPERVISES: Student assistants

DUTIES:

40% *Catalog and classify new slides and photographs purchased and/or produced by the library:* (1) Check new orders against holdings for possible duplication. (2) Complete and verify information required to identify images; when necessary translate information from foreign languages. (3) Determine appropriate classification for images and assign call numbers, descriptive cataloging, cross-references, and subject indexing. (4) Reclassify areas of the collection. (5) Recommend new classifications and subject headings for material not appropriate to existing historical organization. (6) Prepare cataloged material for typist.

15% *Collection maintenance:* (1) File new slides, photographs, and shelflist cards into collection. (2) Spot and correct errors on labels; weed damaged or worn slides from the collection for cleaning, repair, or replacement. (3) Identify and search for lost items. (4) Assist in annual shift of collection ensuring ease of access to materials.

20% *Public service:* (1) Act as telephone and walk-in receptionist. (2) Provide information and reference in the form of orientations for new users and assistance in locating images for patrons. (3) Advise faculty, students, and other patrons on use of visual materials in lectures and operation of audiovisual equipment.

10% *Circulation control:* (1) Notify borrowers of overdue slides, projectors, and trays and advise curator when replacements are necessary. (2) Compile statistics for circulation and production.

10% *Supervision:* (1) Assist curator in training student assistants to sort, refile, mount, and label slides and photographs; assign and supervise daily work in curator's absence. (2) Act as head of the unit in curator's absence.

5% *Miscellaneous work:* (1) Create graphics for collection services and special projects. (2) Assist as needed in mounting and labeling slides, typing labels, xeroxing slides for shelflist cards, and sorting and filing circulated slides. (3) Assist with office maintenance.

TECHNICAL SERVICES

EXAMPLE A

TITLE: Slide Librarian for Audiovisual Services

REPORTS TO: Curator of Visual Arts

SUPERVISES: Student assistants (2)

ORGANIZATIONAL UNIT: Art Department

BASIC DESCRIPTION: To assist the Curator in the routine operations of the slide and photograph collection, including in particular the management and scheduling of the department's audiovisual equipment.

QUALIFICATIONS:

Knowledge, skills, and abilities: Thorough knowledge of the operation of audiovisual equipment, particularly 35mm automatic slide projectors, dissolve units, 8mm and 16mm movie projectors, videocassette recorders, video projectors, video cameras and editing equipment, audiotaping equipment, and public address systems. Ability to do minor maintenance checks and repairs on such equipment.

Education and training: BA level degree, preferably in art or subject related to media production.

Experience: Understanding of uses of audiovisual equipment in art classes, lecture, and special performances. Experience in audio and video recording and operating slide and motion picture projectors.

DUTIES:

Routine departmental services: Provide a semester schedule of all scheduled classes using audiovisual equipment on a regularly basis. Maintain a weekly calendar of nonroutine audiovisual equipment requirements. Assure that all requested equipment is available and set up at the requested times and places.

Special lectures, programs, and performances: Coordinate and keep a weekly schedule for necessary audiovisual equipment for all special events.

Maintenance of audiovisual equipment: Receive and check-out all reports of audiovisual equipment malfunctions. Make minor repairs when possible. Arrange for all repairs as well as an annual preventive maintenance check for all audiovisual equipment.

Training and orientations: Instruct special guest lecturers, new faculty, and students in the use of department's audiovisual equipment, as well as policies and procedures for its use.

Inventory and reports: Maintain a complete inventory list of all departmental audiovisual equipment under the jurisdiction of the slide and photograph collection. Maintain inventory of all audiovisual supplies and advise curator when to reorder. Keep maintenance record on each piece of equipment. Make recommendations to the curator on purchase of new equipment and on development of policies and procedures for use of equipment.

EXAMPLE B

TITLE: Slide Librarian for Technical Services

REPORTS TO: Curator of Visual Arts

SUPERVISES: Half-time data entry assistant (1)

ORGANIZATIONAL UNIT: Art Department

BASIC PURPOSE: To assist curator in development and maintenance of all computer automated systems in the visual resources collection. These duties include program development, documentation, and modifications; staff proficiency training; and recommendations on and coordination of computer equipment and software purchases. Standard visual resources collection duties include accessioning and cataloging of new slide acquisitions into collection holdings; overseeing various aspects of daily operation, including training and supervision of part-time staff; and general assistance to patrons in the collection.

QUALIFICATIONS:

Knowledge, skills, and abilities: Proficiency in microcomputer operations and BASIC programming language. Ability to get along well with faculty and students alike; good supervisory skills. Research ability. Proficient in written and verbal communications.

Education and training: BA in art history required. MA preferred. Reading knowledge of at least two European languages.

Experience: Previous work experience in slide and photo collection and/or library.

PRIMARY DUTIES AND RESPONSIBILITIES:

60% *Administration of computer automation projects and activities.* Includes research, innovative development, and modification of commercial software packages and development and documentation of additional programs to automate various manual procedures in the collection; maintenance and administration of a database of slide collection holdings, and an automated statistical gathering system; work with curator to develop plans and strategies and write proposals for long-term automation goals; train and supervise collection staff in use of computer; order and maintain supplies appropriate for automation projects; stay abreast of current technologies and related projects at other institutions.

30% *Accessioning and cataloging* of new materials into the holdings of the collection; assist in maintaining accuracy of previously cataloged materials; training and supervision of part-time assistants in cataloging, accessioning, and circulation procedures.

10% *Supervise daily operation* of circulation desk, including patron assistance and reference questions; maintenance of a file of users of the collection; explanation of circulation and usage policies and procedures to users.

Appendix B — Sample Job Descriptions / 109

EXAMPLE C

TITLE: Laboratory Assistant

WORKING TITLE: Photographer

IMMEDIATE SUPERVISOR: Head Curator

ORGANIZATIONAL UNIT: Art History Department

DUTIES AND RESPONSIBILITIES:
Responsible for all the technical aspects of slide production for the art history slide collection. Maintains a photocopy laboratory and is responsible for the production of approximately 6,000 color and black-and-white 35mm slides annually. Duties include the scheduling of materials to be processed in order to meet departmental deadlines; photocopying of these materials using color film and the in-house processing of black-and-white slides; and the review of the finished slides to maintain quality standards. In addition, follows new developments in the field of photography and makes recommendations regarding material and equipment purchases.

EXAMPLE D

TITLE: Photographer

REPORTS TO: Slide Librarian

QUALIFICATIONS:

Education and training: One year training at professional school of photography, or two years' professional experience, or an equivalent combination of education and experience.

Knowledge, skills, and abilities: Ability to operate a variety of photographic processing equipment; determine lens settings, filters, types of films, shutter speeds, color tests, exposure times, etc. Ability to maintain photographic equipment in working condition. Be familiar with a wide range of equipment and material and photographic literature.

Experience: Fully experienced as a copy photographer.

EXAMPLES OF DUTIES AND RESPONSIBILITIES:
- Responsible for the production of all visual instruction requests on a weekly production schedule.
- Shoots, develops, and prints 35mm slides and 8-by-10-inch prints weekly.
- Responsible for oversize work, rush jobs, architectural model photography, and transfer of images between all formats (35mm, 4x5, lantern, print).
- Advises the Slide Librarian on new photographic technologies, creation of new procedures, and ordering photographic supplies and equipment.

EXAMPLE E

TITLE: Photographer/Technician/Darkroom Supervisor

REPORTS TO: Curator

110 / APPENDIX B – SAMPLE JOB DESCRIPTIONS

QUALIFICATIONS:

Education and Training: At least one year's training in professional photography or equivalent experience.

Knowledge, skills, and abilities: Knowledge of a wide range of photographic techniques to include copy photography, slide duplication, black-and-white reversal processes, photographic printing. Abilities with and knowledge of a wide range of audiovisual equipment, operation, and minor maintenance.

CATEGORIES OF DUTIES AND PERCENT TIME FOR EACH:

35% *Photographer*

1. Photographing two-dimensional work selected by curator and college faculty.
2. Duplicating slides.
3. Processing the above photographic materials in the appropriate chemistry.
4. Experimenting with new photographic materials and development processes.

30% *Technician*

1. Maintain college-owned audiovisual equipment. This includes:
   a. Checking equipment periodically to determine proper working condition.
   b. Performing minor repairs.
   c. Sending equipment for repairs when necessary.
   d. Instructing others in the proper use of college-owned equipment.
2. Maintain college-owned darkroom equipment. This includes:
   a. Checking equipment periodically to determine if it is in proper working order.
   b. Performing minor repairs and functional improvements.
   c. Sending equipment for repairs when necessary.
   d. Instructing students, faculty, and darkroom workers in the proper use of darkroom equipment.

30% *Darkroom supervisor*

1. Supervising the darkroom to make sure that it opens and closes as scheduled and that the areas are kept clean and supplied with the appropriate chemistry.
2. Taking inventories to maintain proper chemical and supply levels.
3. Policing the area. This includes:
   a. Asking unauthorized users to leave.
   b. Keeping theft and abuse of equipment to a minimum.
   c. Instructing in proper use of equipment.
4. Maintaining schedule of darkroom hours including opening dates, extra hours at the semester's end, and class reservations.

5% *Publicity photographer*

1. Photographing college-sponsored events, including conferences, lectures, and other gatherings.

CLERICAL SERVICES

EXAMPLE A

TITLE: Student Worker

QUALIFICATIONS:
   Knowledge, skills, and abilities: Manual dexterity, visual perception, ability to follow specific instructions and directions, care in accuracy and cleanliness; ability to type and use computer.

EXAMPLES OF DUTIES:
   - File and mount 35mm slides.
   - Perform basic computer entry, type labels, and project slides for art history classes.
   - Work at circulation desk signing in and out slides and audiovisual equipment.

EXAMPLE B

TITLE: Slide Room Assistant

QUALIFICATIONS:
   Art or architecture major or other, with a knowledge of art history, in order to understand the organization of the slide room and to execute tasks expeditiously. Reading knowledge of a foreign language preferred. Expected to perform duties as accurately and neatly as possible. It would be most desirable for assistants to have the academic background that would enable them to assist in cataloging and classifying slides and research.

SUMMARY:
   Assists Slide Curator in the operation of the slide collection on a part-time basis.

DUTIES:
   Performs technical and clerical duties as assigned, including processing slides into the collection by entering slide information into the database, masking and mounting slides, filing slides, circulating slides, and instructing patrons in the use of the collection.

Appendix C
Glossary

accession(s) — Item(s) added to the collection.

accession book or record — A master list in which are recorded, in order of receipt, slides and other formats added to the collection, with information concerning them, such as date of acquisition, source, cost, requestors, etc.

accession number — The unique number assigned to an item showing the order of its acquisition and, in some cases, the year acquired. (*See also* acquisition number.)

acquisition number — Unique identification number assigned to each item acquired. (*See also* accession number.)

acquisition(s) — Item(s) acquired or gained.

administration — (1) The active management of the visual resources collection; (2) type or area of visual resources service comprising determination of policy and program, financial management, personnel coordination and supervision, and public relations for the visual resources collection.

audiovisual specialist — Staff member of the visual resources collection responsible for activities related to the acquisition, use, and care of audiovisual equipment and to the techniques of presentation through the use of audiovisual equipment and materials.

authority list — A list of standardized terms or names approved for use in image descriptions. (*See also* thesaurus).

binding and rebinding — The process of mounting transparencies in glass binders or mounts, or the restoration of an old or damaged slide mount. Binding refers to all steps in the process, from cleaning and assembling the glass and frames and placing directional marks or signal dots on the frames, to the actual masking, cleaning and framing the transparency, and final inspection.

budget — An estimate of proposed expenditures for a given period or purpose and the proposed means of funding them.

capital expenditures — Expenditures which result in the acquisition of fixed or permanent assets such as slide or photo storage files, slide viewers/sorters, slide projectors and other audiovisual equipment, computers, and typewriters. (In some situations this category can also include purchased slides and photographs.)

114 / APPENDIX C—GLOSSARY

catalog — A list or file which records and describes the holdings of the visual resources collection organized in a meaningful way.

cataloged material — Material that has been identified in a catalog which records, describes, and indexes the resources in a visual resources collection.

cataloging — (1) The act of identifying in a list or file the holdings of the visual resources collection; (2) the act of assigning codes or "catalog numbers" (call numbers) to items (slides or photographs) to enable their "shelving" or "filing" in a predetermined order.

cataloging corrections — Minor modifications made in the call number, such as correcting a Cutter number or country designation, etc.

circulation — The activity of lending resources (slides, photographs, other formats, audiovisual equipment) to users/borrowers.

classification — A system of categorization of the field of art for the purpose of arranging images or other material in like groups; systematic grouping of like items together.

classification system — The plan or order utilized for categorization for the purpose of arranging images or other material in like groups.

clientele — Users of the visual resources collection services. (Also known as patrons or users.)

collection — An accumulated group of materials having a common characteristic.

College Work Study Program (C.W.S.P.) — Federally funded program providing funds to create jobs for qualified full-time students. The federal program usually provides 60 to 80 percent of the students' salaries.

copy photography — Production of photographic images (usually slides) from images in books, magazines, postcards, or other art reproductions.

copy stand — Equipment consisting of a camera, a horizontal platform with an upright at right angles equipped with a tripod attachment to attach the camera, and lights that can be adjusted for the purpose of making photographic reproductions of images from two-dimensional sources.

cost group — All the expenditures associated with a particular collection activity.

curator — A person having the responsibility of the care and supervision of something; a manager or director.

database — A collection of records related to the collection and accessible through computer hardware and software.

database management system — A computer software program that accomplishes the tasks of creating, accessing, and maintaining the database for the collection.

donation — Additions to the collection that are acquired at no cost (except for the processing into the collection); a gift.

dry mount — Method of attaching a photograph or other photographic reproduction to a support surface with the use of "dry mount tissue" (a bonding material) and heat. (Some bonding materials are cold adhesive processes.)

duplication, slide — The process of rephotographing a slide onto transparency film.

encumbrance — An outstanding bill or debt, a financial commitment made before it is actually paid for.

equipment — Items of a nonexpendable nature which retain their basic identity and utility over a period of time.

exchange — The acquisition of visual resources by exchange with another collection.

facilities — A visual resources collection's quarters and its equipment.

field — A location in a data record where a specified item of information regarding an image is stored.

file — (1) Any equipment, such as a slide file or vertical file, in which slides, mounted photographs, microfiche, filmstrips, catalogs, etc., can be stored; (2) a collection of cards, brochures, etc., arranged systematically for reference.

filing slides — The process of arranging slides in classes, and returning them to their proper location in the storage cabinets or files. May also include cleaning the slides, marking them to show usage and removing coded circulation cards, if they are used. This process also includes time utilized to correct misfilings discovered and to rearrange the physical location of the materials to ease the spacing of the slides in the file drawers or the racks, when necessary.

film, photographic — A thin, flexible sheet of cellulose triacetate or polyester coated with a light sensitive emulsion for taking pictures. (Historical materials may include cellulose nitrate, which is highly combustible.)

fiscal period — Any period at the end of which financial condition and the results of operations are determined, whereupon its books are closed. It is usually a year, but not necessarily a calendar year.

floor space — The total area in the visual resources collection devoted to collections and services and to the working activities of the staff. (This includes space under cabinets, occupied by closets, and built-in storage units.)

full-time equivalent (FTE) — Part-time staff hours equal in time value to full-time staff.

full-time position — A position, the duties for which require the incumbent to be on the job the standard work week of the visual resources collection, usually 40 hours per week.

gift — The acquisition of visual resources material by gift, or donation. (*See also* donation.)

hours of service — Those hours during the week when the collection is open and available for service to its users.

indexing — Activities included in the preparation of lists, card files, or other form of an array of references to topics, artists, sites, titles of images, etc.

in-house production — Photography done by the staff of the collection.

in-service training — Informal education taken by staff, often consisting of seminars or workshops; staff or professional development.

inventory — (1) Detailed list showing quantities, descriptions, date of acquisitions, and original cost of property; (2) a shelf reading.

microfiche — A microfilm sheet containing multiple images in a grid pattern.

microfilm — A strip of film containing photographic images, usually too small to be read without magnification.

mounting — *See* binding and rebinding; dry mount.

operating expenditures — Costs necessary to the rendering of services.

patrons — Persons who use the collection services and holdings. (*See also* users; clientele.)

personnel costs — A category of expenditures comprising items related to the staffing of the collection, including salaries and wages.

photograph collection — An accumulated group of photographs.

professional positions — Those positions which require training and skill in a specific field and carry broad responsibilities for independent judgment regarding the overall functions of the unit.

public (user) area — The area open to patrons/clientele, furnished with tables and chairs, viewers/slide sorters, card catalog, and the area in which the collection holdings are usually found.

reclassifications — Complete changes of the classification for an image or group of images.

record — A group of data elements which pertain to a particular item in the collection.

reference question — Any request for information or aid which requires use of one or more sources to determine the answer, or which utilizes the knowledge and professional judgment of the curator.

reference work — Activity performed by the professional staff in seeking to locate and supply specific information or images requested by clientele.

replacements, slides or photographs — New slides or photographs acquired to take the place of damaged, deteriorated, or lost slides or photographs.

report — An official or formal record, as from a special investigation, the activities of a particular unit, or a time period.

salary range — The lowest and the highest salaries actually paid to incumbents of a given position classification.

salary scale — The span in salary from the highest to the lowest which has been authorized for a given position.

seating capacity — The number of chairs or other seating units available within the area reserved for clientele while they are using the materials.

shelf reading — Process of comparing the items in the files with the shelflist for the purpose of identifying missing, misfield, or lost materials.

slide duplication — *See* duplication, slide.

slide mounting or slide binding — *See* binding and rebinding.

slide storage area — Space in the visual resources collection allocated for the files or cabinets housing the slide collection.

Appendix C—Glossary / 117

special collection — A collection within a visual resources collection of material of a certain format, on a certain subject, of a certain period or geographical area, or gathered together for a particular reason in a collection which is more or less general in character.

staff — The group of persons who carry on the activities of a visual resources collection under the direction of the person responsible for the operation.

standards — (1) Objective, observable, and usually quantitative measures of achievement set up as ideals of service with which a particular collection can be compared; (2) agreed upon usage of terms, procedures, policies.

storage area — (1) That portion of the total floor space of the collection quarters allocated to the storage of materials, supplies, and equipment not in immediate use; (2) area of total space which houses slide and/or photograph storage files.

storage capacity — Number of items (slides) that can be accommodated in a particular style or model of storage unit.

student assistant — A student employed part-time, usually in a university, college, or school to perform nontechnical or nonprofessional duties under the supervision of the professional staff and paid on an hourly basis.

supplies — Material items of an expendable nature that are consumed, wear out, or deteriorate through use.

survey — A scientifically conducted study through which data are gathered according to a definite schedule and are presented in a statistical, tabulated, or summary form.

technical services — Activities inherent in producing or preparing images for use in the collection.

technical staff — Employers whose primary responsibilities involve photographic production, audiovisual equipment, or computer automation.

thesaurus — A standard list of authorized terms showing relationships (i.e., synonymous, broader, narrower) of related terms to the preferred terms.

transparency — Image on film viewed by light shining through.

unexpended balance — That portion of current funds which is not spent or pledged to a particular purpose. Such funds may revert to the appropriating unit, or become part of the expendable funds for the succeeding fiscal period.

unit cost — The cost of producing a unit of product or rendering a unit of service.

users — People who use the collection and its services.

weeding — The process of removing a slide or photograph and all entries that refer to the item from active use.

work area — That portion of the collection's total floor space allocated for use by staff members in performing their work duties.

visual resources — Images in various formats utilizing vision to enhance or promote instruction, research, or documentation, such as photographs, slides, motion pictures, maps, models, perspective drawings or plans, videotapes, videodisks, microfiche, etc.

visual resources collection — An accumulated group of images as described above.

Appendix D
Miscellaneous Administrative Forms

PHOTOGRAPHIC SERVICES FORMS

ART DEPT. SLIDE REQUEST FORM

NAME .... DATE IN ....
SPEC. INSTR .... DATE NEEDED ....
Call No.   AUTHOR ....
....   TITLE ....
....   PLATES / PAGES / FIGURES ....

bibl. .... date ret'd. .... date ret'd. ....
date shot .... date acc'd ....
roll no. .... acc'd by ....

[white - requestor's 1st. notification]

date shot .... date acc'd ....
roll no. .... acc'd by ....

[yellow - notification that slides are in collection]

date shot .... date acc'd ....
roll no. .... acc'd by ....

[card - collection's file copy]

120 / APPENDIX D—MISCELLANEOUS ADMINISTRATIVE FORMS

RETURN TO: ___ LIBRARY   DATE NEEDED _____
             ___ OTHER _____

SLIDE ORDER FORM

AUTHOR: _____

TITLE: _____

CALL NO.: _____

ORDERED BY: _____

DATE: _____   TOTAL: COLOR _____   ENTERED? _____
                        B&W   _____   intial

COLOR		**BLACK & WHITE**	
Page plate / fig	Page plate / fig	Page plate / fig	Page plate / fig

Appendix D — Miscellaneous Administrative Forms / 121

SLIDE REQUEST FORM

Submitted by: ....
Date: ....

Description of image / set: ....
....
....

Possible source: ....
....
....
....

Term / Date needed: ....
Course name: ....

Reason for request:
/ / Collection's slide is lost
    Cat #

/ / Collection's slide should be replaced because:
    Cat #

/ / Collection development

INSTRUCTIONAL RESOURCE CENTER
SLIDE RECOMMENDATION REQUEST FORM

Instructor: ....
Course: ....
# of Slides: ....

Please use this form as marker in book or magazine and to provide as much information as possible about slides to be made.

Source (Book, Magazine, other): ....
....

Author: ....

Date of Pub.: ....

Page #: ....

[spine]

Please mark X to show location on page.

Architect / Artist / Site
Period: ....
....
....

Title / Project: ....
....
....
....
....
....
....
....

Today's Date: ....

122 / APPENDIX D—MISCELLANEOUS ADMINISTRATIVE FORMS

SLIDE ORDER

Date Needed: ....

Author ....

Title ....

Call No ....

ORDERED BY ....

DATE .... TOTAL SLIDES

color .... b/w ....

Page Plate / Fig.	Page Plate / Fig.
COLOR	B/W

USE FOR RUSH ORDER ONLY!
SLIDE ORDER

Date Needed: ....

Author ....

Title ....

Call No ....

ORDERED BY ....

DATE .... TOTAL SLIDES

color .... b/w ....

Page Plate / Fig.	Page Plate / Fig.

PLEASE NOTE
Rush Order LIMIT: 10 slides

STAFF-RELATED FORMS

STAFF PERFORMANCE EVALUATION FORM

NAME: _____ JOB TITLE: _____
DEPARTMENT: _____ SUPERVISOR: _____
EVALUATION PERIOD: _____

JOB DESCRIPTION: (list main elements)
_____
_____

JOB SKILLS: (rate by checking the appropriate box)

	SUPERIOR	VERY GOOD	SATIS-FACTORY	UNSATIS-FACTORY
Work habits: (punctual, follows instructions)				
Quality of Work: (neat, accurate)				
Amount of Work: (commensurate with task)				
Cooperation: (works well with employer and others)				
Intuitive: (self-motivated)				

RATING KEY: SUPERIOR: Exceptionally good worker in all respects.
VERY GOOD: Above average performance in most respects.
SATISFACTORY: Meets minimum acceptable standards.
UNSATISFACTORY: Performance below average; needs improvement.

SUPERVISOR'S REMARKS:
_____
_____

Supervisor's Signature:_____ Date:_____

I have reviewed this document and my signature does not necessarily imply that I agree with this evaluation.

Employee Signature:_____ Date:_____
Additional Employee Remarks:_____
_____

ART DEPT. SLIDE COLLECTION
PART-TIME ASSISTANT WORK SCHEDULE

NAME: _____

ADDRESS: _____ PHONE #: _____

SEMESTER: _____

Please indicate the hours you are available to work. We prefer 3-hour time blocks.

Hours	Monday	Tuesday	Wednesday	Thursday	Friday
8-9					
9-10					
10-11					
11-12					
12-1					
1-2					
2-3					
3-4					
4-5					

ASSIGNMENT HOURS REPORT
Fiscal Year _____

WEEK OF:	TECHNICAL / CLERICAL					CIRCULATION					CURATORIAL							GRAND TOTAL
	A	B	C	D	Total	E	F	G	H	Total	I	J	K	L	M	O	P	Total	

TECHNICAL / CLERICAL

A = SLIDE BINDING
B = RE-BINDING
C = MOUNTING / SLEEVING PHOTOS
D = FILING SHELF and ACCESSION CARDS

CIRCULATION

E = FRONT DESK DUTY
F = FILING NEW SLIDES / PHOTOS
G = REFILING CIRCULATED SLIDES / PHOTOS
H = SPACING and SHIFTING FILES

CURATORIAL

I = ACCESSIONING / IDENTIFICATION
J = DATA ENTRY
K = CATALOGING
L = RECATALOGING
M = CORRECTIONS
O = COLLECTION DEVELOPMENT
P = FILING PUBLIC FILE CARDS

PART-TIME HELP WEEKLY TIME CHART

Semester: _____ Week of: _____

Name:	Monday	Tuesday	Wednesday	Thursday	Friday	TOTAL
hrs./wk.: total appt.: bal.as of ____:____						hrs.: new bal.:
hrs./wk.: total appt.: bal.as of ____:____						hrs.: new bal.:
hrs./wk.: total appt.: bal.as of ____:____						hrs.: new bal.:
hrs./wk.: total appt.: bal.as of ____:____						hrs.: new bal.:
hrs./wk.: total appt.: bal.as of ____:____						hrs.: new bal.:
hrs./wk.: total appt.: bal.as of ____:____						hrs.: new bal.:
hrs./wk.: total appt.: bal.as of ____:____						hrs.: new bal.:
hrs./wk.: total appt.: bal.as of ____:____						hrs.: new bal.:
hrs./wk.: total appt.: bal.as of ____:____						hrs.: new bal.:

ART DEPARTMENT
SLIDE COLLECTION   Date:_____
Application for Part-Time Employment

Name:_____ SS#_____

Address (Austin)_____ Phone_____

Permanent Address_____ City_____

Semester for which you wish employment: Fall_____ Spring_____
                                         Summer(1)_____ Summer (2)_____

How many hours a week do you wish to work?_____
How many hours of coursework will you be registered for?_____

Class Rank	School or College	Major	Degrees

Total hours complete: Studio_____ Art History_____ Art Ed._____
Are you currently employed by the University of Texas? Yes_____ No_____
If so, complete the following:
Department_____ Position_____
Supervisor _____ No. of Hours/Week_____

Are you related to any employee of the University of Texas? Yes_____ No_____
If so, state their name, relationship, position, and department.
_____

Following is a list of duties performed by Slide Collection employees. Please indicate any of those you would be interested in doing and for which you might be qualified.

_____Slide Binding   _____Numerical Filing   _____Alphabetical Filing
_____Slide Filing   _____Label Pasting   _____Typing (WPM____)

Previous experience in Slide and Photo Collections? ___Y ___N
Please describe, briefly, previous work experience:

List three faculty references:
1._____
2._____
3._____

> Submit this application with a completed schedule of possible work times indicating 3 hour time blocks per work session.

128 / APPENDIX D—MISCELLANEOUS ADMINISTRATIVE FORMS

STATISTICS FORMS

**Department of Art
Slide & Photo Collection
PHOTOGRAPHER'S   STATISTICS**
MONTH_____

Photo Services Requests [   ]

Copy Photography [   ]

Slide Duplication (Images) [   ]

Prints Requested [   ]

Rolls of Film Used:
Color Copy film [   ]
B & W Reversal film [   ]
Slide Duplicating film [   ]

Black & White Prints [   ]

Copy Stand Use [   ]

SLIDE COLLECTION

BINDING STATISTICS

NAME _____ DATE FOR WEEK _____

	Monday	Tuesday	Wednesday	Thursday	Friday
Total number of slides bound					
Number of rebinds					
Number of hours spent binding					
Box number or project					

APPENDIX D — MISCELLANEOUS ADMINISTRATIVE FORMS

FILER _____ DATE (for the week) _____

Faculty / Color Card	MON	TUES	WED	THURS	FRI	TOTAL
(Art History Faculty) / color card						
" " "						
" " "						
" " "						
" " "						
" " "						
STUDIO						
ART EDUCATION FACULTY						
Art History Students						
Art Ed. Students						
Other Departments						
Professors Emeriti						
Box #:						
New Slides						
In-House: (including Rebinds, Misfiled, etc.)						
					TOTALS:	

Appendix D – Miscellaneous Administrative Forms / 131

Department of Art
Slide & Photo Collection
Accessions Log (Slides)

CODES
(column 5)
A - Pre-Columb./Primitive/Pre-Hist.
    No.Am. Indian
B - Egyptian, Roman, Greek
C - Medieval, Byz., Rmsq., Gothic
D - Renaissance, Baroque
E - 18c., 19c.
F - 20c.
G - Islamic
H - Oriental, S.E. Asian
I - Student work J - Didactic

(column 8)
1 - Commercial
   1A - Replacement
2 - In-House Replacement
   2A - Copy Photography
   2B - Slide Duplication
   2C - Original Photography
       1 - Replacements
3 - U.T. Art Museum
4 - Donations

(column 10)
5 - Art History
6 - Studio
7 - Art Education
8 - Slide Collection

1. Date	2. Accession #'s	3. No. of slides	4. Medium	5. Century	6. Country	7. Source	8. Type	9. Requestor	10. Area	11. Accessor	12. Box #

Sources: Commercial: ____ Areas: Art History: ____
Produced Here: ____ Studio: ____
Donations: ____ Art Ed.: ____
TOTAL: ____ Slide Library: ____

Appendix E
Audiovisual Circulation Forms

PHOTOGRAPH CHARGES

Date _____ Due _____

Name _____ ☐ Faculty ☐ GTF ☐ Student

Student's I.D. # _____ No. of Photos _____

Supervising Instructor _____ Home phone _____

Faculty's Department _____ Office phone _____

Call Number:

Line 1	Line 2	Line 3	Line 4	Line 5	Filing number(s)
[723]	[Fr]	[C84]	[Sa9]		[1,4,15,24] = sample

By completing this form the borrower agrees not to copy in any way the items listed above. This restriction is required under the provisions of the Copyright Law.

134 / APPENDIX E – AUDIOVISUAL CIRCULATION FORMS

CIRCULATION FORM
SLIDE AND PHOTOGRAPH COLLECTION

NAME _____ SUPERVISING FACULTY _____ DEPARTMENT _____
PHONE _____ ADDRESS _____ COLOR / LETTER CARD USED _____

DATE ISSUED _____ HOLD FOR (DATE) _____ (HOUR) _____ DATE RETURNED _____
NUMBER OF SLIDES _____ EXPECTED _____ (HOUR) _____ NUMBER OF SLIDES _____
ISSUED BY _____ RETURN (DATE) _____ (HOUR) _____ RECEIVED BY _____

<u>Copyright</u>: No slides borrowed from this collection are to be reproduced in any form.
<u>Conservation</u>: Heat and moisture are harmful to slides. Please keep them in a cool, dry place at all times. Never project a slide for more than one minute. Please determine in advance if the projection equipment you plan to use is safe for glass mounted slides.

<u>Circulation policy</u>: Up to 50 slides may be borrowed for the <u>length of time of the lecture only</u>. Slides are due back immediately following the lecture. Slides may be placed on reserve in the Slide Collection and held for up to two weeks. Please return slides to the circulation desk during regular hours: Monday through Friday, 8 AM through 5 PM. On this circulation form, please list accession number (in parenthesis on slide label) and subject (either name of artist or in the case of architecture, the name of the city). See example at left.

373 HOLBEIN, HANS.
H723 Portrait of Charles
Ho2A de Solier.

1534/5. (o/wd). Dresden
(87-05287)

Slide number:	Subject:	Slide number:	Subject:	Slide number:	Subject:

Appendix E — Audiovisual Circulation Forms / 135

PLEASE FILL OUT COMPLETELY!!! THIS INFORMATION IS CRITICAL FOR OUR CIRCULATION RECORDS

NAME: _____ DATE: _____ TOTAL # _____

_____ FACULTY _____ T.A. _____ STUDENT (PROFESSOR: _____ CLASS: _____)
I.D. # _____

PHONE NUMBER: _____ NUMBER OF CAROUSEL TRAYS _____

STAFF: ENTERED? _____

136 / APPENDIX E – AUDIOVISUAL CIRCULATION FORMS

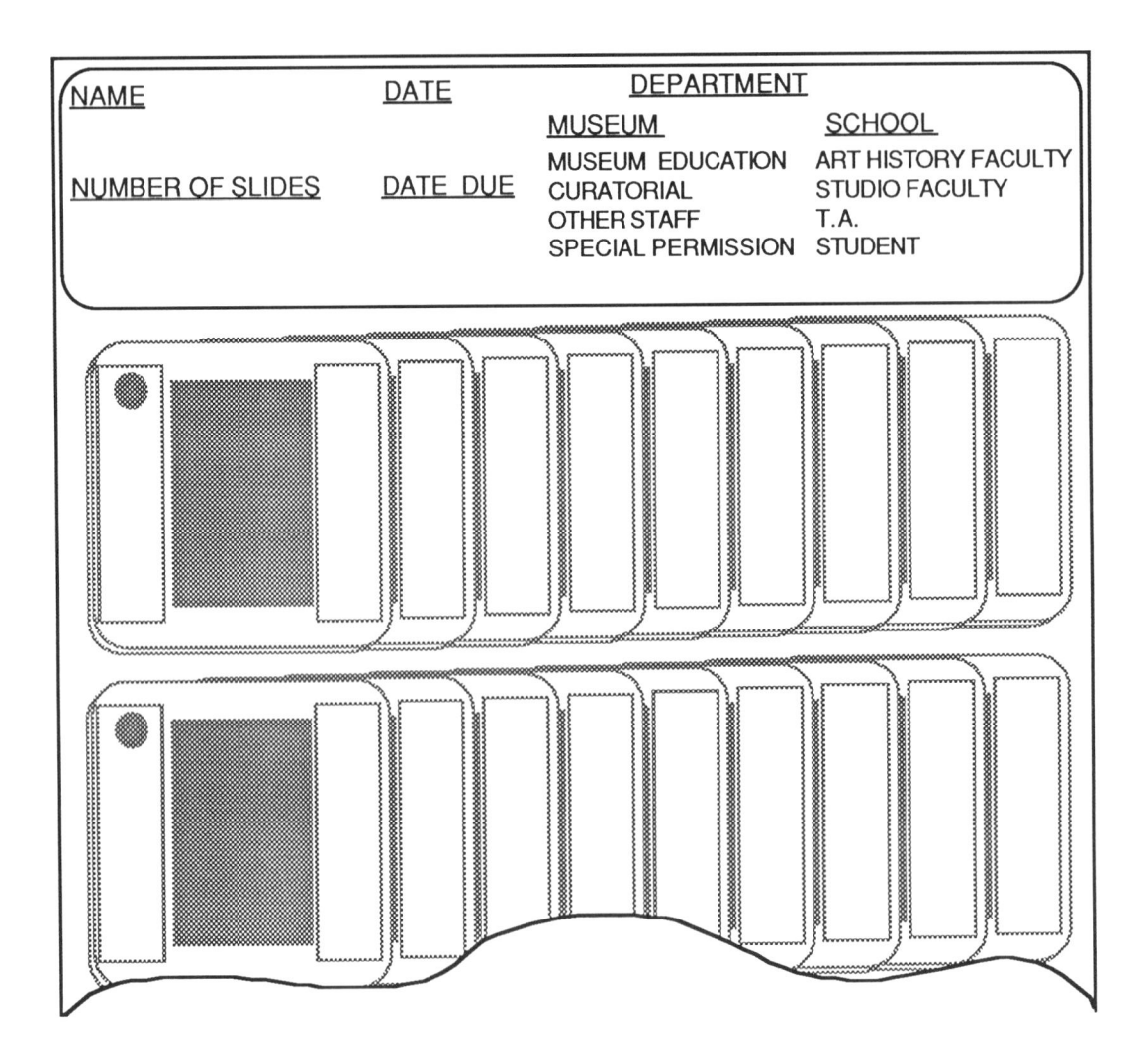

NAME	DATE	DEPARTMENT	
		MUSEUM	SCHOOL
NUMBER OF SLIDES	DATE DUE	MUSEUM EDUCATION CURATORIAL OTHER STAFF SPECIAL PERMISSION	ART HISTORY FACULTY STUDIO FACULTY T.A. STUDENT

Appendix E — Audiovisual Circulation Forms / 137

FACULTY: _____
DEPARTMENT: _____
Office: _____ Ext: _____

Pls. enter the total number of slides checked out and the date. When returning slides, be sure to have correct number and date recorded on this card. Numbers of carousels should also be entered.

ALL MATERIALS MUST BE RETURNED BY LAST DAY OF QUARTER

Date	No. Out.	No. Ret.	Date

CAROUSELS - Box #	Returned	Date

(Over)

- INSTRUCTIONAL RESOURCE CENTER -

BORROWERS' AUTHORIZATION

NAME:_____ DATE:_____

                                                               PHONE:_____(home)

ADDRESS:_____ _____(office)

SLIDE CIRCULATION RULES

    Students are authorized to borrow slides for use only in an in-class presentation which is part of an official museum or university course. Slides will not be lent to students for any other purposes. They are not to be used as research or review material, nor is browsing permitted in the Slide Collection.

    Staff from the teaching program may borrow slides for use only in official university or museum activities.

    Slides may not be reproduced in any form. It is implicit in the lending that the borrower agrees not to authorize duplication or reproduction of any slides and assumes all responsibility for that restriction.

CATEGORY OF BORROWER

_____Graduate teaching assistant. Fall____Spring____(check one only)

    Loan period: two weeks. Subject to fines.

_____Student project (assigned by a faculty member for in-class presentation.)

    Loan period: one day. (Slides may be put on reserve up to 3 days in advance of borrowing date.)

    Limit: 60 slides. Subject to fines.

_____Teaching staff

    Loan period: two weeks. Subject to fines.

FINE SCHEDULE

    $5.00   Overdue slides

    $2.00   Per slide with broken mount or glass

    $10.00 Per slide lost or with damage to film.

NOTE

    Students may borrow only one group of slides at a time. Previous loans must be returned and outstanding fines paid before additional slides may be borrowed. Slides must be returned during working hours (Monday-Friday, before 4:30 PM).

    Course credit will be withheld until all records are cleared and fines paid.

AUTHORIZATION

_____   _____   _____

Name of faculty member   Signature of same   Course No.

_____   _____

Department   Date

REQUISITION FOR MEDIA AND TECHNICAL SERVICES

Request must be received **3 WORKING DAYS** prior to showdate. Today's date _____

Incomplete forms will not be processed.

Showdate:_____ Requested By:_____
                                Instructor   *Department*   *Course & Section No.*

_____
(List 2 alternates)   Number of students   Office Phone Number   Home Phone Number

FOR OFFICE USE ONLY   Film / Tape starting time (Indicate AM or PM)_____ to_____
Showdate:_____   Bldg. and Room_____

I. EQUIPMENT

Confirmed by AVS

- ☐ 16mm Film Projector (M)
- ☐ 8mm Film Projector (8M)
- ☐ Opaque Projector (OP)
- ☐ Overhead Projector (OV)
- ☐ Filmstrip Projector (FS)
- ☐ Extension Cord (EC)
- ☐ Carousel Slide Projector (C)
- ☐ Screen (SR)
- ☐ Video Tape Playback (1/2") VHS
- ☐ Video Tape Playback (1/2") BETA
- ☐ Video-cassette Playback (3/4") (VC)
- ☐ Other _____
- ☐ Carousel and Cassette with pulse (CCT)
- ☐ Audio Tape Cassette Recorder (CT)
- ☐ Audio Tape Reel to Reel Recorder (T)
- ☐ Phonograph (P)
- ☐ PA System (PA)

II. OPERATOR REQUIRED: YES ☐ NO ☐

III. MEDIA MATERIALS

Confirmed by Film

Title (s)_____

Running time:_____ minutes

Source: ☐ Queens College ☐ Consortium:_____ ☐ My own materials

Rental: Source_____ Price_____

FOR OFFICE USE ONLY

Operator_____

Notes:_____

DELIVERY: ☐ Give to projectionist ☐ Pick up at I Bldg. Room 212

INSTRUCTOR'S SIGNATURE: _____

140 / APPENDIX E — AUDIOVISUAL CIRCULATION FORMS

Equip. I.D. No._____

Type of Equip._____

Name of Borrower
_____

Date Checked Out_____

Date Checked In _____
Remarks_____

Equip. I.D. No._____

Type of Equip._____

Name of Borrower
_____

Date Checked Out_____ Renewal_____
Date Returned_____ Renewal_____
　　　　　　　　　　　　　　 Renewal_____
For Semester Check-out Only　Renewal_____

Art Department audio visual equipment may be used for official education activities only. The user takes responsibility for the repair or replacement of the equipment if it is damaged or lost while in his or her possession.

The equipment I am borrowing is for an educational activity, and I will be responsible for this equipment.

****

NAME / COURSE # / ROOM #   DATE   STUDENT ID

EQUIPMENT:
- ___ Projector w/ zoom lens & case
- ___ Audio cassette player
- ___ Stereo record player
- ___ 16mm projector
- ___ Zoom lens
- ___ 178 mm lens
- ___ 65 mm lens
- ___ EC - 3 remote control / projector
- ___ 2 dissolve unit
- ___ 3 dissolve unit
- ___ Stacker unit for projector
- ___ Sync. cassette player
- ___ Headphones
- ___ Video Cassette Recorder & Monitor
- ___ Video Camera & Porta-pack
- ___ Overhead projector
- ___ Tripod
- ___ Carousel Tray No.____
- ___ Other_____

Appendix F
Sample Standard Record Formats

Example A The University of Texas, Austin, Art Department Slide Collection DataEase® accessions record format and field descriptions. Used with permission.

```
1    10   20   30   40   50   60   70   80
----+----+----+----+----+----+----+----+----+
 ACC#        CAT#       !      !         PC _ CENTURY ____

 MEDIA            :                          DATE _____

 LABEL ENTRY  _____

 CARD ENTRY   _____

 CREATED BY   _____  COUNTRY _____

 TITLE       _____
             _____

 PRESENT LOCATION _____

 SOURCE       _____

 DIMENSIONS   _____  BOX NO. _____ CYCLE NO. __

 X-REF        _____  SLIDE TYPE ___

 X-REF        _____  X-REF  _____
----+----+----+----+----+----+----+----+----+
```

No.	Name	Type	Long	Reqd	In-dex	Uni-que	Der-ived	Range Chk	Record size	offset
1	ACC.NO.	Numeric String	8	Yes	Yes	Yes	No	No	7	5
2	CAT.NO.1	Text	8	No	No	No	No	No	8	12
3	CAT.NO.2	Text	8	No	No	No	No	No	8	20
4	CAT.NO.3	Text	12	No	No	No	No	No	12	28
5	PC	Choice	1	No	No	No	No	No	1	40

    Choice field type name :
      Choice 1: Y
      Choice 2: N

No.	Name	Type	Long	Reqd	In-dex	Uni-que	Der-ived	Range Chk	Record size	offset
6	CENTURY	Text	5	No	No	No	No	No	5	41
7	MEDIUM	Text	12	No	No	No	No	Yes	12	46
8	DESCRIPTION	Text	28	No	No	No	No	No	28	58
9	DATE/CENTURY	Text	15	No	No	No	No	No	15	86
10	MAIN ENTRY	Text	56	Yes	No	No	No	No	56	101
11	MAIN ENTRY (CARDS)	Text	56	No	No	No	No	No	56	157
12	CREATED BY	Text	31	No	No	No	No	No	31	213
13	COUNTRY	Text	15	No	No	No	No	No	15	244
14	TITLE	Text	69	Yes	No	No	No	No	69	259
15	PRESENT LOCATION	Text	51	No	No	No	No	No	51	328
16	SOURCE	Text	61	Yes	No	No	No	No	61	379
17	DIMENSIONS	Text	25	No	No	No	No	No	25	440
18	BOX NO.	Text	6	Yes	Yes	No	No	No	6	465
19	CYCLE	Number	2	Yes	No	No	No	No	1	471
20	REF-1	Text	46	No	No	No	No	No	46	472
21	SLIDE TYPE	Choice	5	Yes	No	No	No	No	1	518

    Choice field type name :
      Choice 1: color
      Choice 2: b/w

No.	Name	Type	Long	Reqd	In-dex	Uni-que	Der-ived	Range Chk	Record size	offset
22	REF-2	Text	26	No	No	No	No	No	26	519
23	REF-3	Text	26	No	No	No	No	No	26	545

Record size 571

144 / APPENDIX F—SAMPLE STANDARD RECORD FORMATS

Example B University of Oregon, Architecture and Allied Arts Slide Collection standard form for accessions and field descriptions. Courtesy of Christine L. Sundt, University of Oregon, Architecture and Allied Arts Library Slide and Photograph Collection.

```
1        10        20        30        40        50        60        70        80
----+----+----+----+----+----+----+----+----+----+----+----+----+----+----+----+
         N E W -- A C C E S S I O N S -- UO-AAA Slide/Photo Collection
                         CARD TYPE
    ACCESSION NO._____      _____   CATALOG NO._____ _____ _____ _____ _____

    LABEL HEADING    _____
       MAIN ENTRY    _____  (Artist/Site)
      DESCRIPTION    _____  (Title/Description)
                     _____    /   /   /   /
                     _____  (medium; dimensions)
                     _____  (Museum/Architect)

        SUBJECT CODE _____       CENTURY CODE _____
        PAGE/PLATE/SLIDE NO. _____     FILM TYPE _____   DATE ENTERED _____

        SOURCE: _____  _____

        ACQUISITION TYPE _____   VALUE _____   REQUESTOR _____   RECORDER ___


----+----+----+----+----+----+----+----+----+----+----+----+----+----+----+----+
1        10        20        30        40        50        60        70        80

         FIELD DESCRIPTIONS
         ------------------

No. Name                    Type          Long Reqd In-  Uni- Der-  Rng Pre- Record
                                                    dex  que  ived  Chk vent size offset

  1 Accession Number        Num.String       7 Yes  Yes  Yes  No    No  No     6     5
    Field Display Attribute: Highlight 1
  2 Card Type               Choice          12 Yes  No   No   No    No  No     1    11
    Choice field type name : Card
         Choice   1: regular
         Choice   2: architecture
  3 CN1                     Text             5 Yes  No   No   No    No  No     5    12
  4 CN2                     Text             5 No   No   No   No    No  No     5    17
  5 CN3                     Text             5 No   No   No   No    No  No     5    22
  6 CN4                     Text             5 No   No   No   No    No  No     5    27
  7 CN5                     Text             5 No   No   No   No    No  No     5    32
  8 Label Heading           Text            19 No   No   No   Yes   No  No    19    37
    Field calculation formula : lookup codes Heading
  9 Main Entry              Text            31 No   Yes  No   No    No  No    31    56
 10 Desc1                   Text            31 No   No   No   No    No  No    31    87
 11 Desc2                   Text            31 No   No   No   No    No  No    31   118
 12 Desc3                   Text            31 No   No   No   No    No  No    31   149
 13 Desc4                   Text            28 No   Yes  No   No    No  No    28   180
 14 Subject Code            Choice          41 No   No   No   No    No  No     1   208
         Choice   1: Planning
         Choice   2: Landscape
         Choice   3: Religious
         Choice   4: Residential
         Choice   5: Civic
         Choice   6: Educational
         Choice   7: Business
```

Appendix F — Sample Standard Record Formats / 145

```
Choice   8: Other
Choice   9: C10 Self-portrait
Choice  10: C11 Male Portrait
Choice  11: C14 Female Portrait
Choice  12: C17 Group Portrait
Choice  13: C21 Eastern Religions
Choice  14: C21.1 Hindu
Choice  15: C21.2 Buddhist
Choice  16: C21.3 Confucianism
Choice  17: C21.4 Taoism
Choice  18: C21.5 Shintoism
Choice  19: C21.6 Jain
Choice  20: C21.7 Islam
Choice  21: C22 Old Testament
Choice  22: C23 New Testament
Choice  23: C24 Virgin Subject
Choice  24: C26 Christ Subject
Choice  25: C28 Saint/Angel
Choice  26: C29 Non-Traditional Religion
Choice  27: C30 History
Choice  28: C33 Mythology
Choice  29: C36 Allegory
Choice  30: C38 Literary
Choice  31: C40 Abstraction
Choice  32: C50 Interior
Choice  33: C55 Interior with figure
Choice  34: C60 Exterior/Landscape
Choice  35: C61 Marine
Choice  36: C65 Exterior with figure
Choice  37: C70 Animal/Fantastic Creature
Choice  38: C80 Still Life
Choice  39: C90 Cycle, Series
Choice  40: C99 Comparison
Choice  41: S10 Male Head/Bust
Choice  42: S12 Male Figure
Choice  43: S15 Female Head/Bust
Choice  44: S17 Female Figure
Choice  45: S19 Group
Choice  46: S20 Relief
Choice  47: S25 Stele/Slab
Choice  48: S30 Funerary Container
Choice  49: S35 Sarcophagus
Choice  50: S40 Exterior Architectural (in situ)
Choice  51: S50 Interior Architectural (in situ)
Choice  52: S70 Animal
Choice  53: S80 Abstraction
Choice  54: S90 Conceptual (Installation/Performance)
Choice  55: T01 Chart/Document
Choice  56: T05 Groupings of diverse objects
Choice  57: T08 Architecture
Choice  58: T15 Architectural elements
Choice  59: T21 Armor
Choice  60: T23 Weapon
Choice  61: T31 Tool/Utensil/Paddle
Choice  62: T33 Vessel/Receptacle
Choice  63: T35 Basket
Choice  64: T41 Textile
Choice  65: T43 Costume/Accessory
Choice  66: T45 Mask/Headdress
Choice  67: T47 Ceremonial/Ritual Object
Choice  68: T49 Body Painting/Scarring
Choice  69: T50 Figure/Head (general)
Choice  70: T51 Male Figure
Choice  71: T52 Female Figure
Choice  72: T53 Group
Choice  73: T57 Plant
```

146 / APPENDIX F—SAMPLE STANDARD RECORD FORMATS

```
               Choice    74:  T58 Animal
               Choice    75:  T59 Fantastic Creature
               Choice    76:  T60 Musical Instrument
               Choice    77:  T75 Furniture
               Choice    78:  T80 Transportation
               Choice    79:  T90 Miscellaneous/Other
               Choice    80:  Text/Calligraphy
               Choice    81:  Maps/Charts/Diagrams
               Choice    82:  T10 Murals/Petroglyphs/Tablets
15 Century Code           Number      5 No   Yes No  No   No   No    4   209
      Number Type : Fixed point
      Digits to left of decimal = 3
16 Page/Plate/Slide No. Text          8 No    No No  No   No   No    8   213
17 Film Type              Choice      5 No    No No  No   No   No    1   221
      Choice field type name : type
      Choice    1:  color
      Choice    2:  b/w
18 Date Entered           Date        8 No    No No  Yes  No   No    6   222
      Field calculation formula : ??/??/??
19 Source1                Text       24 No    No No  No   No   No   24   228
20 Source2                Text       30 No    No No  No   No   No   30   252
21 Copy/Purchase/Gift     Choice      8 Yes   No No  No   No   No    1   282
      Choice    1:  copy
      Choice    2:  purchase
      Choice    3:  gift
22 Value                  Number      6 No    No No  No   No   No    4   283
      Number Type : Fixed point
      Digits to left of decimal = 3
23 Requestor              Choice      6 Yes   No No  No   No   No    1   287
      Choice    1:  AAA
      Choice    2:  ArH
      Choice    3:  Arch
      Choice    4:  LA
      Choice    5:  PPPM
      Choice    6:  FAA
      Choice    7:  ArE
      Choice    8:  ColDev
      Choice    9:  Lib
      Choice   10:  other
24 Recorder               Text        3 Yes   No No  No   No   No    3   288
```

Record size 291

Appendix F — Sample Standard Record Formats / 147

Example C Arizona State University, School of Art, Slide and Photograph Collection sample data entry forms. Used with permission.

```
SOURCE
TITLE    THE LOST WORLD OF THE IMPRESSIONISTS
AUTHOR
CALL #
```

Sample labels:

GENERAL INFO:
- N/G = information not given
- ND = no known date
- / = no information in field

WESTERN ART (Medieval through Modern):

```
ACCESSION # 85.05880  PG 160   PL        DECADE 18.7
MEDIA       P              WEST PER/STYL MDN    REGION
COUNTRY     FR             DYN/2nd CHRON        SUB-REGION
SUBJECT     LAND           DATE 1873
ARTIST      CEZANNE, Paul
TITLE 1     La Maison du Pendu
TITLE 2     —
TITLE 3     —
TITLE 4     —
MEDIA:SIZE  o/c: 92.3 x 78 cm
LOCATION/ 1 Paris: Louvre
MUSEUM    2
ADD. INFO.  —
```

```
P     CEZANNE, Paul
MDN   La Maison du Pendu
FR
LAND                    1873
o/c: 92.3 x 78 cm
Paris: Louvre
                        85.05880
```

```
ACCESSION # 85.05881  PG 225   PL        DECADE 18.6
MEDIA                      WEST PER/STYL         REGION
COUNTRY                    DYN/2nd CHRON         SUB-REGION
SUBJECT                    DATE 1867-9
ARTIST
TITLE 1     The Jas de Bouffan
TITLE 2     —
TITLE 3     —
TITLE 4     —
MEDIA:SIZE  o/c: 54 x 31 cm
LOCATION/ 1 London: Tate
MUSEUM    2
ADD. INFO.
```

```
P     CEZANNE, Paul
MDN   The Jas de Bouffan
FR
LAND                    1867-9
o/c: 54 x 31 cm
London: Tate
                        85.05881
```

```
ACCESSION # 85.01703  PG 52    PL 15     DECADE 16.5
MEDIA       P              WEST PER/STYL BAR    REGION
COUNTRY     NE             DYN/2nd CHRON        SUB-REGION
SUBJECT     STILL          DATE 1658
ARTIST      KALF, Willem
TITLE 1     Still-life with the
TITLE 2     Drinking Horn of the
TITLE 3     S. Sebastian
TITLE 4     Archer's Guild, Lobster + Glass
MEDIA:SIZE  o/c: 50 x 30 cm
LOCATION/ 1 London
MUSEUM    2
ADD. INFO.
```

```
P       KALF, Willem
BAR     Still-Life with the
NE      Drinking Horn of the
STILL   S. Sebastian   1658
Archer's Guild, Lobster & Glass
o/c: 50 x 30 cm
London: Nat Gall
                        85.01703
```

WESTERN ARCHITECTURE:

```
ACCESSION # 85.06542  PG       PL        DECADE 19.3
MEDIA       A              WEST PER/STYL MDN    REGION
COUNTRY     US             DYN/2nd CHRON        SUB-REGION
SUBJECT     DWEL.4         DATE 1937
ARTIST      WRIGHT, Frank Lloyd
TITLE 1     Taliesin West
TITLE 2     General view of exter-
TITLE 3     ior
TITLE 4     —
MEDIA:SIZE  —
LOCATION/ 1 AZ SCOTTSDALE
MUSEUM    2
ADD. INFO.
```

```
A       AZ SCOTTSDALE
MDN     Taliesin West
US      General view of ext-
DWEL.4  erior          1937

Arch: WRIGHT, Frank Lloyd
                        85.06542
```

148 / APPENDIX F — SAMPLE STANDARD RECORD FORMATS

ANCIENT WESTERN (Egyptian through Early Medieval):

```
ACCESSION # 85.01805  PG ___  PL ___  DECADE 05.0
MEDIA       SC         WEST PER/STYL EX/BYZ  REGION ___
COUNTRY     ___        DYN/2nd CHRON COPTIC  SUB-REGION ___
SUBJECT     ARCH.1     DATE          6C
ARTIST      ANON
TITLE 1     Portion of Frieze
TITLE 2     —
TITLE 3     —
TITLE 4     —
MEDIA:SIZE  Stone
LOCATION/ 1 Monastery of S. Jeremiah
MUSEUM    2 Cairo: Coptic Mus
ADD. INFO.  —
```

```
SC      ANON
EX/BYZ  Monastery of S.Jeremiah
COPTIC  Portion of Frieze
ARCH.1                    6C

Stone
Cairo: Coptic Mus
                       85.01805
```

WESTERN MISCELLANEOUS ARTS, Stained Glass:

```
ACCESSION # 85.05321  PG ___  PL ___  DECADE 11.0
MEDIA       Mgl        WEST PER/STYL MED     REGION ___
COUNTRY     FR         DYN/2nd CHRON —       SUB-REGION ___
SUBJECT     ARCH       DATE          12C
ARTIST      ANON
TITLE 1     Rose Window
TITLE 2     —
TITLE 3     —
TITLE 4     —
MEDIA:SIZE  Stained glass
LOCATION/ 1 Paris: S. Chapelle
MUSEUM    2 —
ADD. INFO.  —
```

```
Mgl   ANON
MED   Paris: S. Chapelle
FR    Rose Window
ARCH                      12C

Stained glass
                       85.05321
```

WESTERN ILLUMINATED MANUSCRIPTS:

```
ACCESSION # 85.03411  PG ___  PL ___  DECADE 08.0
MEDIA       MSS        WEST PER/STYL E.MED   REGION ___
COUNTRY     ___        DYN/2nd CHRON H-S     SUB-REGION ___
SUBJECT     GOSPEL     DATE
ARTIST      ANON
TITLE 1     BOOK OF KELLS
TITLE 2     f.21r: Breves causae of
TITLE 3     Luke, cover-
TITLE 4     ing Chapter XVIII,33-IX,60
MEDIA:SIZE  —
LOCATION/ 1 Dublin: Trinity College
MUSEUM    2 A.I.6, no 58
ADD. INFO.  —
```

```
MSS     BOOK OF KELLS
E.MED   Dublin: Trinity Colle
H-S     A.I.6, no 58
GOSPEL  f.21r: Breves causae
        of Luke, cover-   8-9C
        ing chapter XVIII,33-IX,5C

ANON                   85.03411
```

ISLAMIC ART:

```
ACCESSION # 85.02430  PG ___  PL ___  DECADE 11.0
MEDIA       Mmt        WEST PER/STYL —       REGION ___
COUNTRY     I/PER      DYN/2nd CHRON SELJUK  SUB-REGION ___
SUBJECT     LAMP       DATE          12C
ARTIST      ANON
TITLE 1     Incense Burner
TITLE 2     —
TITLE 3     —
TITLE 4     —
MEDIA:SIZE  Pierced bronze, H:20 cm
LOCATION/ 1 Berlin: Staatl Mus
MUSEUM    2 —
ADD. INFO.  —
```

```
I/PER   ANON
SELJUK  Incense Burner
Mmt
LAMP                      12C

Pierced bronze, H:20 cm
Berlin: Staatl Mus
                       85.02430
```

ORIENTAL:

```
ACCESSION # 85.01705  PG ___  PL ___  DECADE 09.0
MEDIA       SC         WEST PER/STYL —       REGION ___
COUNTRY     O/IND      DYN/2nd CHRON HIN.9   SUB-REGION ___
SUBJECT     FIG.62     DATE          10-11C
ARTIST      ANON
TITLE 1     Nataraja, from Tamil-
TITLE 2     nadu (Shiva as Lord of
TITLE 3     the Dance)
TITLE 4     —
MEDIA:SIZE  Bronze: 98 x 83 x 27 cm
LOCATION/ 1 New Delhi: Nat Mus
MUSEUM    2 —
ADD. INFO.  —
```

```
O/IND   ANON
SC      Nataraia, from Tamil-
HIN.9   nadu (Shiva as Lord
FIG.62  of the Dance)  10-11C

Bronze: 98 x 83 x 27 cm
New Delhi: Nat Mus
                       85.01705
```

Appendix F—Sample Standard Record Formats / 149

AMERICAS, General:

```
ACCESSION # 85.04331 PG___ PL___ DECADE -.
MEDIA      Mce       WEST PER/STYL -    REGION     AM/S
COUNTRY    ANDES     DYN/2nd CHRON M.HOR  SUB-REGION -
SUBJECT    HUARI     DATE  nd
ARTIST     Keros, from Supe Valley
TITLE 1    -
TITLE 2    -
TITLE 3    -
TITLE 4    -
MEDIA:SIZE H: 15.5 to 17.8 cm
LOCATION/ 1 Berkeley, CA: Lowie Mus of Anthr
MUSEUM   2 -
ADD. INFO. -
```

AM/S   HUARI
ANDES   Keros, from Supe
M.HOR   Valley
Mce   nd

H:15.5 to 17.8 cm
Berkeley,CA:Lowie Mus of
Anthr   85.04331

With Sub-region (North American Indian only):

```
ACCESSION # 85.02930 PG___ PL___ DECADE -.
MEDIA      COST      WEST PER/STYL -    REGION     AM/N
COUNTRY              DYN/2nd CHRON HIST  SUB-REGION PLAINS
SUBJECT              DATE  nd
ARTIST     CROW
TITLE 1    Ritual Medicine Hoop
TITLE 2    -
TITLE 3    -
TITLE 4    -
MEDIA:SIZE n/a
LOCATION/ 1 New York, NY: Mus Amer Indian
MUSEUM   2 -
ADD. INFO. -
```

AM/N   CROW
PLAINS Ritual Medicine Hoop
HIST
COST   nd

N/G
New York,NY:Mus Amer Indian
                85.02930

Architecture

```
ACCESSION # 85.02340 PG___ PL___ DECADE -.
MEDIA      A         WEST PER/STYL -    REGION     AM/M
COUNTRY              DYN/2nd CHRON CL    SUB-REGION -
SUBJECT    RELG,4    DATE  nd
ARTIST     MAYAN
TITLE 1    Eagle-Jaguar Platform
TITLE 2    Ballcourt + Tzompantli
TITLE 3    (skull rack)
TITLE 4    -
MEDIA:SIZE -
LOCATION/ 1 CHICHEN ITZA
MUSEUM   2 -
ADD. INFO. -
```

AM/M   MAYAN
        CHICHEN ITZA
CL   Eagle-Jaguar Platform
A   Ballcourt & Tzompantl
        (skull rack)   nd

                85.02340

AFRICA, OCEANIA:

```
ACCESSION # 85.04560 PG___ PL___ DECADE -.
MEDIA      SC        WEST PER/STYL -    REGION     OC
COUNTRY    MELAN     DYN/2nd CHRON HIST  SUB-REGION -
SUBJECT    RE        DATE  nd
ARTIST     NEW HEBRIDES (RAGA)
TITLE 1    Rain charm
TITLE 2    -
TITLE 3    -
TITLE 4    -
MEDIA:SIZE Stone, H:18 cm
LOCATION/ 1 Paris: Mus de l'Homme
MUSEUM   2 -
ADD. INFO. -
```

OC   NEW HEBRIDES (RAGA)
MELAN   Rain Charm
HIST
SC   nd

Stone,H:18 cm
Paris:Mus de l'Homme
                85.04560

Bibliography

GENERAL

Bakewell, Elizabeth, et al. *Object Image Inquiry*. Santa Monica, CA: Getty Art History Program, 1988.

Bunting, Christine. *Reference Tools for Fine Arts Visual Resources Collections*. Occasional Papers, no. 4. Tucson, AZ: Art Libraries Society of North America, 1984.

Cashman, Norine, ed. *Slide Buyers' Guide*, 5th ed. Littleton, CO: Libraries Unlimited, 1985.

Cook, Michael. *Archives Administration*. Folkestone, England: Dawson, 1977.

Gracy, David. *Archives and Manuscripts: Arrangement and Description*. Chicago: Society of American Archivists, 1977.

Irvine, Betty Jo. *Slide Libraries*, 2d ed. Littleton, CO: Libraries Unlimited, 1979.

Kirkpatrick, Nancy. "Major Issues of the Past Ten Years in Visual Resources Curatorship." *Art Libraries Journal* 7, no. 4 (Winter 1982): 30+.

Ritzenthaler, M. L., G. J. Munoff, and M. W. Long. *Archives and Manuscripts: Administration of Photograph Collections*. Chicago: Society of American Archivists, 1984.

Roberts, Helene. "Art History and Visual Documentation: The Interplay of Two Evolutions." *International Bulletin for Photographic Documentation of the Visual Arts* 10, no. 4 (1983). Supplement.

Sunderland, John. "Image Collections: Librarians, Users, and Their Needs." *Art Libraries Journal* 7, no. 2 (Summer 1982): 41-49.

FACILITIES PLANNING

Cohen, Aaron, and Elaine Cohen. *Designing and Space Planning for Libraries: A Behavioral Guide*. New York and London: Bowker, 1979.

Eastman Kodak. *Preservation of Photographs*. Rochester, NY: Eastman Kodak Company, 1979.

Holt, Raymond M. *Wisconsin Library Building Project Handbook*. Bulletin #8268. Madison, WI: Bureau of Cooperative and Library Services, Division for Library Services, Wisconsin Department of Public Instruction, 1961.

Lodewycks, K. A. *Essentials of Library Planning*. Melbourne, Australia: University of Melbourne Library, 1961.

Lushington, Nolan, and Willis N. Mills, Jr. *Libraries Designed for Users: A Planning Handbook*. Hamden, CT: Library Professional Publications, 1980.

Metcalf, Keyes D. *Planning Academic and Research Library Buildings*. New York: McGraw-Hill, 1965.

Munther, Richard, and John D. Wheeler. *Simplified Systematic Layout Planning*. Kansas City, MO: Management and Industrial Research Publications, 1977.

Nolan, Margaret P. "The Metropolitan Museum of Art Slide Library." In *Planning the Special Library*, edited by Ellis Mount, 101-3. New York: Special Libraries Association, 1972.

Vance, David. "Planning Ahead: The Registrar's Role in a Building Program." *Museum News* 58, no. 4 (March/April 1980): 60+.

BUDGETING

Hillman, Howard, and Marjorie Chamberlain. *The Art of Winning Corporate Grants*. New York: Vanguard, 1980.

Lefferts, Robert. *How to Prepare Charts and Graphs for Effective Reports*. New York: Harper, 1982.

Ramsey, Inez L., and Jackson E. Ramsey. *Library Planning and Budgeting*. New York: Watts, 1986.

Spiro, Herbert T. *Finance for the Nonfinancial Manager*, 2d ed. New York: Wiley, 1982.

Sweeney, H. W., and Robert Rachlin. *Handbook of Budgeting: Systems and Control for Financial Management*. New York: Ronald, 1981.

Trumpeter, Margo C., and Richard S. Rounds. *Basic Budgeting Practices for Libraries*. Chicago: American Library Association, 1985.

STAFFING

Art Libraries Society of North America. *Standards for Art Libraries and Fine Arts Slide Collections*. Occasional Papers, no. 2. Tucson, AZ: ARLIS/NA, 1983.

Atkinson, Hugh C. "The Importance of Good Supervision in Libraries." In *Supervising Employees in Libraries*, edited by Rolland Stevens. Allerton Park Institute, no. 24. Urbana-Champaign, IL: University of Illinois Graduate School of Library Science, 1979.

Chapman, Edward, Paul L. St. Pierre, and John Lubans. *Library Systems Analysis Guidelines*. New York: Wiley-Intersciences, 1970.

Creth, Sheila. "Conducting an Effective Employment Interview." *Journal of Academic Librarianship* 4, no. 5 (November 1978): 357-58.

Creth, Sheila, and Frederick Duda. *Personnel Administration in Libraries.* New York: Neal-Schuman Publishers, Inc., 1981.

De-Cotiis, Thomas A., and Richard A. Morano. "Applying Job Analysis to Training." *Training and Development Journal* 31, no. 7 (1977): 20-24.

Downs, Robert B., and Robert F. Dezell. "Professional Duties in University Libraries." *College and Research Libraries* 26 (1965): 30-39.

Drake, John D. *Interviewing for Managers.* New York: AMACO, 1982.

Durey, Peter. *Staff Management in University and College Libraries.* Oxford: Pergamon Press, 1976.

Ferguson, Anthony W., and John R. Taylor. "'What *Are* You Doing?' An Analysis of Public Service Librarians at a Medium-Sized Research Library." *Journal of Academic Librarianship* 4, no. 5 (November 1978): 24-29.

Fry, Eileen, and Nancy S. Schuller. "Visual Resources Job Information." *Mid-America College Art Association Newsletter* 4, no. 1 (1977): 4.

Harlow, Neal. "Misused Librarians." *Ontario Library Review* 49 (November 1965): 170-72.

Hoort, Rebecca J. "Upgrading Professional Status through Fair Pay: Equal Pay for Equal Worth Issue." *Visual Resources* 4, no. 2 (1987): 191-200.

Imundo, Louis V. *The Effective Supervisor's Handbook.* New York: AMACO, 1980.

———. *Employee Discipline: How to Do It Right.* Belmont, CA: Wadsworth Publishers, 1985.

Johnson, Robert G. *The Appraisal Interview Guide.* New York: AMACO, 1979.

Jones, Noragh, and Peter Jordan. *Staff Management in Library and Information Work.* Hampshire, England: Grove Books, 1982.

Library Association of London, Research and Development Committee. *Professional and Non-professional Duties in Libraries.* London: The Library Association, 1974.

Pell, Arthur R. *Recruiting, Training and Motivating Volunteer Workers.* New York: Pilot Books, 1972.

Rothenberg, L. "A Job-Task Index for Evaluating Professional Staff Utilized in Libraries." *Library Quarterly* 41 (October 1971): 320-28.

Schaffer, Dale Eugene. *A Guide to Writing Library Job Descriptions.* Salem, OH: Schaffer, 1981.

United States. Equal Employment Opportunity Commission. *Affirmative Action and Equal Employment: A Guidebook for Employers.* Washington, DC: EEOC, 1974.

REPORTS AND STATISTICS

American Library Association. *A Handbook of Concepts, Definitions, and Terminology.* Chicago: ALA, 1966.

American National Standards Institute. *American National Standards for Library Statistics.* Washington, DC: ANSI, 1968 (reaffirmed 1978).

Beasley, Kenneth E. *A Statistical Reporting System for Local Public Librarians*. Monograph no. 3. Philadelphia, PA: Pennsylvania State Library, 1964.

Carpenter, Ray L., and Ellen Story Vasu. *Statistical Methods for Librarians*. Chicago: American Library Association, 1978.

Gross, Dean C. "A More Meaningful Statistical Report." *Wilson Library Bulletin* 32 (December 1957): 297.

Hoadley, Irene, and Helen Clarke, eds. *Quantitative Methods in Librarianship: Standards, Research Management*. Westport, CT: Greenwood Press, 1972.

POLICIES AND PROCEDURES MANUALS

Eastman Kodak. *Conservation of Photographs*. Publication no. F-40. Rochester, NY: Eastman Kodak Co., 1985.

_____. *Mounting Slides in Glass*. Publication no. AE-36. Rochester, NY: Eastman Kodak Co., 1971.

_____. *Preservation of Photographs*. Publication no. F-30. Rochester, NY: Eastman Kodak Co., 1979.

Malaro, Marle C. "Collections Management Policies." *Museum News* 58, no. 2 (November/December 1979): 57-61.

Scott, Gillian, ed. *Guide to Equipment for Slide Maintenance and Viewing*. Albuquerque, NM: Mid-America College Art Association, 1978.

Sundt, Christine L. "Mounting Slide Film between Glass—For Preservation or Destruction?" *Visual Resources* 2, nos. 1-3 (1981-1982): 35-62.

Tull, A. G. "Film Transparencies between Glass." *British Journal of Photography* 125 (1978): 322-23, 349-51, 353.

_____. "Hazards of Mounting Slides." *Photographic Journal* 114 (1974): 184-85, 232-35.

Wykle, Helen H. "Collection Development Policies for Academic Visual Resources Collections." *Art Documentation* 7, no. 1 (Spring 1988): 22-25.

CIRCULATION AND CONTROL

Bahr, Alice Harrison. *Automated Circulation Systems, 1979-80*. White Plains, NY: Knowledge Industries Publications, Inc., 1979.

Block, Carol. "Automated Circulation Systems Using PCs and Codes." Paper presented at the annual meeting of the Visual Resources Association, Boston, February 1987.

George Fry and Associates, Inc. *Study of Circulation Control Systems*. Chicago: LTP/American Library Association, 1961.

Gore, Daniel. "Let Them Eat Cake While Reading Catalog Cards, An Essay on the Availability Problem." *Library Journal* 100 (January 1975): 93-98.

Hubbard, William J. *Stack Management: A Practical Guide to Shelving and Maintaining Library Collections.* Chicago: American Library Association, 1981.

Lewis, Elizabeth M. "Control without Cards." *ARLIS/NA Newsletter* 1, nos. 3/4 (Summer 1973): 17.

Morse, Yvonne. "CASTLE Automation System at the Ringling School of Art," *Art Documentation* 15, no. 2 (1988): 26-27.

Murphy, Marcy, and Claude J. Johns, Jr. *Handbook of Library Regulations.* New York and Basel: Marcel Dekker, Inc., 1977.

Pope, Nolan F. *Microcomputers for Library Circulation Control.* Indianapolis, IN: Indiana Co-operative Library Services Authority, 1984.

Randall, G. E. "Inventory of a Special Library Collection." *Special Libraries* 63 (March 1972): 130-34.

Segal, Joseph P. *Evaluation and Weeding Collections in Small and Medium-Sized Public Libraries, The CREW Method.* Chicago: American Library Association, 1980.

Thomason, Nevada Wallis. *Circulation Systems for School Library Media Centers.* Littleton, CO: Libraries Unlimited, 1985.

Walker, Leslie. "Slide Filing and Control." *College Art Journal* 16 (1957): 325-29.

MICROCOMPUTERS

General

Anderson, Eric. "Seminar on Microcomputers." *International Bulletin for Photographic Documentation for the Visual Arts* 10, no. 2 (June 1983): 12.

Barnett, Patricia, and Amey E. Lucker, eds. *Procedural Guide to Automating an Art Library.* Occasional Papers, no. 7. Tucson, AZ: Art Libraries Society of North America, 1987.

Beetham, Donald W. "Flexible Formatting: The Rutgers Automation Project." *International Bulletin for Photographic Documentation of the Visual Arts* 49, no. 1 (1985 Supplement): 7-11.

Boss, Richard. *The Library Manager's Guide to Automation*, 2d ed. White Plains, NY: Knowledge Industries Publications, Inc., 1984.

———. "Retrospective Conversion: Investing in the Future." *Wilson Library Bulletin* (November 1984): 173-78.

Chenhall, Robert. *Museum Cataloging for a Computer Age.* Nashville, TN: American Association for State and Local History, 1975.

Chenhall, Robert, and David Vance. *Museum Collections and Today's Computers.* New York: Greenwood Press, 1988.

Collins, Jane D., "Planning for Retrospective Conversion." *Art Documentation* 1, nos. 3-4 (Summer 1982): 92-94.

156 / BIBLIOGRAPHY

Computers and Cultural Materials Conference. Conference held at the North Carolina Museum of History, Raleigh, North Carolina Museum of History, 1982.

Culbertson, Martine, "Cataloging Slides Bit by Bit: Managing a Slide Collection with dBase II." *International Bulletin for Photographic Documentation of the Visual Arts* 11, no. 1 (Spring 1984 Supplement): 19-22.

Culver, Joanne P. "Computers and the Visual Resources Environment." *International Bulletin for Photographic Documentation of the Visual Arts* 11, no. 1 (Spring 1984 Supplement): 16-17.

First International Conference of Automatic Processing of Art History Data and Documents. *Conference Transactions* 1 (4-7 September 1978).

Flott, Nancy. "Microcomputers and the Visual Resource Collection." *International Bulletin for Photographic Documentation of the Visual Arts* 11, no. 1 (Spring 1984): 11-13.

Gibbs, Andrea, and Pat Stevens. "MARC and the Computerization of the National Gallery of Art Photographic Archives." *Visual Resources* 3 (1985): 185-208.

Giral, Angela. "Architectural Drawings: An Automated Indexing and Retrieval." *Art Documentation* (Spring 1986): 11-13.

Hayes, Robert M., and Joseph Becker. *Handbook of Data Processing for Libraries*, 2d ed. New York: John Wiley and Sons, 1984.

International Association of Art Critics. *Automation Takes Command: Art History in the Age of Computers* (A special issue of AICARC Bulletin). Zurich: AICARC, 1984.

Kesner, Richard M. *Automation for Archivists and Records Managers: Planning and Implementing Strategies*. Chicago: American Library Association, 1984.

Maddox, Brent F. "Automating the Getty Photo Archive." *Art Documentation* 4, no. 4 (Winter 1986): 170-71.

Markey, Karen. "Visual Arts Resources and Computers." *Annual Review of Information Science and Technology* 19 (1984): 271-309.

Muller, Karen, ed. *Authority Control Symposium*. Occasional Papers, no. 6. Tucson, AZ: Art Libraries Society of North America, 1987.

Richardson, Zelda, and Sheila Hannah. *Introduction to Visual Resources Library Automation*. Albuquerque, NM: Mid-America College Art Association, 1980.

Roberts, Helene. "The Image Library." *Art Libraries Journal* 3 (Winter 1978): 25+.

Rorvig, Mark E. *Microcomputers and Libraries: A Guide to Technology, Products, and Applications*. White Plains, NY: Knowledge Industries Publications, Inc., 1982.

Saal, Harry J. "Local Area Networks: Possibilities for Personal Computers." *Byte* 6, no. 10 (October 1981): 92-112.

Scuola Normale Superiore. *First International Conference on Automatic Processing of Art Historical Data and Documents, September 4-7, 1978*. Pisa: Scuola Normale Superiore, 1978.

_____. *Second International Conference on Automatic Processing of Art Historical Data and Documents, September 24-27, 1984*. Pisa: Scuola Normale Superiore, 1984.

Seloff, Gary. "Directory of Microcomputer Users in Visual Resource Collections." *International Bulletin for Photographic Documentation of the Visual Arts* 13, no. 2 (Fall 1986): 10-11.

―――. "LABLPRINT." *International Bulletin for Photographic Documentation of the Visual Arts* 11, no. 4 (Winter 1984): 16.

―――. "Tailoring Microcomputer Software for the VR Collection." *International Bulletin for Photographic Documentation of the Visual Arts* 12, no. 1 (1985 Supplement): 12-14.

Simpson, George A. *Microcomputers in Library Automation*. McLean, VA: The Mitre Corp., 1978.

Sunderland, John, and Catherine Gordon. "The Witt Computer Index." Paper read at the International Congress for Historians of Art, Washington, D.C., 1986.

Sundt, Christine. "P-C File III―A Program for Slide Labels ... and More." *International Bulletin for Photographic Documentation of the Visual Arts* 11, no. 3 (Fall 1984): 7-8.

―――. "Public Domain and User-Supported Software for the IBM-PC." *International Bulletin for Photographic Documentation of the Visual Arts* 11, no. 2 (Summer 1984): 7.

Walton, Robert. *Microcomputers and the Library: A Planning Guide for Managers*. Austin, TX: Texas State Library, Department of Library Development, 1982.

Warden, William H., and Bette M. Warden. "Microcomputers for Libraries: Features, Descriptions, Evaluations." *Library Hi Tech* 1, no. 1 (Summer 1983): 25-39.

Welsh, Peter H., and Steven A. LeBlanc. "Computer Literacy and Collection Management." *Museum News* 65, no. 5 (June 1957): 42-51.

Woods, Lawrence A., and Nolan F. Pope. *The Librarian's Guide to Microcomputer Technology and Applications*. White Plains, NY: Knowledge Industries Publications, Inc., 1983.

Authorities and Subject Access

American National Standards Institute. *Guidelines for Thesaurus Structure, Construction, and Use: Approved June 30, 1980*. New York: ANSI, 1980. ANSI no. Z39.19-1980.

Avram, H. C. *MARC, Its History and Implications*. Washington, DC: Library of Congress, 1975.

Barnett, Patricia J. "The Art and Architecture Thesaurus as a Faceted MARC Format." *Visual Resources* 4, no. 3 (Autumn 1987): 247-59.

Burger, Robert H. *Authority Work: The Creation, Use, Maintenance and Evaluation of Authority Records and Files*. Littleton, CO: Libraries Unlimited, 1985.

Chenhall, Robert. *Nomenclature for Museum Cataloging*. Nashville, TN: American Association for State and Local History, 1978.

Clark, Doris Hargett. "Authority Control: Issues and Answers." *Technical Series Quarterly* 3, nos. 1-2 (1984-1985): 127-40.

Delroy, Stephen H. "Data Standards." *SPECTRA* 14, no. 3 (Fall 1987): 3-6.

BIBLIOGRAPHY

De SaRego, Stella, and Richard Spector. "IMAGES." *International Bulletin for Photographic Documentation of the Visual Arts* 15, no. 1 (Spring 1988): 20-30.

Eskind, Andres H., and Deborah Bassel. "IMP/GEH Conventions for Cataloging Photographs." *Image* 21, no. 4 (December 1978): entire issue.

Fawcett, Trevor. "Control of Text and Images, Tradition and Innovation." *Art Libraries Journal* 7, no. 2 (Summer 1982): 7-16.

_____. "Subject Indexing in the Visual Arts." *Art Libraries Journal* 4, no. 1 (Spring 1979): 5-17.

Fink, Eleanor, and Christine Hennessy. "A National Database for Information on Sculpture in Public and Private Collections throughout the US and Abroad." *SPECTRA* 15, no. 1 (1988): 11-13.

Foskett, A. C. *The Subject Approach to Information*, 3d ed. London: Clive Bingley; Hamden, CT: Linnet Books, 1977.

Hennessey, Christine. "The Status of Name Authority Control in the Cataloging of Original Art Objects." *Art Documentation* 5, no. 1 (Spring 1986): 3-10.

Lucker, Amy, "The Right Words: Controlled Vocabulary and Standards." *Art Documentation* 7, no. 1 (1988): 19-20.

Maddox, Brett. "To VIM with VIGOR." *International Bulletin for Photographic Documentation of the Visual Arts* 15, no. 3 (Fall 1988): 18-20.

Markey, Karen. *Subject Access to Visual Resource Collections*. Westport, CT: Greenwood Press, 1986.

McCaffrey, Rosanne. "FACETS: An Innovative Approach to Subject Access at the Historic New Orleans Collection." *SPECTRA* 15, no. 1 (1988): 1-3.

Olhgren, Thomas. "Subject Indexing of Visual Resources: A Survey." *Visual Resources* 1, no. 1 (Spring 1980): 7-73.

Parker-Betz, Elizabeth, ed. *Graphic Materials: Rules for Describing Original Items and Historical Collections*. Washington, DC: Library of Congress, 1982.

_____. *LC Thesaurus for Graphic Materials, Topical Terms for Subject Access*. Washington, DC: Library of Congress, 1987.

_____. *Subject Headings Used in the Library of Congress Prints and Photographs Division*. Washington, DC: Library of Congress, 1982.

Parker-Betz, Elizabeth, and Helena Zinkhan. *Descriptive Terms for Graphic Materials: Genre and Physical Characteristic Headings*. Washington, DC: Library of Congress, 1986.

Petersen, Toni. "The AAT: A Model for the Restructuring of LCSH." *Journal of Academic Librarianship* 9, no. 4 (September 1983): 207-10.

_____. "The AAT and Museum Object Cataloging." *SPECTRA* 14, no. 2 (Summer 1987): 3.

_____. "Computer-aided Indexing in the Arts: The Case for a Thesaurus of Terms." *Art Libraries Journal* (Autumn 1983): 6-11.

_____. "The Role of the AAT in Automated Data Retrieval." In *Automatic Processing of Art History Data and Documents*, vol. 1: 317-18. Pisa: Scuola Normale Superiore, 1984.

Roberts, Helene. "The Image Library." *Art Libraries Journal* 2 (Winter 1978): 25+.

Roddy, Kevin. "The Belmont Conference on Subject Access." *Visual Resources* 2, nos. 1-3 (1981-1982): 101-11.

Rogers, Donna, and Jeffrey Hamm. "Compiling an Authority List on a PC." *International Bulletin for Photographic Documentation of the Visual Arts* 14, no. 3 (Fall 1987): 11-13.

Sarasan, Lenore. "Visual Content Access: An Approach to the Automated Retrieval of Visual Information." In *Automatic Processing of Art History Data and Documents*, 389-406. Pisa: Scuola Normale Superiore, 1984.

Schuller, Nancy S. *Standard Abbreviations for Image Descriptions Used in Visual Resources Collections.* Special Bulletin, no. 2. Ann Arbor, MI: Visual Resources Association, 1988.

Sobinski-Smith, Mary Jane. "The Yale Center for British Art: The Photograph Archive and Iconographic Access." *Visual Resources* 1, nos. 2-3 (1980): 173-87.

Stam, Deidre C. "Factors Affecting Authority Work in Art Historical Information Systems: A Report of Findings from a Study Undertaken for the Comité International d'Histoire de l'Art (CIHA), Project: Thesaurus Artis Universalis (TAU)." *Visual Resources* 4 (1987): 25-49.

Interactive Videodisk, Optical Disk Use

Boss, Richard W., and Judy McQueen. *Videodisc and Optical Digital Disk Technologies and Their Applications in Libraries.* Chicago: American Library Association, 1985.

Bui, Dominic. "The Videodisk: Technology, Applications and Some Implications for Archives." *American Archivist* (Fall 1984): 418-29.

Cash, Joan. "Spinning toward the Future: The Museum on Laser Videodisk." *Museum News* 63 (August 1985): 19-43.

Caswell, James O. "Video Disc Project at the University of British Columbia, Vancouver." Factsheet and news release, 1984.

Davisson, Darrell. "A Look at Some Forthcoming Resources in Optical Disc Storage." *Visual Resources* 3, no. 4 (Winter 1987): 287-315.

Daynes, Rod. "Interactive Videodisc Design and Production." *Byte* 7 (June 1982): 48-55.

_____. "The Videodisc Interfacing Primer." *Byte* 7 (June 1982): 56-59.

DePopolo, Margaret. "Video Disk: Study Aid/Teaching Tool." Paper presented at the Symposium, Architecture Libraries of the Future, sponsored by the School of Architecture, University of Michigan, Ann Arbor, Michigan, January 1987. (Publication forthcoming.)

Femenias, Blenda, and Patricia Mansfield. "Museum Management and Collection Access, Using ARTSearch, and Interactive Videodisc-computer Systems." *Visual Resources* 3 (1985): 209-26.

Gale, John. "Use of Optical Disks for Information Storage and Retrieval." *Information Technology and Libraries* 3 (December 1984): 379-82.

Hastings, Angela. "Interactive Videodisc Project at University College, Dublin." *Art Libraries Journal* 3, no. 4 (1986).

Ison, Mary. "Preserving Architectural Drawings: The Optical Disk Experience." Paper presented at the Symposium Architecture Libraries of the Future, Sponsored by the School of Architecture, University of Michigan, Ann Arbor, Michigan, January 1987. (Publication forthcoming.)

Kamisher, Lisa M. "The Images System: Videodisc and Database Integration for Architecture." *Optical Information Systems* 6, no. 6 (December 1986): 501-3.

McMillan, Tom. "Teaching Tomorrow's Architects." *Computer Graphics World* 9 (August 1986): 40-44.

Michel, Steve. "Shedding Light on Optical Storage." *MacWEEK* (27 October 1987): 1+.

Okun, Henry. "Picassofile, or Using a Computer to Look at Picasso." *Picturescope* 31, no. 4 (1985): 114-18.

Parker-Betz, Elizabeth. "The Library of Congress Non-Print Optical Disc Pilot Program." *Information Technology and Libraries* 4 (December 1985): 289-99.

Purcell, Patrick, and Henry Okun. "Information Technology and Visual Images: Two Case Studies." *Art Libraries Journal* 7 (Autumn 1983): 43-48.

Sorkow, Janice. "Videodiscs and Art Documentation." *Art Libraries Journal* (Autumn 1983): 27-33.

Sustik, Joan M., "Art History Interactive Videodisc Project at the University of Iowa." *Videodisc/Teletext* 1, no. 2 (Spring 1981): 78-85.

_____. *An Art History Interactive Videodisc Project at the University of Iowa, A Report*. Iowa City, IA: Weeg Computing Center, University of Iowa, 1981.

Urbach, Peter. "The Video Patsearch System: An Interview with Peter Urbach." *Videodisc/Videotex* 2, no. 1 (Winter 1982): 30-37.

Vance, David. "Optical Disk Technology." *SPECTRA* 12, no. 4 (Winter 1985): 1-2.

Index

Abbreviations standards, 86
Abodia slide racks, 7
Absence transaction system. *See* Transaction system
Academic fine arts slide collections, 71
Access, 1, 71, 72
   and security, 19, 71
   chart(s), 16
   visual and textual, 87
Accessibility plan, 16
Accession
   cards, 63
   logs, 63
   forms, 131
   numbers, 58, 72, 73, 74, 75, 82
   records, 58, 63
Accessioning procedures, 63, 64-65
Accounting system. *See* Encumbering accounting system
Accoustical requirements, 10
Accrual system. *See* Encumbering accounting system
Acoustics, 3, 19
Acquisitions
   and collection development, 1, 51, 52, 54, 57, 80, 83, 85
   equipment, 54
   routine procedures, 64-65
   sources, 54
   statistics, 59
   subject areas, 57
   teaching areas, 61
Activities
   analysis, 5, 83
   annual, 66-67
   format, 5
   monthly chart, 86-87
   nonquantitative, 51
   peaks and valleys, 49
   quantitative, 51

Activity areas, graphic analysis, 15
   units, 56, 57
Administrative
   and curatorial job descriptions, 97-103
   authorities and responsibilities, 1
   duties, 37
   forms, 119-32
   functions, 6, 66-67, 83
   responsibility, 35
Air-conditioning, 6
Aisle passages, 7
Allen, Helen L., Textile Collection, University of Wisconsin, 87
American National Standards Institute (ANSI), 50
Analysis
   activities, 5
   of staff and users, 4
Annual
   activities, 49, 61
   budget cycles, 33
   elements of, 51
   outlines for, 51
   reports, 49, 66-67
Applicant rating chart, 44
Application forms, 68
Appraisals, performance, 2
   staff, 46
Architectural features, 4, 6
Architecture Machine Group, Massachusetts Institute of Technology, 87
Arizona State University, Art Slide Collection, 75
   standard record format of, 147-49
Art and Architecture Thesaurus (AAT), 83, 86
Art Bibliographies Modern, 86
Art Libraries Society of North America (ARLIS), 39, 40, 42, 50, 52, 71, 81
ARTSearch, University of Wisconsin, Helen L. Allen Textile Collection, 87
Assistants, student, 39

161

162 / INDEX

Audiovisual
  circulation forms, 133-41
  equipment, 6, 10, 53, 54, 62
    management, 38, 83
    storage, 14, 16, 17
  services, 38, 51
  supplies, 53
Authorities and responsibilities
  administrative, 1
  curatorial, 2
  data, 86
Authority
  files, 82
  lists, 87
Authorization forms, users', 138
Automated systems, 85
  capabilities of, 82
  circulation systems, 62, 73
  shelflists, 75
Automation procedures, 85

Bar codes, 74, 82
Behavior patterns, 4
Belmont Conference on Subject Access, 87
Borrowers. *See* Users
Brochures, orientation, 10
Bubble diagrams, 16, 17
Budget(s), 1, 26
  allocations, 52
  defenses, 33, 34
  management, 34
  planning cycles, 32, 33
  projections, 31
  proposals, 49, 66-67
  reports, 49
  systems, 26
    four-year line item, 27
    line item, 26, 52
    lump sum, 26
    program, 28
    zero base, 28, 29
Budgeting, 26-34
  and microcomputers, 34
  bibliography, 152

Calculation of spaces, 9
California Polytechnic State University, School of Architecture and Environmental Design, Instructional Resources Center, 94
Call numbers, 75
Camera equipment. *See* Photographic equipment
Capacities (physical), 5
  storage and seating, 6
Capital expenses, 29, 53
  outlays, 29
Capitalization and depreciation, 30, 31
Carrels, 6, 9
Categorical or designated expenses, 31

Catalog production, 80
Central processing units, 83
Change orders, 20
Charge sheet, 72
Charts
  access, 16
  flow, 16
  monthly activities, 66-67
  organizational, 61
  processing slides, 63, 64-65
Charting method, 18
Checklist, time line, 61
Circulation, 1, 5, 50, 51, 54, 61, 62, 71, 73, 80, 82, 83
  and controls, 71-79
  areas, 10, 15, 18
  bibliography, 155
  charge sheets, 72
  counters, 10, 16, 17, 18, 71, 74
    design for, 11
  drop cards, 54, 73
  figures, 54, 57
  files, 10, 17
  forms, 10, 62, 133-41
  management, 38
  manuals, 72
  policies, 62, 71, 72, 74
  procedures, 71, 78
  records, 58, 78
  return bailers, 54
  statistics, 72
Circulation systems
  automated, 56, 62, 73
  objectives, 72
  transaction and absence systems, 72, 73
Classification and cataloging, 63, 77, 80, 83
  manuals, 56
  schemes (system), 61, 62, 75
Clerical (or general) staff, 36, 37, 39, 55
  job descriptions, 111
Closed stack storage, 77
Cold storage, 6
Collecting information, 119
Collections
  access, 37, 62
  aims and objectives, interpretation of, 37
  arrangements, 62
  committees, 66-67
  controls, 9, 74
  counting the, 38
  databases, 74
  descriptions, general, 62
  development and acquisitions, 1, 37, 48, 54, 74, 76, 80
    statement, 62
  evaluations, 76
  goals, 26, 52, 87
  holdings, quality/quantity, 58
  hours, 62
  income, 52
  maintenance and controls, 74

Index / 163

materials, production of, 38
physical arrangements, 74
purposes of, 78
replacements, 74
requirements, statement of, 3
strengths and weaknesses, 52, 56, 75
types, 52, 61, 62
weeding, 74
College Art Association (CAA), 42
College Work Study Program (CWSP), 41, 55, 66-67
Commercial software, 84, 86
Committees, planning, 3
policy, 72
Communications, 47
outlets, 6
staff, 35, 47, 48
Computers, 9
capacity requirements, 84
database development, 56, 59
equipment, 5
hardware, 83
linked with videodisk, 87
programs, development and management of, 38
services, 38
software, 81, 83, 84
spreadsheet programs, 34
system documentations, 86
technicians, job description, 108
terminals, 10, 84, 86
vendors, 84
work stations, space requirements, 12
Conservation and maintenance, 61
procedures, 63
Content standards, 86
Controls, 1, 71
environmental, 4, 6
humidity, 6
intellectual, 80, 82, 83
noise, 4
physical, 80, 82, 83
temperature, 6
Cooling, 4
Copy photography, 13
Copy stand, 6, 62
Copy studio. *See* Darkrooms
Copyright statement, 61, 133
Correspondence, 61
Cost accounting system, 31
Cost groups, 29
Counting the collection, 58
Critique of physical facilities, 24
Cross-references, 74
Curators
assistant, 39
authorities, 2
offices, 13, 16, 17, 18
professional, chief, 39
responsibilities, 2
Curatorial and curatorial assistants, job descriptions, 103-7

Darkrooms, 13, 16
DataEase®, 143
Data
entry, 10, 87, 63, 67
fields, 85
formats, 59
processing, 61
standards, 84, 86
Databases
additions to, 63
collections, 74
developments, 56, 59
fields, 85
functions, documentation of, 63
inventories, 73
management systems, 82, 83
records, 85
updates of, 63
searchable, 81
Deaccessioning and replacing, 62
Definition of requirements, 2
Delegation, 2
Depreciation and capitalization, 30, 31
Designs, physical, 3
Designated expenses, 29, 31
Development
computer database, 56
staff, 2, 48, 52, 55
Diagrams
bubble, 16
equipment inventory, 21
for numbering slide storage files, 24
furniture inventory, 22
Dimensions, area, 6
"Directory of Microcomputer Users," *International Bulletin for Photographic Documentation of the Visual Arts*, 84
Discrimination in interviews, 44
Document cases, 8
Documentation, 1, 86
Donations, 59, 62
Doors, light-tight, 13
Drymount presses, 9
Duplication of materials, 62
Duties
administrative, 37
clerical, 38, 39
professional, 36
technical, 38

Efficiency evaluations, 49
Electrical and communications outlets, 6, 9, 20
Electrical requirements, 4
Electricity, 19
Encumbering accounting system, 31, 32
Encyclopedia of World Art, 86
Environmental controls, 3, 4, 6, 20
Environmentally safe storage, 10

Equal Employment Opportunity Commission (EEOC), 45
Equipment, 4, 20
   acquisitions, 54
   and furniture specifications, 23
   audiovisual, 6, 10
   computer, 6
   inventory diagram, 21
   required, 69
   usage, 1
Establishing priorities, 83
Evaluations
   efficiency, 49
   job, 36
   staff, 35
Expendable supplies, 52
Expenditures, 51, 52, 57
Expenses
   capital, 29
   categorical, 31
   designated, 29, 31
   operating, 29
   types of, 29

Facilities
   bibliography, 151-52
   physical, 57, 58
   planning, 3-25
   program, 4
Facilities, projection, 10
Facilities, use, 1
Fields, data, 85
Filers, training for, 63, 71
Files
   arrangement, 74, 78
   circulation, 6
   (drawer) storage, 7
   legal-sized, 8
   reference, 6
   slide, 6
Filing
   instructions, 63
   procedures, 75
   statistics, 50, 63
   verifications, 76
Final plans, 19, 20
Financial reports, 59
Fines, 62, 78
Fire specifications, 19
Fixed fields, 85
Flat storage systems, 8
Floors
   covering, 4
   loads, 6, 7
   plans, 14, 23, 89-96
Flow charts, 16
   budget planning, 33
Fluorescent lights, 19

Formats
   data entry, 59
   standard record, examples, 143-49
Formats (holdings), 5
Forms, 119-41
   accessions, 131
   applications, staff, 127
   circulation, 62, 133-41
   evaluations, staff, 123
   photographic services, 119-22
   staff schedules, 124, 126
   statistics, collection of, 126, 128-30
Full-time equivalents (FTE), 58
Functions, visual resources collections, 36
Funds, travel, 53
Furniture, 3, 4, 20
Furniture inventory diagrams, 22
Furniture and equipment specifications, 23
Future trends, 87

Getty Center for the History of Art and Humanities, Photograph Archive, 85
Getty Foundation, 83
Glossary of terms, 50, 56, 113-18
Goals
   collection, 26, 87
   setting, 2
   short- and long-range, 52, 56
Grants, 2
Graphic analysis of activity areas, 15
Graphics, 3
Growth projections, 4
Growth restrictions, 59
Guide cards, use of, 63, 76

Hannah, Sheila, and Zelda Richardson, *Guide to Automation in Visual Resources Collections*, 81
Hardware, computer, 83, 84
Harlow, Neal, 36
Heating, 4
Holdings (formats), 5
Housings, projection, 10
Humidity controls, 6
Hydrothermographs, 19

Iconographical retrieval, 87
Identification of images, 62
Image identification data, 82
Implementing computer activities, 84
Income, 51, 52, 57
Index production, 80, 82, 83, 87
Indexed fields, 85
Indexing and retrieving, 81, 87
Information and reference areas, 10
In-house computer system, 85, 86

Instructions
  filing, 63
  slide and photograph binding and mounting, 63
  users, 10
Intellectual controls, 80, 81, 82, 83
Interfiled shelflists, 75
Interior architectural features, 18
International Bulletin for Photographic Documentation of the Visual Arts, 77, 81, 84, 86
Interviews
  budget, 33
  questions for, 43
Interviewing, 41
  discrimination in, 44
  staff, 35
  volunteers, 47
Inventories
  collection, 75
  control system, 71, 73
  database, 73
  furniture and equipment, 20-22, 66-67
  lists, 74, 82
  spaces, 5

Job(s)
  analyses, 40
  classification, 40
    specialist, 40
  descriptions, 35, 40-41, 61, 97-111
    formats, 30, 41
    reviews, 40
    revisions, 41
  evaluations, 36
  titles, 40, 48

Keyword searching, 85

Labels
  and index production, 83
  production, 82, 85
  typing, 10
Leslie, Philip, 87
Letters, samples, to candidates, 45
Library Bureau slide files, 7
Library of Congress
  Prints and Photographs Division, 87
  Subject Headings for Prints and Photographs, 83
  Terms for Graphic Materials, 86
Lighting, 3, 4, 19, 20
  requirements, 6
Light-tight doors, revolving, 13
  diagram of, 14
Lights, 19
Line item budgets, 26, 52
  four year, 27
"Live loads," 7
Load limits, floors, 6

Loan periods, 62, 72
Lost or damaged materials, 72, 78
Lump sum budgets, 26
Luxor slide files, 7

Mainframe
  computers, 80, 81
  projects, 81
Maintenance
  and control of collection, 74
  preventative, 53
Management
  responsibilities, 2
  storage file, 74
Mandatory fields, 85
Manuals
  classification and cataloging, 56
  policies and procedures, 56
  procedures and services, 82, 84, 85
MARC
  format, 85
  VIM format, 85
Markey, Karen, "Visual Arts Resources and Computers," 81
Massachusetts Institute of Technology, School of Architecture, Architecture Machine Group, 87
Meetings
  professional, 2
  staff, 47
Methodology and terminology, 49
Microcomputer applications, 80-88
  bibliography, 155-60
Microcomputers
  budgeting, 34
  circulation systems with, 73
  selection, 83
Mid-America College Art Association (MACAA), 35
Monitoring collection files, 78
Monthly reports, 49
Mounting boards, 9
Moving day plans, 4
Multi-purpose work areas, 10
Multiplex slide storage racks, 7
Munther Charting Method, 18
Munther, Richard, 18
Museum fine arts slide collections, 71

National Gallery of Art, Photograph Archives, 85
National Organization for Women (NOW), 45
Needs assessments, 82
Networking, 81
Neumade slide files, 6, 7
Newsletters, 48
Noise controls, 4, 19
Nonquantative activities, 51, 55
Notification of candidates, 45
Numeric rating for candidate qualifications, 44

Objectives and purposes, statements of, 1, 4
Offices, curators', 13
Operating expenses, 29
Optical video disk players, 87
Orientations
 brochures, 10
 schedules, 68
 slide and tape, 10
 users, 10, 66-67, 71, 72, 74
Outlets, electrical and communications, 6, 9
Outline for policies and procedures manuals, 61
Overdues, 62, 72, 78, 82
Overdue notices, 68, 74

Part-time staff, encumbrance systems, 32
Patterns
 staffing, 35
 traffic, 3
Performances
 appraisals, 2
 evaluations, sample, 46
 responsibilities, 46
 standards, 35, 46
Personal budget interviews, 33
Personnel, 57
 management, 37
 wages and salaries, 53
Photocopying of label information, 73
Photographers
 job descriptions for, 109, 110
 staff, 39, 52
Photographic
 darkroom, 6
 equipment, 54, 62
 services, 38, 51, 59, 62, 83
  forms for, 83, 119-22
Photographs
 archives, 16
 charge sheets, 133
 collection, storage for, 8, 15
 collection, technical services, 9
 collection user areas, 15
 mounting and sleeving methods, 50, 62
Physical
 arrangement of collections, 74, 77
 controls, 80, 82, 83
 designs, 3
 facilities, statistics, 57, 58
 proximity and accessibility plans, 4, 16
 requirements, 3
PICASSOFILE, Architecture Machine Group, Massachusetts Institute of Technology, 87
Planning, 2
 committees, 3
 program facilities, 4
 worksheets, 4, 82, 83

Plans
 accessibility, 4, 16
 final, 19, 20
 floor, 14, 89-96
 moving day, 4
Plumbing requirements, 19
Policies, circulation, 62
Policies and procedures, 1, 61-70, 71
 bibliography, 154
 collection evaluation and weeding, 76
 formulations, 37
 manuals, 56, 61, 69, 71
Policy committee, 1
Printing, 63, 82
 and duplicating, 53
Private collections, 10
Procedures
 and policies, 1
 sorting and filing, 74
 standardized, 81
 uniform, 81
Processing routines, 61
Professional
 activities, 55
 and curatorial staff, 55
 curator, chief, 39
 development, 37, 53
 duties, 36
 meetings (conferences), 2, 53
 organizations, 53
 positions, 42
 recognitions, 48
 responsibilities, 36
 status, 48
Program budgets, 28
Projection housing and facilities, 10
Projects, special, 52
Proofing, 63
Proposals and reports, 1
Proximity plans, 6
Psychological spaces, 10
Public library fine arts slide collections, 71
Purchases, 52, 56

Qualifications, applicants', 43
 assessing, 44
Quantitative activities, 51, 52, 54, 56

Rack storage, slides, 7
Reading the collection, 75
Recalls, 72
Reclassifications and corrections, 63
Recommended space per worker, 10
Record volume, database, 84
Records and reports, 61, 68
Recruiting tactics, 47
Recruitment, staff, 1, 41

Reference
  files, 6
  information areas, 10
  materials, 53
  questions, 10
Remington Rand files, 7
Remote storage, 77
Renewals, 72
Renovations, 3
Replacements for collections, 74, 76
Reports
  and proposals, 1
  and statistics, 39, 49-60, 82
  annual, 49
  bibliography, 153-54
  financial, 59
  forms, refiled slides, 54
  monthly, 49
  standard formats for, 68
Requirements
  accoustical, 10
  collection, 3
  definitions of, 2
  lighting, 6
  physical, 3
  space, 4
Reserve materials, 10, 72
Responsibilities
  and authorities, 1
  curatorial, 2
  management, 2
Retrieval, iconographical, 87
Review slides and photographs, 62
Reward reviews, staff, 46
Richardson, Zelda, and Sheila Hannah, *Guide to Automation in Visual Resources Collections*, 81
Roddy, Kevin, 87
Rogers, Donna, 86
Routines for processing, 61

Salaries, staff, 58
Salary reviews, 46
Search and retrieval, 80, 83
Search committees, 42
Seating, 9
  and storage capacities, 4
Secure storage areas, 14
Security, 3, 10, 74, 78
  and access, 10, 20, 71
Services
  and repairs, 53
  audiovisual, 38
  capabilities, 59
  computer, 38
  photographic, 38
  provided, 62
  required, 69
Shared information (networking), 81

Shelf
  order, 75
  reading, annual, 66-67, 75
Shelf cards (list), 63, 71, 74-75
Shelflist
  automated, 75
  interfiled, 75, 82
Sign-out procedures, 72
Signs, 4
Slides
  and tape orientations, 10
  binding for, 62, 64-65
    area, 13
    instructions, 63
    methods, 50
    statistics, 57, 59
  circulation forms, 132-38
  collections, 71
  containers, 10
  exchanges, 77
  mounting. *See* Slides, binding for
  projectors, 10
  replacements, 73
  sorters, 6
  sorting, 10
  storage
    areas, 6, 15, 16, 18
    files and units, 6, 23, 24
  trays, 10
  user areas, 15
  viewers, 9
  viewing and sorting spaces, 9
Smithsonian Institution, National Museum of American Art, 85
Software programs
  commercial, 84
  computer, 81, 83, 84, 87
  customized, 84
  upgrades, 84
Sorting and filing procedures, 62, 74, 75
Sources for supplies, equipment, services, 61
Spaces
  calculations, 9
  designs, 3
  inventory, 5
  psychological, 10
  requirements, 4, 6, 9
    computer work stations, 12
    racks vs. files, 8
  shapes, 4
  slide viewing and sorting, 9
  staff, calculation of, 11
  storage, 10
  summary, 15
  support, 6, 13
  work, 9
Spatial relationships, 17
Special income, 52
  projects, 52, 55

168 / INDEX

Specifications
  furniture and equipment, 23
  list, 4
  space, 6
Spreadsheet programs, 83
Square footage, 6
Staff
  additions, 48
  administrative responsibilities to, 35
  and users analysis, 4
  application forms, 68
  appraisals, 46
  benefits descriptions, 68
  charts to describe, 55
  communications, 35, 47, 48
  development, 2, 48, 52, 55
  evaluations, 35
  filers, 71
  full-time equivalent (FTE), 58
  interviews, 35
  management, 47
  meetings, 47
  organizational charts, 61, 65
  part-time, budget systems, 32
  rules and regulations, 68
  salaries, 58
  satisfaction of, 36
  schedules, 68
  size of, 39, 52, 54
  spaces, 6, 10, 18
    calculation of, 11
  supervision, 2, 35
  timesheets, 68
  training, 35, 46, 61, 68, 74, 86
  volunteers, 35
  work schedules, 68
Staffing, 35-48, 51, 68
  administrative and professional, 36, 39
  bibliography, 152-53
  categories, 35, 36
  clerical and general, 36, 37, 38, 39
  curatorial, 36, 37, 39
  job evaluations, 38, 68
  needs, 54
  patterns, 35
  standards, 37
  survey (MACAA), 35
  technical, 36, 37, 39
Staff-related forms, 123-27
Standard authority lists, 83
Standardized procedures, 81
Standards
  data entry, 84
  formats for reports, 68, 84
  indexing vocabulary, 81
  performance, 35, 46
  record formats, 84, 85, 143-47
  staffing, 39, 40
  terminology, 50, 56, 83, 86

Statements
  collection requirements, 3
  objectives, 1
Statistics
  acquisitions, 59
  and reports, 49
  collection and uses of, 56, 57, 80
  filing, 50, 63
  forms, 128-31
  methodology for gathering, 56
  monthly, 66-67
  objectives and purposes, 4
  photograph mounting and sleeving, 57
  physical facilities, 57
  reports, 39, 48
  slide binding, 57
Storage, 3
  audiovisual equipment, 14
  capacities, 4, 7
  environmentally safe, 10
  file labels, 76
  file management, 74
  image, 71
  photographs, 8
  secure, 14
  slides, 7
  space, 10
  supplies, 9
Structural load limits, 6
Student assistants, 39
Subject thesauri, 83
Subscriptions, 53
Sundt, Christine L., 25, 144
Supervision
  filers, 76
  staff, 1, 2, 35
Supplies
  and equipment for maintenance, 53
  records, 69
Support spaces, 6, 13
Surfaces, 6
Surveys, staffing, 35
System documentations, 86

Technical
  duties, 38
  facilities, 3
  job descriptions, 107-10
  requisition forms, 139
  services, 38, 39
    area, 10, 18
  staff, 36, 37, 39, 55
Temperature controls, 6
Terminals, computer, 10, 84, 86
Terminology
  and methodology, 40, 56
  standard, 50, 56
Textual and visual access, 87

Thermohydrograph, 19
Thesauri, 83, 87
Thieme-Becker, *Kunstler-Lexikon*, 86
Timeline checklist, 61
Tracking slide use, 77
Traffic flow, 16
Traffic patterns, 3
Training, staff, 1, 35, 46
Transaction and absence system, 72, 73
Travel funds, 53
Trends, future, 87

Ultraviolet lights, 19
Unit costs, 29, 30
University of Houston, College of Architecture, Slide Library, 92
University of Iowa, School of Art and Art History, 87
University of Missouri at Kansas City, Slide Library, 93
University of New Mexico, Albuquerque, Special Collections Photograph Archive of the General Library, 85
University of Oregon, Architecture and Allied Arts Slide Collection, standard record format, 144
University of Texas at Austin, Art Department, Slide and Photograph Collection, 73, 96
  filing statistics, 50
  standard record format, 143
University of Wisconsin, Helen L. Allen Textile Collection, ARTSearch, 87
Updating databases, 63
Users
  areas, 9, 16, 18
  authorized, 62, 72
  groups, 1
  information, 62, 73
  instructions, 10
  occasional, 17
  orientations, 10, 62, 72
  patterns, 54

registration, 72
regular, 17
spaces, 6

Variable fields, 85
Venting, 4
Videodisk projects, 87
Videodisks, 87
  computer linked, 87
Viewers, 6
Views, outside, 4
Visual and textual access, 87
Visual Resources Association, 42
  International Bulletin for Photographic Documentation of the Visual Arts, 77, 81, 84, 86
  Standards Committee, 86
Vollmer, *Lexikon der Bildenden Kunstler des II Jahrhunderts*, 86
Volumes of records, 84
Volunteer staff, 35, 47, 54
Volunteers, interviews form, 47

Wages and salaries, 53
Warburg and Courtauld Institute, 71
Weeding, collection, 76, 87
Weight distribution, 8
Wheeler, John D., 18
Withdrawals, 62
Witt Library, 71
Wordprocessing programs, 69, 83
Work
  space, 3, 9
  stations, 6
  surfaces, recommended, 10
Works in progress, 10
Worksheets, planning, 4

Zero base budgets, 28, 29

2680-25